Dinosaurs, Volcanoes, and Holy Writ

Dinosaurs, Volcanoes, and Holy Writ

*A Boy-Turned-Scientist Journeys
from Fundamentalism to Faith*

JAMES L. HAYWARD

RESOURCE *Publications* · Eugene, Oregon

DINOSAURS, VOLCANOES, AND HOLY WRIT
A Boy-Turned-Scientist Journeys from Fundamentalism to Faith

Copyright © 2020 James L. Hayward. All rights reserved. Except for brief quotations in critical publications or reviews, no part of this book may be reproduced in any manner without prior written permission from the publisher. Write: Permissions, Wipf and Stock Publishers, 199 W. 8th Ave., Suite 3, Eugene, OR 97401.

Scriptural quotations without attribution are from the Authorized King James Version (KJV). Other scriptural quotations are from the New Revised Standard Version Bible (NRSV), copyright © 1989, by the Division of Christian Education of the National Council of the Churches of Christ in the U.S.A., and are used by permission. All rights reserved.

Cover painting, "Dinosaur Museum" by Eric Dowdle, copyright © 2020 by Americana Art Enterprises. Used by permission.

Resource Publications
An Imprint of Wipf and Stock Publishers
199 W. 8th Ave., Suite 3
Eugene, OR 97401

www.wipfandstock.com

PAPERBACK ISBN: 978-1-7252-5769-6
HARDCOVER ISBN: 978-1-7252-5770-2
EBOOK ISBN: 978-1-7252-5771-9

Manufactured in the U.S.A.   04/27/20

To my brother, John William Hayward—
kind, thoughtful, insightful, helpful, generous, considerate,
intelligent, witty. We have traveled much of this road together.

Contents

Prologue   ix

PART ONE: EARLY YEARS

1 | When I Was a Child   3
2 | Adolescent Adventist   14
3 | Young Creationist   27
4 | Learning to Think   41

PART TWO: LIFE SCIENTIST

5 | Chasing Credentials   53
6 | Teaching Life   68
7 | Learning Firsthand   84

PART THREE: EVIDENCE

8 | Parsing the Word   105
9 | Dividing the Earth   120
10 | Gauging Time   135
11 | History Writ Large   147
12 | What about Home?   161
13 | Life Changes   171

PART FOUR: CONCLUSION

14 | Voyage of Discovery   191

Acknowledgments   205
Bibliography   207
Index   225

Prologue

"If the task of the first half of life is to put yourself out there, the task of the second half is to make sense of where you've been."

—Susan Cain[1]

An explosion, deep and rumbling, disrupted the morning peace. Startled, I paused and glanced about. Seeing no danger, I continued measuring the eggs laid by ring-billed and California gulls nesting on this tiny island in an eastern Washington lake.

Two hours later a bank of fierce-looking clouds appeared in the southwest. Last week similar-looking clouds in the southwest spawned a short-lived tornado that roiled fields of wheat and sagebrush. Apparently another storm was brewing.

Except for the explosion and approaching inclement weather, this May 18 morning had been delightful—blue sky, pleasant temperatures, and a slight breeze. By noon, however, the oncoming shroud enveloped the island, making me feel edgy. The gulls appeared nervous as well, oddly swimming about in the eerie calm of the surrounding lake.

By 1:30 pm it was too dark to read the scale on the calipers I was using to measure the eggs.

"The storm could hit us at any moment," I told Calvin Hill, who had come to help for the weekend. "Let's head back to the mainland. We need to be off the island before it hits."

We gathered our gear, hurried to the fiberglass boat awaiting us on the south side of the island, and rowed the quarter mile back to the mainland.

---

1. Cain, *Quiet*, 318.

As we pulled the boat ashore, we heard crickets singing in the gathering midday darkness. Two fishermen at the landing were packing their tackle.

"Looks like quite a storm!" I exclaimed, glancing at the angry sky overhead.

"You haven't heard? Mount St. Helens erupted. This is the ash cloud."

I was stunned. For the past several weeks I had listened to reports about the rumbling volcano, but I never dreamed an eruption would affect us here in eastern Washington. I now understood the source of the earlier explosion—and why, at midday, it seemed as if we had entered twilight.

"We're part of a geologic event!" I exclaimed to Calvin as the strange reality sank in. "Let's see how the premature darkness affects the behavior of the gulls!"

We had no flashlight or radio, so I drove the six miles back to our rented cabin at the lake's east end to fetch them, while Calvin stayed with the boat. The batteries in the portable radio were dead, so I drove another two miles to the little town of Sprague to purchase replacements.

As I emerged from the variety store, gray dust tickled my nose. I had never experienced a volcanic eruption and naively assumed the dark cloud from a volcano 200 miles away would, like most clouds, simply pass overhead—that would be it. But no, these clouds were collapsing.

Heart pounding, I drove back west toward the boat landing and stirred up ever thickening clouds of volcanic ash dusting the road. I turned down the unpaved lane to the lake. The boat was there but Calvin was not. With mounting anxiety I yanked the boat onto the trailer, jumped into the pickup, and hurried back to the main road.

By now the ashfall was a blizzard with ten-foot or less visibility. The center line was covered with ash and the margins of the road were barely visible. Boat-in-tow, heart-in-throat, I drove back toward the cabin, half expecting a head-on collision.

I barely recognized the turnoff to Sprague Lake Resort at the east end of the lake. Seeing my lights, a wide-eyed Calvin met me as I stopped the truck. He had hitched a ride back in the bed of another pickup and was covered with ash.

"This is serious!" I exclaimed, my initial excitement now displaced by a deep sense of foreboding. We pulled the boat from the trailer, flipped it over, and took shelter in the old dilapidated cabin.

Complete darkness enveloped us by mid-afternoon. We listened to news reports about damaged engines, ash-burdened roofs, and mounting casualties. Authorities thought the ash might be toxic.

How long would the ash fall? How deep would it get? Was it dangerous to breathe? What would it do to the truck? Would it kill the gulls? Would I need to begin a new project for my PhD dissertation? Was my family okay back in Walla Walla? These and other questions plagued me the rest of the day.

AFTER AN UNEXPECTEDLY GOOD night's rest, we awoke to a well-lit, albeit hazy, horizon. The ashfall was over. We wrapped the truck's air filter, loaded the boat onto the trailer, and drove back over an ash-laden road to the landing.

As we rowed toward the island, carp groped for oxygen at the surface. How could any unsheltered organism have survived the suffocating ordeal? Anxious, I braced for the worst.

We landed and made our way up the slope toward the gull colony. An inch and a half of ash, the consistency and hue of dry plaster of Paris, covered the ground. I expected to see dead and dying gulls splayed over the colony surface.

We peered over the crest onto a moon-like terrain. As we did, virtually all the gulls took flight. They were more edgy than usual, but surprisingly there were no casualties. They soon settled back on their territories.

Most of the hundreds of eggs that had been laid were now buried beneath the ash, but a few, mostly those of California gulls, had been excavated by the parents. Many California gulls had "black eyes"—ash sticking to fluid oozing from irritated eyes. Curiously, no ring-billed gulls displayed this sign. Perhaps in the process of excavating their eggs California gulls had soiled their eyes.

This day, May 19, was not only the day after the ashfall, but it also was the first day of hatching. Many of the chicks that hatched survived. A few, however, swallowed ash and choked to death.

Over the first few post-eruption days, more and more nests were excavated from beneath the ash, mostly by California gulls. Although some of the ring-billed gulls followed suit, many members of this species built new nests over the buried nests and laid new sets of eggs.[2]

MOUNT ST. HELENS' 1980 eruption was a pivotal event for many of us. Although it resulted in a tragic loss of life, both human and nonhuman, it provided scientists with an unprecedented opportunity to study the workings of an active volcano, a study that would help save lives in the future. It

---

2. Previously published descriptions of this event include Hayward et al., "Mount St. Helens Ash," 623–31; Hayward et al., "Volcanic Ash Fallout," 141; Hayward, "Breath of Vulcan," 4–8.

also provided an unparalleled chance to monitor and describe ecosystem recovery following such an occurrence.[3]

My concerns about how the ashfall would impact my graduate degree proved groundless. The data I collected transformed a rather mundane dissertation into a fascinating story.[4] I had been keenly interested in both biology and geology since I was a kid. I trained as a biologist, but I always kept an eye open for interesting rocks and fossils. Mount St. Helens afforded a spectacular opportunity to combine my professional interest in birds with my avocational interest in earth science.

Sadly, for some the eruption was a disaster. Luckily for me, it was a serendipity—the people I have met, the places I have visited, and the knowledge I have gained have been remarkable. I developed a more nuanced understanding of earth and life processes. I began to think more deeply about life on earth than was before possible. I was forced to ask questions I might not otherwise have asked.

The eruption occurred during a period of personal reassessment. I had been raised in a loving home by fundamentalist parents.[5] My father, a Seventh-day Adventist pastor and church administrator, read the Bible literally. He also believed that the writings of the church's nineteenth-century prophet, Ellen G. White, were historically and scientifically accurate. She wrote that life on earth is only about 6,000 years old, Adam and Eve were twice as tall as people today, and volcanoes are caused by burning coal formed from plants buried by the flood.[6] Raised as a fundamentalist believer, yet trained as a scientist to value physical evidence, I had much to think about.

---

3. Olson, *Eruption*; Parchman, *Echoes of Fury*; Waitt, *In the Path of Destruction*.

4. Hayward, "Effects of Nest Habitat, Behavior, and Volcanic Ash," 1–58.

5. Seventh-day Adventists have never formally identified themselves as "Fundamentalists," Christians who subscribe to five fundamentals of belief codified in 1910, the first of which was the "infallibility of scripture" (see Marsden, *Fundamentalism and American Culture*, 117). Adventists, by contrast, hold that the "writers of the Bible were God's penmen not His pen" (White, *Selected Messages*, Book One, 21), a view that makes allowance for some human influence on the wording of the biblical text. In practice, however, many conservative Adventists function as "literalists" in their interpretation of the Bible and the writings of church prophet, Ellen G. White. I use the term "fundamentalist," here and throughout the book, in the informal sense it is applied to any conservative Buddhist, Hindu, Jew, Muslim, or Christian who emphasizes his or her distinctiveness by adhering to rigid, literalistic interpretations of sacred texts and strict observances of religious practices.

6. White, *Spiritual Gifts*, 34, 79, 92. Today Seventh-day Adventists, like members of many other religious groups, subscribe to an enormously broad spectrum of religious beliefs, attitudes, and customs, ranging from fervent nineteenth-century-style apocalypticism to agnosticism. For a description of the diversity of Adventist beliefs, see Schwarz and Greenleaf, *Light Bearers*, 607–47; see also Wehtje, "Too Adventist to be Adventist," 16–25.

In addition to my personal struggles, the 1970s and 1980s were troubled times for my church. Seventh-day Adventism was reeling from financial scandal, traditional Adventist interpretations of scripture were challenged by leading Adventist scholars, and Ellen White was accused of plagiarism. Books were written, official denouncements and counter denouncements published, congregations split, and careers destroyed. Some of this turmoil involved issues related to the history of earth and life. The Seventh-day Adventist Church, which had for the most part remained quietly out of the headlines, now found its troubles featured on the pages of *Time* magazine, the *Los Angeles Times*, and the *Washington Post*. Adventism was experiencing its own eruption.[7]

FUNDAMENTALISTS OF ALL STRIPES, Christian and non-Christian, share many characteristics, including an antirelativistic "quest for certainty, exclusiveness, and unambiguous boundaries where the 'other' is the enemy demonized."[8] Although the strand of Seventh-day Adventism from which I emerged shares these characteristics, it will be helpful for me to describe the major historical underpinnings of this rapidly-growing and complex denomination.

The Seventh-day Adventist Church was established in 1863. It emerged from the ashes of the mid-nineteenth-century Millerite movement after its thrice-failed prediction that the Second Coming of Christ would occur in March 1843, April 1843, and finally on October 22, 1844.[9] William Miller, the movement's founder, based his predictions on Dan 8:14: "Unto two thousand and three hundred days; then shall the sanctuary be cleansed." According to Miller's interpretation, the "sanctuary" was the earth and its cleansing would be the Second Coming.[10]

Seventh-day Adventists rescued Miller's prediction from obscurity by claiming that the timing of the third prediction was correct but the event was wrong. They claimed the sanctuary to be cleansed was not on earth but in heaven. The "cleansing of the heavenly sanctuary" begun in 1844 was a judgment by Jesus who started reviewing the names of earthly inhabitants to determine who would be saved and who would be lost. He would remove—or "cleanse"—the names of the lost out of the "Book of Life." Once

---

7. Anonymous, "Prophet or Plagiarist?" 43; Dart, "Seventh-day Adventist Prophet White Is Called Plagiarist"; Hyer, "Adventists Facing Financial Crisis."

8. Nagata, "Beyond Theology," 481.

9. Jonathan M. Butler, "The Making of a New Order," 195–96.

10. Godfrey T. Anderson, "Sectarianism and Organization," 36–65; Bull and Lockhart, *Seeking a Sanctuary*, 1–4, 52.

this task was complete, Jesus would return to earth to claim the redeemed. This "sanctuary doctrine," tied to a hope in the soon Second Coming of Jesus, became of central importance to Seventh-day Adventists,[11] and it drove the spread of Adventism throughout the world, much like the expectation of Jesus' soon return drove the expansion of Christianity during the time of St. Paul.

A second touchstone of the early Seventh-day Adventist movement was the Sabbath. Adventists believed that some of the Old Testament Jewish laws, especially the Ten Commandments, were to be kept forever. The Sabbath commandment states that "Six days shalt thou labour, and do all thy work, but the seventh day is the Sabbath of the Lord thy God; in it thou shalt not do any work" (Exod 20:9–10). The Jewish Sabbath, Saturday, should be kept holy. Keeping this day holy meant not only attending church, but celebrating the entire day as "holy time," a rest day away from the mundane activities that fill the rest of the week. It also meant an emphasis on holism—that as a created being, one should live simply and in harmony with nature, keeping one's body and mind strong and healthy, remaining free of harmful substances and habits.

The Sabbath, however, was more than a rest day to Adventists. It was seen as a sign of commitment to God. Because Genesis reports that God rested on the seventh day of creation week, Adventists believed they should do the same. Indeed, Sabbath-keeping would become a test of one's commitment just before the Second Coming. Those saved would be those who "keep the commandments of God, and the faith of Jesus" (Rev 14:12). Seventh-day Adventists self-identified as members of that group.[12]

The connection between the Sabbath and creation was of particular significance to Adventists. They saw the weekly cycle as beginning at creation and maintained by Adam and Eve and all their descendants without missing a beat. If, as evolutionists taught, the development of earth and life occurred gradually over a span of millions of years with no humans around to keep track, the Sabbath, they said, would lose its significance.[13] Thus Adventists were the vanguards of modern creationism, parsing every word of the Genesis creation account, shoehorning every scrap of scientific data

---

11. Anonymous, *Seventh-day Adventists Believe*, 312–31.

12. Andrews, *History of the Sabbath*, 14–32, 44–50; Damsteegt, *Foundations of the Seventh-day Adventist Message*, 140–3; Anonymous, *Seventh-day Adventists Believe*, 248–66.

13. Price, *Genesis Vindicated*, 304–5; Coffin, *Creation—Accident or Design?*, 15–19; Zinke, "Theistic Evolution," 159–71; Numbers, *The Creationists*, 90, 104, 156.

they could into a six-day creation several thousand years ago, and discounting or ignoring the rest.[14]

A third major component of Adventism, one that overshadowed and shaped all other aspects, was the influence of the visionary reformer, Ellen G. White. Her writings on everything from biblical interpretation to music, sex, geology, and tree planting, influenced traditional Adventist thought on nearly every imaginable topic.[15] She made healthful living, education, and compassion for the needy spiritual responsibilities, obligations that led her church to establish one of the largest private healthcare systems in the world, develop a worldwide educational system, and form an extensive humanitarian organization that promotes sustainable development and responds to needs of the disadvantaged throughout the planet.[16]

Historians have demonstrated that White borrowed heavily from both nineteenth-century culture and Millerite religious fervor, but to conservative Adventists her views were mainlined from heaven via visions, dreams, and impressions.[17] Wielding her powerful "pen of inspiration," she became known as the "messenger of the Lord," a corporeal channel for the "testimony of Jesus" or the "spirit of prophecy" of Rev 19:10.[18] Indeed, her writings today are collectively referred to by Adventists as *the* "Spirit of Prophecy." If Ellen White's name crops up disproportionately in the pages that follow, it is because she exerted a disproportionate influence on my life and the lives of many others brought up within the Seventh-day Adventist tradition.

Apocalypticism, creationism, and the nature of sacred writings—I have wrestled with these and other issues from my past. For a thoughtful Baptist, Latter-day Saint, or Roman Catholic who grew up within a fundamentalist home, the nature of the struggle would be the same even though the specific issues would differ.[19] But struggling with one's past can lead to good things. Just as art, literature, and music emerge out of the experience of war and

14. Numbers, "'Sciences of Satanic Origin'," 17–30. Numbers, *The Creationists*, 88–119, 137–60, 320–28.

15. A glance through the three-volume, 3,216 page index to her writings (Ellen G. White Estate, *Comprehensive Index to the Writings of Ellen G. White*) will establish this fact.

16. Greenleaf and Moon, "Builder," 139; Bull and Lockhart, *Seeking a Sanctuary*, 309; Schwarz and Greenleaf, *Light Bearers*, 458–64.

17. McAdams, "Shifting Views of Inspiration," *Spectrum*, 27–41.

18. While growing up, I often heard each one of these terms applied to White and her writings.

19. Other stories with parallels to my own include Gosse, *Father and Son*; Gardner, *The Flight of Peter Fromm*; Spencer, *Shattered Dreams*; Evans, *Evolving in Monkey Town*; Phelps and Stewart, *Girl on a Wire*; Stott, *In the Days of Rain*; Westover, *Educated*; Armstrong, *Through the Narrow Gate*; and Armstrong, *The Spiral Staircase*.

tragedy, the tensions created by one's fundamentalist past in juxtaposition with a broader reality can serve as a source of originality and creativity.

"WRITING IS THINKING," DAVID McCullough once said.[20] This book is my attempt to think through where I have been. Some readers will find my perspectives appealing, others will find them puzzling, and still others will find them disconcerting. Regardless of how my perspectives are received, it is with an honest and open spirit that I describe my journey, explain why I have come to the conclusions I have, and hope to inspire others to find an intellectual space they can inhabit with peace and integrity. I am critical of views I find untenable, but I eschew ridicule, because I believe most of us think as we do because of our upbringing, education, temperament, exposure to information, and genetic heritage, not as a result of some obstructionist motive.

Although this book is autobiographical, I have left out many important aspects of my life. I focus on my journey from fundamentalism, through a period of exploration and discovery, to a life that is open and nuanced. I write as a scientist about my early life, education, emerging views of scripture, and understanding of earth history as they have interfaced with my belief system and spiritual life. My underlying theme is resilience, the resilience of a research program in face of natural disaster, the resilience of science in the face of anti-intellectual cultural forces, and the resilience of faith that is consistent with physical reality.

---

20. Cole, "The Danger of Historical Amnesia: A Conversation with David McCullough," 4.

PART ONE

Early Years

PART ONE: EARLY YEARS

These beginning chapters chronicle the first two dozen years of my life. I highlight events pivotal to the development of my personality, outlook, and passion for natural history, and I detail aspects of my years growing up within a conservative religious culture and belief system. I experienced the usual childhood and adolescent anxieties and insecurities, but I felt loved by my parents, and I remained hopeful and optimistic about life. I developed a strong sense of integrity, which I came to value above all things. Curiosity and love for the natural world dominated this period, setting me up for a career in science and encouraging me to ask questions about the nature of reality. Unlike many conservative denominations, the Seventh-day Adventist Church placed a high value on education. There was never any question in my home about whether I would obtain a good education.

1

When I Was a Child

"For in every adult there dwells the child that was, and in every child there lies the adult that will be."

—John Connolly[1]

Mountains crumbled. Rocks tumbled. People fled. Frightening music heightened a sense of horror. My seven-year-old heart thumped violently and my stomach revolted. I could take no more. I slid from my seat and beat a hasty retreat to the lobby where I was shielded from the horrible images.

It was 1955. Dad and his fellow Adventist pastors were holding an evangelistic "effort," as they called it, in the Little Theater in downtown Worcester, Massachusetts. The terrifying images depicted events climaxing at the Second Coming. I was a sensitive kid who found the images repulsive.

One of Dad's fellow evangelists at the Little Theater, Pastor Donald R. Goodness, apparently found the images repulsive as well. It wasn't long before he traded his Adventist credentials for the turned collar of the Episcopalian priesthood—and a less apocalyptic theology.[2] Dad, however,

---

1. Connolly, *The Book of Lost Things*, dedication page.
2. Hayward, Sr., *Memoirs*, 35; Donald R. Goodness served as a Seventh-day Adventist pastor from 1953 to 1959, at which time he entered the Episcopal Theological School in Cambridge, Massachusetts. He became an ordained priest in 1962 or 1963 (*New York Times*, January 17, 1972, 35). In 1997 Goodness retired as the tenth rector of

throughout his long life remained true, a person of strong Adventist opinions and firm Adventist convictions. He never understood how Don Goodness or anyone else who knew "The Truth" could turn their back on "God's remnant Church."[3]

Dad grew up dirt poor in Naugatuck, Connecticut. He and his identical twin, John, were the last of ten children. Their father once made a good living as a tool and die maker with the Steele and Johnson Company. But Grandpa's eyesight went bad, so he could no longer see his work. In desperation he took a low-paying job at a Naugatuck plating factory, laboring twelve hours a day, six days a week.[4]

Dad's French Canadian mother was raised Roman Catholic, but she converted to Seventh-day Adventism before giving birth to Dad and his twin brother. Grandma supplemented the meager family income by cleaning houses. She reigned over the family in a four-dollar-per-month clapboard shack at the dead end of a dirt road.[5]

Dad was shy. While other kids played during recess, he and John stood aside, too timid to join in.[6] At Naugatuck High School he refused to read the English assignments because they were "untrue"—Sister Ellen G. White, the Adventist prophet, had warned that novels were "pernicious in their influence," Satan-inspired, and best set ablaze.[7] After three years of hating high school, he dropped out at age seventeen, moved to Stoneham, Massachusetts, and took a job as a kitchen helper and desk clerk at the Adventist-run New England Sanitarium and Hospital. In keeping with Sister White's counsel he converted to vegetarianism.[8]

The nation was in the grip of World War II, and Dad soon was drafted as a conscientious objector. Ironically, the war years seemed among his

---

New York City's The Church of the Ascension, located on Fifth Avenue and founded in 1827 (The Church of the Ascension in the City of New York, "Parish History").

3. James L. Hayward, Sr. served as a Seventh-day Adventist (SDA) pastor and administrator for forty years. During his career he pastored nine churches and served as secretary of Michigan Conference of SDA, president of Wisconsin Conference of SDA, and manager of the Voice of Prophecy radio ministry. After his retirement he served as an interim pastor at nine more churches in Texas and California (Hayward, Sr., *Memoirs*, 74–75).

4. Hayward, Sr., *Memoirs*, 1–2.

5. Hayward, Sr., *Memoirs*, 1–3.

6. Hayward, Sr., *Meniors*, 5, and personal communication.

7. Personal communication; White, *Testimonies for the Church*, Volume 2, 236; White, *The Story of Patriarchs and Prophets*, 459.

8. Hayward, Sr., *Memoirs*, 8, and personal communication.

happiest. He was stationed at a United States Army hospital for the treatment of injured soldiers near the town of Painswick, England. German V-2 rockets made most people nervous; to Dad they meant excitement. He volunteered as a medic to parachute into the Battle of the Bulge; his offer was declined because he refused to carry a sidearm. He volunteered, he said, not primarily because he was patriotic, wanted to save the world from Hitler, or hoped to support his comrades—just for the sheer adventure of it.[9]

After three years in the military and a GED, Dad completed a bachelor's degree and ministerial training at Atlantic Union College in South Lancaster, Massachusetts. He served the Adventist Church for forty years as a talented and much loved pastor and church administrator. He was one of the most honest, hard-working, and courageous people I have known. Most of his days, however, were consumed with attempts to live in harmony with a plethora of nineteenth-century admonitions and warnings by Sister White. It was not unusual for him to begin sentences out of the blue with "She said . . ." "She" was an ever-present specter in our home.[10]

SISTER WHITE'S NINETEENTH-CENTURY COMMENTS on "The Time of the End"—events leading up to the Second Coming—were of particular concern to Dad and served as powerful motivators for his ministry. His meticulously drawn time line of these events was copied, recopied, and delivered to thousands of believers. Once, when he was in his eighties, I voiced skepticism about the feasibility of one of the predicted events happening during the twenty-first century. Dad impatiently retorted "It *has* to happen!" Five years before he died, he proudly published a 623-page tome entitled *The Time of the End: A Study for the Last Days from the Word of God and the Spirit of Prophecy*. The compilation, primarily of thousands of Sister White's statements printed in dense, Bookman type, covers everything from the benefits of country living to the threats of the Mark of the Beast. The legend beneath Dad's picture on the back cover notes that he "was recognized as one of Adventism's leading authorities on Ellen White and the Spirit of Prophecy."[11]

Having grown up in poverty, Dad learned that success is the reward of hard labor and endurance. Throughout life he preferred work to most forms of pleasure. For the most part, his was a simple, practical life which

9. Hayward, Sr., *Memoirs*, 9–25. Twenty-three percent of *Memoirs* is devoted to Dad's recollections of his three-year Army experience. For many years he kept his Army insignia and honors in his top dresser drawer, and he often spoke fondly of his years in "the service." His comment about volunteering to parachute into the Battle of the Bulge was made to me in 2011 or 2012.

10. Hayward, Sr., *Memoirs*, 74–75.

11. Hayward, Sr., *The Time of the End*, back cover.

reflected the common sense realism typical of many New Englanders of his era. I once heard him preach a sermon on philosophy—or "foolosophy" as he called it. The part I remember went like this: "Who am I? I'm Jim Hayward! Where am I from? I'm from Naugatuck, Connecticut! Where am I going? I'm going to heaven!"[12]

MOM AND DAD MARRIED on May 22, 1947, two years after Dad was honorably discharged from the Army. Mom had completed her three-year nursing program at the New England Sanitarium and Hospital in 1946, and I was born on September 30, 1948 at the "San." Both my parents were twenty-four years old at the time and lived on Prescott Street in South Lancaster. Dad was listed as a "student" and Mom as a "housewife." Three years later, my brother, John, was born on July 26, 1951.

Dad's studies at Atlantic Union College were funded by the G.I. Bill, but he had to work three jobs to keep the family afloat—maintenance at the college, pastor at a nearby church, and law enforcement as a policeman for the city of Lancaster. Much of the time he was exhausted. But he managed to complete his bachelor's degree in religion on June 1, 1952.[13]

Dad was required to take a science course at AUC. Mammalogy was the only one that fit his schedule. Mammalogy is concerned with the anatomy, physiology, diversity, ecology, behaviors, and adaptations of mammals, creatures that share with us the possession of hair, three middle ear bones, neocortex, and mammary glands. He enrolled in the course with little enthusiasm. This, after all, was not his area of interest. The instructor, Richard M. Ritland, required two books for students, *Mammals of North America*, by Victor H. Cahalane, and *American Mammals: Their Lives, Habits, and Economic Relations* by W. J. Hamilton, Jr. When I was a boy, I discovered these books in Dad's library and especially enjoyed reading Cahalane's text. These books still occupy a place in my library, and I credit them with encouraging my interest in biology, especially of mammals.

We lived in a little brown, shingled cottage, "Cady's House," one block from campus. My first memories come from that house. I recall pictures of cats on the wall above my crib and playing in a sandbox beside the house. I was impressed by the authority of a little neighbor girl, Gail, even though she sometimes called me "So Po" ("Slow Poke"). Gail liked to pass

---

12. Hayward, Sr., *Memoirs*, 6–7. Dad preached this sermon at the Arizona SDA Conference Camp Meeting, Camp Yavapines, Prescott, Arizona, probably during the summer of 1969.

13. Hayward, Sr., *Memoirs*, 26–28.

interesting bits of information my way. When Mom and Dad tried to caution me against believing everything I heard, I remonstrated, "Gail said so!"

I GREW INTO AN earnest kid who shared Dad's concrete realism and confidence in the absolute truth of Sister White's statements. Through high school and my first three years of college, I studied her "Spirit of Prophecy" books, underlined important points and admonitions, and tried to live up to "The Truth" as she proclaimed it. But while Dad prepared for the end of the world, I was intrigued by its beginnings—creation and the flood.

My earliest concepts of creation and the flood were shaped largely by the first volume of Arthur S. Maxwell's *The Bible Story* series. These lavishly illustrated books told tales from the Bible that appealed to children. I particularly admired the paintings by Harry Anderson. Anderson had been trained as an impressionist, and before joining the Adventist Church he had worked as a prominent magazine illustrator. His "people images" deftly captured facial expressions and moods with an almost mystical quality which imparted to them a life-like vibrancy.[14]

Anderson's painting of Adam with the animals was my favorite. A joyful, naked, male figure stands, arms outstretched, surrounded by a menagerie of newly-created animals. "How happy Adam must have been to have all the animals love to come to him," reads the accompanying legend.[15] I could picture myself as Adam, mingling among the delightful assortment of creatures. I never thought to question why in such a "perfect" creation—one without pain, suffering, and death, and one of exquisite design—the lion in the picture bears canine teeth, the cat stalks the chickens, the dog exhibits carnivorous molars, and Adam sports nipples. These and other questions would come later.

DURING THE 1950S, OUR family often returned to South Lancaster where Dad had attended Atlantic Union College and where Grandma Hayward, his aging mother, lived. Grandma rented a room in a white frame house two blocks from campus and adjacent to the office of Dad's employer, the Southern New England Conference of Seventh-day Adventists. Dr. Guy Winslow owned the house and lived on the main level. He rented out the upstairs rooms to older folks. Upon arrival, we would pass little baskets of organic, home-grown vegetables for sale on the front lawn, enter a large hall decked with colorful wall hangings, ascend the creaky stairs, and knock on

---

14. Stein, "Harry Anderson (1906–1996)."
15. Maxwell, *The Bible Story*, Volume One, 42–43.

Grandma's door just to the right. I remember the smell of the place, not a bad smell, but a distinctive one.

Winslow liked to sit in a rocking chair on his front porch and pass the time of day. My parents would greet him with "Hi, Dr. Winslow," but I don't recall much conversation beyond the greeting. He always seemed a little gruff, although apparently he treated Grandma and the other residents kindly. If one of us needed to use the bathroom during our visit, Grandma would tell us, "Don't flush the toilet, Dear, if it's just void. Dr. Winslow doesn't want us to use too much water." But Grandma had a soft spot in her heart for him. My cousin Richard Coffen remembers she once worried that Winslow had developed colon or prostate cancer after seeing blood-spattered underwear hanging on his clothesline.[16]

It was never clear to me what Winslow did for a living. Everyone addressed him as "Doctor," but he didn't seem to be a medical doctor and he didn't teach at Atlantic Union College. Dad and Mom said very little about him. But a cloud hung over his reputation, something to do with church. All this remained a mystery to me until recently.

In the course of some historical research, I ran across a reference to a 1933 dissertation from Clark University entitled "Ellen Gould White and Seventh-day Adventism" by Guy Herbert Winslow. Clark is only twenty-one miles from South Lancaster, so I wondered if Guy Winslow, my grandmother's landlord, was the Guy Herbert Winslow who authored the dissertation. It turns out he was. James White Library at Andrews University, where I was teaching, contained just about every published item associated with Adventism and its history, and sure enough, Winslow's dissertation was in the stacks.

I checked out his 465-page tome and found it to be highly critical of both Ellen White and Seventh-day Adventist leadership. Winslow claimed that church leaders influenced the prophet to such an extent that her visions and dreams were simply confirmations of their own views, and that they manipulated her "prophetic gift" to support their own political ends. He wrote "There is not the slightest evidence that she at any time in this condition [in vision] learned a single thing that was not well-known before by her associates." He concluded his work by predicting that her "teachings will gradually join the ranks of outgrown and therefore discarded fanatical American religious theories, together with witchcraft, spiritualism and Mormonism; and their author will remain but as a curiosity—like those exhibited by [P. T.] Barnum in the Great American Museum."[17]

---

16. Richard Coffen to JLH (email), August 8, 2017.
17. Winslow, "Ellen Gould White and Seventh-day Adventism," 387.

Further research demonstrated that before attending Clark, Winslow had been a dedicated Seventh-day Adventist. He funded part of his way through Adventist secondary school as a door-to-door peddler of Adventist books in Maine, served as the tent master and cornetist for several Adventist evangelistic meetings, taught biology at South Lancaster Academy, held summer sessions at the Adventist campuses of Union College in Nebraska and Southwestern Union College in Texas, and served as a professor of history at Atlantic Union College until 1929. He was much appreciated by his AUC students, who dedicated their 1929 annual to him. He stood in more than once for the college president when the president was away from campus. By 1930, however, Winslow had transferred to Worcester State College where he taught history, a job he retained until his retirement in 1958.[18]

One can only guess at what transpired to lead a respected and much-loved forty-three-year-old professor to leave AUC, and who then four years later wrote a stridently negative dissertation on Ellen White and Adventist leadership. Was he severed from the college for something he said or did? Did he fail to get along with the new college president installed the year before he left? Did he become aware of things about Ellen White and the Adventist Church that made him angry? The answer may be lost to history. Regardless, there is some irony to the fact that an early and vitriolic critic of Ellen White and the Adventist Church was the long-time landlord for the mother of my dad, a conservative Adventist pastor who eventually would hold the reputation as one of Ellen White's most devoted disciples and staunch defenders.

Winslow apparently retained some respect for his Adventist heritage, at least in relation to health care. A 1968 issue of the *Atlantic Union Gleaner*, a regional Adventist news magazine, pictured the now retired professor, a recent patient at the church's New England Memorial Hospital, donating a check for its building program. He died five years later at age eighty-six.[19]

INSPIRED BY MY COUSIN Richard, I started a life list of birds at age seven. For each new bird I saw, Mom helped me tick off the name in the checklist provided in Roger Tory Peterson's *A Field Guide to Birds*. One of the first names checked was "American goldfinch"—I remember seeing it in its nest

---

18. Winslow's name appears in the SDA church's regional paper, the *Atlantic Union Gleaner*, more than a dozen times between 1908 and 1927, where news notes concerning his book sales, work with evangelistic meetings, faculty appointments, and activities at Atlantic Union College appear. His obituary ("Guy Herbert Winslow," At Rest), noted his faculty appointment at Worcester State College, his gardening, and the year of his retirement.

19. Anonymous, "Patient Donates to Hospital Building Program," 16.

just outside the window of the home of one of Dad's parishioners. Leafing through Peterson's guides, as well as through the Golden Nature Guides edited by Herbert S. Zim, I was introduced to the names of birds, mammals, plants, shells, insects, reptiles and amphibians, rocks, fossils, tracks, weather, and stars and planets—all the wonderful objects that make up the dazzling array we call nature.

I recall trying as a grade schooler to memorize the names of the thirty plus animal phyla—"Porifera," "Cnidaria," "Echinodermata," "Ctenophora," etc. Over and over I practiced the terms. Memorization never came easily or naturally for me, so my intense engagement in the process at this age suggests the value I placed on life's diversity. Years later I would learn the distinguishing features of these groups, their respective positions in the fossil record, and their purported evolutionary relationships, but memorization of their names was an important first step toward understanding.

Mom and Dad encouraged my interest in nature by purchasing nearly every book written by Sam Campbell, the Midwestern naturalist and self-described "Philosopher of the Forest." Sam's books were popular among young Adventist readers during the 1950s and 1960s. I absorbed and re-absorbed his books, and fantasized what it would be like to visit Sam at "Wegimind," his Wisconsin island home. I felt intimately connected with Sam and his friends, both animal and human. If Sam said it, I believed it. Most boys idolized baseball or football stars as their heroes. My hero was Sam Campbell. Sam put a rich, thoughtful, and lovingly humorous face on nature which I deeply relished. More than any other influence, Sam made me want to live the life of a naturalist, to work on an island, and to study the behavior of its creatures.

Year after year Sam came to Atlantic Union College for its Saturday evening lyceum series. During the late 1950s, I watched and listened in delight as he narrated comical films about his animal friends in his friendly, high-pitched voice. At intermissions, he would come out to the lobby, talk and laugh with mobs of adoring kids and adults, and autograph books. He was a joyful, warm-hearted person who loved both nature and people. I longed to meet him but I was too shy, so I gawked from the sidelines. The signed copies of his books we purchased, however, remain prized possessions.

Most Adventists, including my family, had no idea Sam was a Christian Scientist. Christian Scientists, like Adventists, trace their roots to nineteenth-century New England. But unlike Adventists, Christian Scientists consider the material world, including evil, sickness, and death, as illusory. They believe the spiritual world to be the highest reality. Despite his identity as a Christian Scientist, Sam was suspicious of sectarianism. He read broadly, including the Bible and the works of Emerson, Tolstoy, Whitman,

Tennyson, Dante, Longfellow, Bryant, William James, and others. From these influences, and from his experiences with people and with the natural world, he forged an eclectic faith, one he could own with integrity. He fully embraced the material world and spent his adult life writing and lecturing about its importance. His church's belief in the healing virtues of a positive spirit was apparently what attracted him. But to Sam, that positive spirit was achieved through total immersion in a real, physical world.[20]

As I reflect on Sam's writings today, I am bemused at how paternalistic and chauvinistic he was, how he anthropomorphized the animals he wrote about, and how he idealized nature. Nonetheless, the sentiments he expressed, the values he espoused, and the joy he conveyed were qualities that I have carried with me through the years. Sam's upbeat writings served as an antidote to the apocalypticism that pervaded my early years. "Our fears," he wrote, "show us a sort of false world wherein we live a false state of existence."[21]

Although Sam frequently referred to God as the creator of all that is good, "creationism" as we think of it today never appeared in his writings. I learned from him that I could experience warm friendships, the sacredness of life, a worshipful attitude, an appreciation for beauty—the best of life, in other words—without resorting to rigid doctrinal constraints or antiscientific perspectives. He taught me the joy that accompanies the fearless exploration of reality with an honest heart and open mind.

IN 1960, JUST BEFORE I turned twelve, we moved from Boston to Atlanta where Dad became pastor of the Beverly Road Seventh-day Adventist Church. Moving from north to south was an interesting cultural experience. The Civil War centenary, the civil rights movement, and the twenty-fifth anniversary of Margaret Mitchell's *Gone with the Wind* were in full swing. Racially segregated bathrooms, restaurant "sit-ins,"[22] and signs declaring "The South Will Rise Again" were the norm. Accents, foods, and attitudes differed dramatically—although sometimes delightfully so—from what I was used to. Kids ran around barefoot, a practice that seemed oddly primitive to my fully shod and buttoned-up New England sensibilities. Despite my Yankee heritage, though, I made good friends and enjoyed my new surroundings.

One day a grade school classmate at Atlanta Union Academy declared that, it being February 12, we should celebrate Charles Darwin's birthday.

20. Henson, *Sam Campbell*.
21. Campbell, *How's Inky?* 118.
22. Sit-ins were peaceful protests in which groups of black people occupied white-only restaurants until they were served.

Our teacher responded with a disapproving look. I had heard of Darwin and evolution but had paid little attention to the name. I had been taught the Truth about creation since I was knee high, and Darwin's theory was just another one of the deceptions so often spoken about by Dad. Anyway, I was more interested in tending my list of birds than considering arguments about the history of earth and life.

IN MY DAY, MANY Adventist kids were baptized when they reached twelve, which was considered to be their "age of accountability." Thus on December 10, 1960, only four months after arriving in Atlanta, Dad baptized me into the Seventh-day Adventist Church. I stood in front of the congregation before entering the baptismal tank, and Dad questioned me as to whether I believed a list of Adventist tenets; I nodded "yes" to each one. My "Certificate of Baptism," provided that day and signed by Dad, includes a "Summary of Doctrinal Beliefs," two of which allude to the creation: number one refers to Jesus Christ "who created all things," and number fourteen asserts that the seventh-day Sabbath is "the eternal sign of Christ's power as Creator."[23]

Today the Adventist Church's doctrinal summary is considerably more complicated. What is now statement number six declares that God

> created the universe, and in a recent six-day creation the Lord made "the heavens and the earth, the sea, and all that is in them" and rested on the seventh day. Thus He established the Sabbath as a perpetual memorial of the work He performed and completed during six literal days that together with the Sabbath constituted the same unit of time that we call a week today.[24]

The words "recent," "literal," and "same unit of time" were added in 2015, apparently in reaction to burgeoning evidence that both earth and life are billions of years old, evidence perceived to be an existential threat to the church's seventh-day Sabbath doctrine.[25]

Like other Adventist kids, I learned to keep the Sabbath Day holy. For my family that meant faithfully attending "Sabbath School" and church, not playing with non-Adventist neighbor children, not riding my bike, not listening to secular music, not doing chores or homework, not going to the store, and not reading anything unrelated to God. It also meant a peaceful, freshly-cleaned house, visiting with friends at church, and enjoying a

---

23. "Certificate of Baptism," General Conference of Seventh-day Adventists.

24. General Conference of Seventh-day Adventists, *2018 Seventh-day Adventist Yearbook*, 8.

25. Geraty, "How the Adventist Church Changed Its Fundamental Beliefs," 69–72.

delicious after-church meal. And fortunately for me, approved Sabbath-keeping included enjoying nature and reading books by Sam Campbell.

Although Sam Campbell inspired my love of life in the present, he wrote little about life in the past. I don't know what sparked my enthusiasm for historical biology and paleontology. Perhaps it was the Golden Nature Guide on *Fossils* that piqued my interest. But growing up in New England made it unlikely I would find a fossil there—the northeastern states are mostly covered with igneous extrusions, metamorphic rocks, and glacial deposits, generally non-fossil-bearing strata. Fossils are found more commonly in sedimentary rocks like siltstone, shale, and limestone, rocks not so common in the northeast. In the southeastern states where we had moved, however, fossil-bearing rocks are abundant.

During each of the three summers we lived in Atlanta, our family migrated the 120 miles north for a week of "camp meeting" on the campus of Southern Missionary College, located in the beautiful "valleys and ridges" province of southeastern Tennessee. Instead of warming a seat in the "Earliteen" tent, however, I spent much of my time looking for new birds and poking around the natural areas close to campus. Just behind the college buildings loomed White Oak Mountain—not really a mountain, but one of the many crests found in this region. One day I hiked up the side of the ridge, probably looking for a new bird. Not far up the ridge I came to a clearing with a large water tank. As I looked down at the broken, reddish-tan limestone, I spotted my first-ever fossil. The little crinoid fragment stood out clearly from its matrix. I was ecstatic. Within minutes I found many more specimens, trophies I keep as reminders of that day.

I don't recall thinking about the origin of those White Oak Mountain fossils. At thirteen I was more interested in collecting and classifying objects than in thinking about how they got there. I am certain, however, that if asked I would have attributed their origin to Noah's great flood.

2

Adolescent Adventist

"Adolescence is like having only enough light to see the step directly in front of you."

—Sarah Addison Allen[1]

"Imagine, if you can, a new world, coming fresh from the Creator's hand... And on the first 'Friday afternoon' Adam and Eve began their study of the living world around them—they were the first biologists." I carefully underlined the latter sentence in my biology text, proud that I planned to occupy the same profession as the first human pair. An extensive passage from Ellen White followed which described how the first pair was visited by angels, the vigor they experienced from eating fruit from the Tree of Life, and the awesome intellectual powers they enjoyed.[2]

It was the fall of 1963 at Fort Worth Junior Academy, and Ernest S. Booth's *Biology: The Story of Life*, published under the auspices of the Seventh-day Adventist Church, served as my formal introduction to ninth grade biology. The 1950 textbook was already woefully out of date, as was the class. Three years after the book had been published, Rosalind Franklin, James Watson, and Francis Crick determined the structure of DNA and

---

1. Sarah Addison Allen, *The Girl Who Chased the Moon*, 152.
2. Booth, *Biology, the Story of Life*, 1.

identified it as the genetic material. Ten years later, as I sat in my ninth-grade biology class, this discovery—arguably the most important in biology ever—was never mentioned.

IN 1960, DAD HAD accepted an offer to pastor the Fort Worth First Seventh-day Adventist Church in Texas. My brother and I were excited about the prospect of living in what seemed like an exotic land of cowboys and cattle ranches. The opportunity to add new birds to my life list was a big plus—there was even a Peterson Field Guide devoted exclusively to Texas birds—to say nothing of the chance to wear cowboy boots and a ten-gallon hat. This was going to be an adventure.

Dad had enjoyed his three-year tenure as pastor in Atlanta, but his hardline promotion of Ellen White and Spirit of Prophecy-based "standards" cost him popularity with some prominent, "liberal" members of his congregation. He must have been relieved to anticipate a new venue and new start.[3]

We moved to Fort Worth in late summer, just in time for school to begin. I had graduated from Atlanta Union Academy as president of our little eighth grade class, and now, newly situated in Texas, I was ready to start high school. I enrolled in ninth grade at Fort Worth Junior Academy, the local ten-grade Adventist school.

I was a tall, skinny kid who combed my hair with Wave Set, wore my pants high, and carried my lanky frame self-consciously. I had entered a stage of extreme awkwardness. At the slightest hint of embarrassment my face turned pink, red, and then crimson. My desk was close to three pretty girls, Bette, Karen, and Nancy. They tried to get me to talk but I didn't know what to say. They giggled at my discombobulated bouts of blushing. Somehow, though, I survived that first year and even made good friends in the process.

AN AFFABLE MILFORD O. Brown was our ninth grade teacher, and I was excited that biology was one of our subjects. I doubt Brown knew much about biology or about science generally. But he required us to make an insect collection. My specimens were well prepared, accurately labeled, and earned top grade. Had Brown lectured to us about DNA, I might have lost interest in biology; appreciation for the molecular side of life would come later.

I had no idea *Biology, the Story of Life* was so out of date. To me it was inspiring. Ernest S. Booth, the author, seemed like a kindred spirit, a person

---

3. Hayward, Sr., "Memoirs," 45–46.

who loved the out-of-doors, who enjoyed collecting, and who, just like Dad, quoted Ellen White as an authority. I was quite taken with his approach and he became my new hero—more scientifically inclined than my earlier idol, Sam Campbell. Looking back, I realize that Booth's influence, however dated and religiously slanted, transitioned me from an exclusively nature-appreciation stage to one that valued the techniques of science.

Chapter 19 of Booth's text focused on mammals and was the part of the book that especially piqued my interest. The last part of the chapter dealt with ways to study mammals, including photography, trapping, and specimen preparation. Like many kids I was attracted to collecting things. I was especially intrigued by a photograph of students studying mammal skins and skulls in neatly-arranged trays at Walla Walla College where Booth taught. The photo inspired me to want to make my own mammal collection. I decided to start by learning to trap and prepare small mammals as "study skins."[4]

"For best results it will be necessary to learn where to set the traps," I read in Booth's text. "If you merely lay them down anywhere you may catch very few animals, but if you set them by the burrows or nests of the animals you will get many more."[5]

I purchased some Victor mouse and rat traps at the local hardware, some oats for bait, and headed out late one afternoon to a promising grassy area behind Dad's church to set my traps.

Next morning I came back eager with anticipation. But anticipation turned to disappointment when I discovered that all my traps were empty. I tried again and again with no success. I did manage to obtain a black rat collected by a friend, and I salvaged a road-killed Virginia opossum. I practiced making study skins of these and a few other animal corpses I chanced upon, but success in trapping wild rodents eluded me.[6]

So on August 21, 1964, at not quite fifteen years old, I worked up my courage and wrote a letter to my new hero, Ernest Booth. I don't recall how I found his address, but I told him about my trapping difficulties and asked if he could offer some advice.[7]

---

4. Booth, *Biology, the Story of Life*, 248–53. A study skin is a mammal or bird specimen stuffed so as to maximize museum cabinet space, while at the same time preserving important features of the animal for study. It is not positioned in a life-like posture like a taxidermy-mounted specimen.

5. Booth, *Biology, the Story of Life*, 250.

6. I still have the catalogue that lists the mammals and birds I collected and prepared as museum skins and skulls.

7. Although I do not have a copy of my letter to Booth, his response indicates my letter was dated then.

As I BEGAN TENTH grade I waited impatiently for a response. Finally, seven weeks later, the letter appeared. I opened the envelope and discovered a typed, two-page missive on bold letterhead. At the top of the page was a pen-and-ink drawing of an adult and juvenile moose feeding in a shallow pond. A range of craggy peaks appeared in the background. "Outdoor Pictures: Specialists in Natural Color Photography. Publishers of Motion Pictures, Slides, Filmstrips and Books. Ernest S. Booth, Box 1326, Escondido, California" was printed at the top.[8]

"Dear Jim," it began. "Your letter of Aug. 21 was not ignored, but at the time I was in South America collecting animals and making motion pictures. I just got home a week ago and found your letter here for me to answer."

In South America doing what I dreamed I would be doing someday?! The words tumbled quickly from the page into my imagination.

"I'm glad you are interested in mammals," Booth continued, "and if you once get into it you will never want to give up this study. It could become your life work, too, as it did with me. . . I do hope you will keep up your goal of becoming a biology teacher in one of our [Adventist] schools."

I have since been told that my goal at fourteen of becoming a college biology teacher was highly unusual. Even more unusual, I suppose, is the fact that I stuck with that goal through high school, college, and graduate school, and ended up experiencing my boyhood dreams in ways that far surpassed those dreams. I have been most fortunate considering the many college students I've advised who had no idea what they wanted to do when they finished school—no real interests, no passions, no realistic goals.

Booth went on to provide advice on how to achieve success as a biologist, and of more immediate interest, how to successfully collect mammals.

"Trapping and learning to make up museum specimens is very good, but it takes years to learn to do it well—unless you have someone to help you get a good start. My boy is 14, and he does a better job now than I do. . . He earns a lot of money selling his specimens to museums, too."

After telling me about his son, Booth made a business proposition: "I would buy most of what you would want to sell to me too, if you learn to do the job well. Right now I need mammals from your area quite badly. I pay $1.00 each for most small mammals, and more for certain ones—$1.50 for moles, for instance, and $4.00 for skunks, $2.50 for rabbits, $2.00 for flying squirrels, etc."

---

8. Ernest S. Booth to JLH, October 19, 1964.

Really? He wanted me to collect for him? The author of my biology textbook was offering to jump-start my career as a biologist before I was half way through high school? I was ecstatic.

"Best wishes to you," he concluded, "and don't get discouraged. I wish you could work with my boy awhile. It is much easier if you can work with someone, for you learn so much faster. Sincerely, Ernest S. Booth."

After signing off, Booth added a postscript. "By the way," he wrote, "I could show a motion picture program at Fort Worth Nov. 11 if your church would like one of my programs again. . . If you think of it, you might mention this to the person who would have charge of evening programs. I don't know now who might be in charge."

I knew that person very well and immediately lobbied Dad to invite Booth to present a program in our church. November 11 fell on a Wednesday and Dad graciously invited Booth to present his program during the time slot for the midweek "prayer meeting." He also invited Dr. and Mrs. Booth to spend the night at our home.

As promised, the Booths arrived on November 11, and Dr. Booth presented a film at the Wednesday evening meeting. The film featured footage taken at the marine biology field station he had founded ten years earlier at Rosario Beach near Anacortes, Washington. Little did I know that I would spend forty summers based at that field station, taking classes, teaching, and researching seabirds. Had it not been for what I learned that November evening a half century ago, the direction of my life might have been quite different.

We shared dinner with the Booths, after which I happily gave up my bedroom for them. Thursday morning, before they left town, he and I went out to the area behind the church and he taught me where to set my traps. I was walking on air. Thanks to Booth's coaching, I began to experience success at collecting mammals. Over the next two and a half years of high school I collected 129 specimens, not a huge number by any means, but enough for me to learn a great deal about the ecology of mammals and methods for preparing and preserving them as museum specimens.[9] Many of the specimens I collected I sold to Booth for his Outdoor Pictures business. He, in turn, resold them to schools and museums. Years later he told me that, next to his son, I was the best preparer he had.

Texas was an ideal place to study mammals. Not only was the state blessed with a large diversity of species, but there were plenty of natural

---

9. JLH collection catalogue.

or semi-natural areas within which to collect.[10] In addition to trapping, I induced my long-suffering parents to make emergency stops along the highway so I could to pick up road kills. And friends who knew about my hobby passed along animals they had shot—this was Texas, after all, where guns were as plentiful as the "varmints" they targeted.

Our rental house featured a small bar off the family room. The mounted heads of two bucks hung from the wall, pre-conditioning the room as a natural history museum. So that's what I turned it into. I built an airtight storage case, like the ones pictured in Booth's *Biology: The Story of Life*, for my mammal specimens. I displayed my rock and shell collections, and I kept pet black-window spiders and copperhead snakes. My parents must have regretted their early encouragement of my passions when dozens of tiny black-window spider babies escaped from their mother's cage into the family room, and when I prepared road-killed skunks as study skins. But in general I think they were proud of my pursuits, for whenever we had company they showcased my museum.

AT ONE POINT MY interest in mammals got me into trouble. My last two years of high school were spent at Ozark Academy,[11] an Adventist boarding school in Gentry, Arkansas. One day a couple of my friends hiked to a nearby cave where they found a bat. Knowing my interests, they put the tiny animal in the baked bean can they had emptied for lunch. They carried the canned bat back to my dorm room, where they let it free. The poor little animal, now coated with bean juice, tried to fly but could not sustain flight. It dropped to the floor and when I tried to pick it up, it bit my finger and drew blood. Feeling bad for it, I quickly put it out of its misery, and tossed the little corpse out the dorm window. I now regret not finding some way to clean it off and set it free.

The next day one of the dormitory deans heard about my misadventure, reminded me that bats carry rabies, and told me the bat needed to be sent to the state lab for rabies testing. I found the corpse, which by this time had started to decompose. We sent it to the lab, but it was too far gone for proper testing. I was told I needed to undergo a series of rabies shots just in case the bat had been rabid.

I started a long-distance call home that day with a matter-of-fact "Hi Mom—I might be dead in a few days." The greeting didn't set well. When Mom finally calmed down I explained the situation and told her I planned

---

10. Davis, *The Mammals of Texas*. My copy of Davis' book, which now shows much wear and tear, was an important reference for me during those early years of collecting.

11. Now "Ozark Adventist Academy."

to undergo a series of rabies shots at the local doctor's office. I learned from the experience that there are good ways and not so good ways to express unpleasant news to one's parents.

People told me that rabies shots were terribly painful. So it was with a sense of dread—I hated shots—that I visited Dr. Weaver's office in Gentry to begin inoculations. Mercifully, the dread was worse than the reality. Over the next couple weeks I was subjected to a series of fourteen injections around the navel. Fortunately, the tiny sub-cutaneous needles barely hurt. They were much easier to endure than shots in the arm.

Knowing what I know now, it's remarkable I did not succumb to some dread disease from all the animals I had skinned and stuffed. Who knows whether the dead creatures I scraped off the roads were infected with the rabies virus or other debilitating microbes? I never worried about those things back then. Fortunately, I remained healthy despite my cavalier disregard of safety.

Ozark Academy, like many Adventist secondary schools, sought to protect students from the many forms of evil Ellen White had warned against, especially those of the sexual kind. Thus, girls were to wear dresses at all times, except when a dress would not be "modest"; dresses could not be too short or too low-cut; no jewelry of any kind could be worn; shorts were not to be worn on campus; boys were not to use the sidewalk in front of the girls' dormitory, and girls were not to use the walk in front of the boys' dormitory; girls and boys could not enter the same door of the cafeteria, nor could they sit together during church; girlfriends and boyfriends who stood around talking after meals risked being "social bound," a punishment that involved even further restrictions.

During my junior year I was smitten by Linda. She was a quiet, beautiful girl. Printed under her senior picture in the annual were the words, "Softly, smoothly, sweetly she moves through each day"—an apt description of her gentle and unobtrusive persona. Her delightful roommate, Sherry, by contrast, was a wonderfully fun-loving person who liked to tease. "I can find more joy in a day than some folks find in a year," was printed beneath her photo. She called me "lil' Hayward" and took pleasure in my attention to her roommate.

One day toward the end of the school year, Sherry asked a friend to take a photo of the three of us. Sherry led us down to the "Ozark Academy" sign by the main road. I was uncomfortable moving away from the main part of campus with two pretty girls. What if a faculty member saw us? Was this against the rules? I didn't know. What I did know was that I didn't want to get social bound again—that had happened to Linda and me a few weeks before. We had spent too long chatting outside the cafeteria after lunch.

When we arrived at the sign Sherry lined the three of us up in the foreground with me in the middle. "Okay, lil' Hayward, put your arms around us!"

At seventeen, I had only dreamed of putting my arms around a girl. Heaven knows I'd wanted to. I was simply too shy. Linda was the first girl I had ever dated, and given all the campus prohibitions, there was little opportunity to learn how to express affection. Sherry—ever the instigator—helped my timid but desirous left arm to reach around Linda. This provided courage for my right arm to reach around Sherry.

I will never forget the euphoria of that fleeting moment as the picture was snapped. The warm press of two lovely girls—me sandwiched between, my arms reaching round them—was total bliss. I wished it could have lasted forever.

We made it back to the main campus without a problem. I tried my best to retain that warm sensation the rest of the day, but it faded into pleasant memory with the setting sun. Over a half century later, however, I still smile each time I glance at that picture.

DURING MY JUNIOR YEAR at Ozark, trouble was brewing. In May 1966, our dormitory dean informed us about a recent faculty meeting. Some of the Adventist village folk were complaining about student conduct. They said most of the dorm students were smoking, contraband radios were blaring from the dorm on Sabbath, and couples were "making out" down at the church grounds after services. The grossly exaggerated accusations meant that students were going to be placed on a tighter leash than they already were at the highly conservative institution.[12]

A member of this right-wing group was one of our own faculty members, Mr. Johnston (not his real name), a person of slight build, wavy hair, and the intense eyes of someone who believes they know The Truth. I never had a class from him, but those who did said all he talked about were Ellen White's writings.

One Sabbath afternoon I helped prepare religious literature for distribution. Johnston directed the operation. He took the opportunity to indoctrinate us about the "Time of the End" and what we should be doing to prepare. I was about as earnest and sincere an Adventist kid as possible, but I realized there was something wrong with this man.

Recently, a well-known evangelist by the name of Dick Barron had held "week of prayer" meetings at Ozark Academy. At one of the meetings

12. JLH to parents, May 5, 1966.

Barron related the story of what he believed was his miraculous healing from cancer. In the course of telling the story, he mentioned all the prescription drugs he had taken to lessen the unbearable pain associated with his illness.

Johnston told Linda that it was because of sin in Dick Barron's life that he contracted cancer in the first place, and that by taking the meds he was prescribed he had continued his sinful ways. Linda brought up the biblical story of Job who suffered greatly, but whom God declared blameless. Johnston retorted that there didn't need to be a Job in every generation. Linda then told Johnston that God must have healed the evangelist because he was now cancer free. Johnston replied that because the disease had destroyed one of his vertebrae, he wasn't healed; that if God had healed him, he would have replaced the missing bone.[13]

Before his "conversion" experience, Johnston had been an avid photographer. But he had stored away all his expensive photographic gear because pictures were sinful. He refused to sell the gear, however, because he didn't want anyone else to sin.

Johnston was fired at the end of the 1966–1967 year. Ozark Academy was a conservative school, but Johnston had crossed the administration's line into fanaticism. I don't know what he did after that for work. It was rumored, however, that his wife later died because Johnston would not seek medical attention for her when her pregnancy went bad—he took Ellen White's mid-nineteenth-century statement that one should never "dishonor God by applying to earthly physicians"[14] as applicable in the twentieth century. Johnston himself later died from complications from a ladder fall. Sadly, his legacy only confirmed my conviction that fanaticism not only makes one appear odd, but may ultimately lead to one's premature demise.

Seniors at the academy were required to take a "Youth Guidance" course during their final semester. It was taught by the religion teacher, Orlin R. McLean, an earnest fellow, but someone with whom I never felt close. One time he called me to his office to ask if I had looked on someone's paper during an exam. I was mortified. Integrity was and remains of highest priority to me, and cheating was something I had never even thought to do. But I don't know that he believed my denial. The fact that a teacher had questioned

---

13. JLH to parents, May 5, 1966.

14. Ellen G. White, "To Those Who Are Receiving the Seal of the Living God." In 1849, when the "applying to earthly physicians" statement was written, there may have been good reason to avoid the medical establishment. Later in life White strongly supported the work of physicians.

my integrity was highly embarrassing to me. As a result, I have always been extremely careful to make sure I had good evidence before questioning the integrity of any of my own students.

McLean's Youth Guidance course featured topics designed to make us successful, honorable citizens, and to keep us on life-long path of Adventist belief and practice. When it came to the topic of sexuality, I recall him rhapsodizing that one of the most beautiful things about marriage was sexual intercourse, but that we needed to reserve that pleasure for marriage alone. He considered holding hands a dangerous first step toward that pleasure, one far too premature for high school students. During night time social gatherings he always kept his six D-cell flashlight ready to catch touching hands lest adolescent hormones push things too far along that trajectory.

A requirement of Youth Guidance was to write a term paper on our chosen occupation. I typed mine, "Biology as an Occupation," on the old Royal typewriter Dad used to own. Under the gender-biased subheading "The Biologist—His History and Future" I parroted Ellen White and Ernest Booth: "Adam was the world's first biologist and probably its greatest . . . It was his privilege to study nature in its perfect state, just as it had come from the hands of the Creator, untarnished by the curse of sin as it is today."[15]

It would not be long, however, before I would begin to wonder about the meaning of "perfect" and "the curse of sin" relative to living things. The more I learned about life, the less helpful these concepts would become. But I was an eighteen-year-old high school fundamentalist who hadn't thought deeply about sin, perfection—or really much of anything.

Another requirement of Youth Guidance at Ozark was completion of a correspondence course called "Prophetic Guidance in the Advent Movement." We worked through twenty-four lessons based on the life and writings of Ellen G. White. The textbook was *The Spirit of Prophecy Treasure Chest: An Advent Source Collection of Materials Relating to the Gift of Prophecy in the Remnant Church and the Life and Ministry of Ellen G. White*. The cover contained a little pen-and-ink drawing of a man holding a lantern above an open treasure chest he had just dug up from what appeared to be the floor of a cave. On the inside cover was "A Message to You from Sister White": "We are homeward bound," she began. "A little longer, and the strife will be over. May we who stand in the heat of the conflict, ever keep before us a vision of things unseen"—not the most prescient or encouraging remark for adolescents on the threshold of college, love, marriage, and a

---

15. James L. Hayward, "The Biologist—His History and Future."

career, especially from someone who had been moldering in the grave for fifty years.¹⁶

The Spirit of Prophecy Treasure Chest featured a series of seventy short, hagiographic articles by church leaders, White Estate officials, and other endorsers of White's "prophetic gift." They described her visions of the future which allegedly had come true, characterized her use of literary sources, lauded the uniqueness of what she wrote, depicted the work of the White Trustees and Estate, and recalled what the prophet was like as a person. A facsimile of her handwriting was included, along with excerpts from her books. Many of the articles were followed by the initials "A.L.W."— for Arthur L. White, secretary of the Ellen G. White Estate, Ellen's grandson, and burnisher-in-chief of her reputation. The book must have been his creation, although no one was listed on the title page as editor.

Following successful completion of the twenty-four lessons, I was awarded a certificate signed by Arthur White stating that I had "satisfactorily completed" the course.¹⁷

MUSIC HAS ALWAYS BEEN a big deal to Adventists. Few things can split an Adventist congregation more quickly than disagreements over the type of music and the instruments used at worship services. Ellen White weighed in on this topic multiple times, noting, for example, that "No one who has an indwelling Saviour will dishonor Him before others by producing strains from a musical instrument which call the mind from God and Heaven to light and trifling things."¹⁸

Steve, one of my senior classmates at Ozark, played the electric guitar. In the 1960s electric guitars were suspect; the Beatles, Rolling Stones, and other rock groups played them as extensions of their bodies. The whining, screeching, and thumping sounds they produced were unique, wild, and sensed all the way to one's bones. They were perfectly suited for '60s rock-and-roll, and they had taken some of the heat reserved in earlier days for the saxophone.¹⁹

---

16. Ellen G. White Estate, *The Spirit of Prophecy Treasure Chest*. Ellen White died in 1915.

17. My certificate from the Prophetic Guidance in the Advent Movement: A Seventh-day Adventist Correspondence Course states: "This is to certify that James Hayward has satisfactorily completed the twenty-four lessons of the Prophetic Guidance Course on the life and writings of Ellen G. White. Issued at Glendale California, April 5, 1967. Arthur L. White, Ellen G. White Publications, Ione Lawrance, Instructor."

18. White, *Testimonies for the Church*, Volume one, 510.

19. Segell, *The Devil's Horn*. The saxophone was banned in Japan, and in 1903 Pope Pius X condemned it for its capacity to foment "disgust or scandal."

One day word got around the dorms, surreptitiously, that Steve was going to play his version of "Wipe Out," a fast-paced, pulsating instrumental first recorded in 1963 by "The Surfaris," and later rendered by the famous "Ventures." Surfing was wildly popular during the 1960s and "wipe out" referred to the tumble taken by an out-of-control surfer.

Dozens of us heard about the plan and moved quietly, but with eager anticipation, to an outdoor amphitheater between the girls' and boys' dorms. Steve had set up his amplifier and speakers. The excitement was palpable. What would happen? Would the deans be all over Steve as soon as he played the first few bars? Would he be kicked out of school for such an act? Would *we* be disciplined for attending the one-song concert?

Steve began to play. Everyone held their breath. I think our dormitory dean may have been present, but no one tried to stop Steve. He made it through to the end to an enthusiastic round of applause.

I never heard if Steve was disciplined for this breach of official Adventist campus etiquette, but those of us who attended that day's impromptu concert enjoyed three minutes of release from the otherwise staid atmosphere of Ozark Academy.

DURING THE LAST SEMESTER of my senior year I was one of twenty Ozark students selected as delegates to attend a regional Bible Conference at the Flaming Arrow YMCA Camp in Kerr County, Texas. This was to be a five-day affair, including one travel day each way. We left Ozark at 3:30 a.m. on Wednesday, April 19, 1967, and we arrived in time for the evening meeting.[20]

Most of the meetings involved the entire student assemblage, but Sabbath afternoon we divided into discussion groups consisting of just a few students each. Ours was located in a small tent. There were not enough chairs to go around, so I sat on a folded mattress at the sidelines of the discussion. An older gentleman walked in late and joined me on the mattress. I looked over and saw that it was Arthur L. White, Ellen White's grandson. He was sixty years old, but he seemed much older. Adventist ministers had a way, at least back then, of appearing more ancient than they really were. They talked in an unctuous, concerned manner, all the while staring deeply into your eyes as if they understood your deepest longings and concerns. They typically dressed in dark suits, white shirts, and ties. I don't recall how Arthur was dressed that day, but he was very pleasant, asked my name, and of course, knew Dad.

Eleven years earlier, when Dad pastored in historic New Bedford, Massachusetts, one of Arthur's older twin brothers—Henry or Herbert, I

20. JLH to parents, March 14, 1967 and April 17, 1967.

don't recall which—came to visit our church. It must have been on a Sunday that we followed him to an outdoor location where we watched him plant a small tree. He explained that he would give the tree a good start by applying "Grandma's dressing." Grandma's dressing was Ellen White's recipe for mulch. Her grandson mixed up the mulch with just the right proportions of decaying leaves, manure, soil, sand, etc., carefully placed the tree in the hole that had been prepared for it, and added the dressing.[21] Our lesson that day was that Sister White's inspired wisdom extended even to the composition of mulch. I'm sure we expected that little tree to grow more vigorously than any other little tree in New Bedford.

I WAS ATTENDING "CAMP meeting" in Keene, Texas, home of Southwestern Union College. I knew I would be headed to this campus for college, so I decided to check out the biology building. The creaky old place was unlocked so I walked in. I wandered the halls and found an open biology lab. Nobody was around, so I snuck into an adjacent storage room. The shelves were filled with jars of pickled marine invertebrates, frogs, and other curiosities. I was in my element. I had no idea that, before long, I would be responsible for curating these very same specimens.

---

21. A description of the use of "Grandma's dressing" is found in Ellen G. White, *Selected Messages*, Book 3, 328. Under the heading "Specific Light on Gardening" and "Ellen G. White Instructed in Planting Fruit Trees," an excerpt from a 1907 letter of White's is printed: "The man of whom we purchased our peach trees told me that he would be pleased to have me observe the way they were planted. I then asked him to let me show him how it had been represented in the night season [a divinely inspired dream] that they should be planted. I ordered my hired man to dig a deep cavity in the ground, then put in rich dirt, then stones, then rich dirt. After this he put in layers of earth and dressing until the hole was filled. I told the nursery man that I had planted in this way in the rocky soil in America. . . He said to me, 'You need no lesson from me to teach you how to plant the trees.'"

3

Young Creationist

"The trick of reason is to get the imagination to seize the actual world—if only from time to time."

—Annie Dillard[1]

I stepped off the road and descended the slope to the nearly dry Paluxy River bed near Glen Rose, Texas. The usually peaceful watercourse and riparian woodland was buzzing with activity on this October 1969 afternoon. A crew, directed by the Reverend Stanley E. Taylor from Peoria, Illinois, was filming a fossilized dinosaur trackway alongside a series of depressions Taylor imagined to be human footprints pressed into the limestone riverbed. Taylor believed his film would provide proof that dinosaurs and humans walked the earth together.

The series of depressions running beside the dinosaur trackway indeed seemed spaced as though made by a human. As I looked more closely, however, I observed that the film crew had painted each depression with oil in the shape of a human foot. The oil stains gave the illusion the depressions had more of a human shape than they really did. Minus the oil, the hollows appeared to be either heavily eroded dinosaur tracks, or craters in the limestone carved by swirling eddies. I was a conservative creationist, but I

---

1. Dillard, *An American Childhood*, 20.

was deeply skeptical of Taylor's interpretation—and put off by what seemed to be his lack of integrity. Taylor's film, "Footprints in Stone," would become a creationist classic.[2]

WHEN TAYLOR WAS MAKING his film, I was a junior biology major at Southwestern Union College located about thirty miles from the dinosaur trackways. It was a thrill to be close to such an amazing but still undeveloped fossil site. Not only was it a great place to spend a free afternoon, but it also got me thinking more about dinosaurs and earth history. Ernest Booth's *Biology, the Story of Life*, my high school text, had little to say about dinosaurs, except that they "roamed the earth before the Flood, some four thousand years ago." And because, according to Booth, humans were created about six thousand years ago, it seemed reasonable to me that, despite the questionable Paluxy River evidence, trackways of dinosaurs and humans could occur together.[3]

Today the Paluxy River dinosaur trackways are the focal point of Dinosaur Valley State Park, operated by the Texas Parks and Wildlife Department. When water in the river is low, trackways of three-toad *Acrocanthosaurus* dinosaurs are easy to see in the limestone. The thirty-foot long theropods, now thought to be close cousins of our modern birds, hunted on their hind legs just like their considerably larger *T. rex* relatives. They left their footprints while walking through firm, limy, mud along an ancient seashore. The mud hardened into limestone and was covered by different sediment which eventually formed shale. The river eroded away the soft shale, revealing the beautifully exposed dinosaur trackways. In addition to the more common theropod tracks, one can see wash-tub-sized tracks made by an enormous sauropod.[4]

Roland T. Bird, a vertebrate paleontologist with New York City's American Museum of Natural History, brought these tracks to the public's

---

2. The original "Footprints in Stone," produced by Taylor in 1972, is no longer available. An updated "Footprints in Stone: Forbidden History II" was released in 2014 by Restoring Genesis Ministries. The organization continues to promote the view that the "human" tracks Taylor found were genuine. At least two creationist investigators, however, reexamined Taylor's presumed human tracks and determined they were not of human origin (see Notes 35 and 36 below). A website accompanying the 2014 film notes that "pressure" resulting from these reexaminations "was enough to cause Paul Taylor, son of Stanley Taylor and Head of Films for Christ, to pull the [original 1972] movie 'Footprints in Stone' out of circulation" (Footprints in Stone, "The Controversy").

3. Booth, *Biology, the Story of Life*, 182. On page 1 of his text, after referring to the creation of Adam and Eve, Booth refers to "the almost six thousand years of time that have elapsed since Creation Week."

4. Farlow et al., "Dinosaur Tracksites of the Paluxy River Valley."

attention back in the 1930s. At the end of a fossil-hunting season in the American Southwest, Bird stopped at an Native American trading post in Gallup, New Mexico, where he spotted a set of fifteen-inch long, human-like footprints in limestone displayed in the storefront window. He could scarcely believe his eyes. He entered the store and inspected the prints more closely, which convinced him the tracks were fake. The clerk told him, however, that the trading post owner had a dinosaur track collected from the same locality as the "human tracks." This piqued Bird's interest. Unlike the "human tracks," the dinosaur track exhibited all the features of a real fossil footprint. Both types of tracks, he was told, came from the Paluxy River bed.

After visiting the Paluxy tracks himself, Bird published an article about his experience in the May 1939 issue of *Natural History* magazine.[5] His article contained photographs of the dinosaur trackway, but also, as a point of interest, a photo of the "human tracks" he had seen in the New Mexico store window. The article captured the attention of many people, especially creationists.

One such creationist was Clifford Burdick, a self-styled, Seventh-day Adventist consulting geologist who had inflated his educational credentials, made untrustworthy claims about geology and paleontology, and taken part in quixotic expeditions to search for Noah's Ark in the Mount Ararat region of Turkey.[6] It was a 1958 article by Burdick in the Adventist magazine, *Signs of the Times*, that had attracted the interest of Reverend Taylor, the filmmaker, in the dinosaur and supposed human tracks of the Paluxy River.[7]

WHEN I ARRIVED AS a freshman at Southwestern Union College in 1967, Dexter Beary, chair of the science division, learned of my interest in natural history and hired me to take responsibility for the museum. The museum, a disorganized collection of poorly tended specimens, was located in the basement of Scales Hall, the new science building. I got busy replenishing formalin in the jars, sprucing up the unfinished basement room, and organizing the collection. I had my own desk, which provided a quiet place to study when I wasn't clocked in. I liked the location, isolated as it was from the bustle in the rest of the building.

I soon convinced Beary we needed a mammal collection, so he provided me with funds to build an airtight cabinet for specimens. My woodworking

---

5. Bird, "Thunder in His Footsteps," 254–61.

6. Numbers, *The Creationists*, 141, 287–88, 291–93, 478–79, note 8; Arthur V. Chadwick, "Precambrian Pollen in the Grand Canyon," 7–12; Burdick, "Ararat," 5–12.

7. Burdick, "Were the First Americans Giants?" 23–24; Numbers, *The Creationists*, 293.

skills came in handy, and soon we had an attractive, new cabinet which I had modeled after the Lane cabinets used in many large museums. I furnished the cabinet with my personal collection, and I was able to add to the assemblage from time to time as specimens became available.

Field trips highlighted my experience at Southwestern. In November 1968, for example, Beary took our Invertebrate Zoology class to the Texas coast where we saw Portuguese man-o-wars, strange, floating, jelly-like creatures, each of which appears to be an individual, but in reality is a colony of animals with different functions. We also learned about oysters and their appeal to the palates of the locals. Our guide that day pried one open, scooped out the contents, and swallowed the slimy thing live and whole. But it was the small flock of whooping cranes feeding on their wintering grounds at Aransas National Wildlife Refuge that for me was the highlight of the trip. Fewer than fifty of these birds were alive in the wild at the time.[8]

On another partial-day trip we visited a stretch of privately-owned land between Dallas and Fort Worth where fossil shark's teeth littered the ground surface. Shark's teeth are relatively common in ancient marine sediments because, unlike the soft cartilaginous skeletons of sharks, their teeth were very hard and resistant to destruction. Within a few minutes, I discovered several beautiful specimens of the shiny, dark brown, sharply serrated fossils which had eroded out of the local Cretaceous strata.

Our most exciting trip, however, was to Acapulco, Mexico in January 1969. We stayed at an American doctor's family's home and enjoyed the most delicious fruits and tortillas I had ever tasted. We took an excursion to a forested region forty miles south of town where we hiked to a pond and saw northern jacanas, polyandrous birds with enormously long toes which allow them to walk on lily pads. It was beastly hot that day and I was desperate for something to drink. We came to a small store, and the only drink available was Pepsi Cola. I was twenty years old and had never sipped a caffeinated drink—Ellen White had warned against the sin of imbibing caffeinated beverages.[9] It didn't take me long, however, to decide which was the lesser of two evils: collapsing from dehydration or downing an ice-cold Pepsi.

THE DECADE OF THE 1960S, when I started college, was an important one for creationists. In February 1961, two fundamentalist academics, John C. Whitcomb, Jr., an Old Testament biblical scholar, and Henry M. Morris, a hydrological engineer, published *The Genesis Flood*. Their book was written to counter arguments made in 1954 by evangelical philosopher and

---

8. Nedelman et al., "The Statistical Demography of Whooping Cranes," 1401–11.
9. White, *Counsels on Diet and Foods*, 419–31.

theologian Bernard Ramm. His book, *The Christian View of Science and Scripture*, was highly critical of George McCready Price, the Seventh-day Adventist architect of twentieth-century flood geology.[10] Ramm argued that the Bible should not be read as a scientific document, that the days of creation were symbolic, and that the flood story could not account for the world's geological evidence.[11] Whitcomb and Morris were disturbed by Ramm's approach to scripture, believing he had sold out to evolutionary uniformitarianism.[12] *The Genesis Flood* was an instant hit among fundamentalists, and now five decades later it remains in print.

I purchased the ninth printing of Whitcomb and Morris's *The Genesis Flood*. As trained academicians, Whitcomb and Morris had produced a text with all the accouterments of a scholarly work: technical jargon, detailed footnotes, meticulous referencing, subheadings, professionally prepared figures, and a comprehensive index. Arguments for a universal flood accompanied detailed discussions which explained how the size of the ark was adequate to house representatives of all the "created kinds"[13] of land-living animals, how God miraculously redistributed organisms after the Flood, and how evidence from geology is consistent with belief in a universal flood. Arguments against the notion of an evolutionary progression of fossils in the geologic column reflected those of Price, whose works I was beginning to read as well. A foreword by Christian geologist John C. McCampbell, a geology professor at the University of Southwestern Louisiana, stated that "God has given us the Bible not only to guide our faith but also to provide a framework of revelation within which to interpret the mysteries of the earth's origin and destiny." I underlined these words which fit comfortably within my fundamentalist mindset.[14]

Of particular interest to me in the book were photographs by Clifford Burdick of purported fossil human footprints from the Paluxy River. The first figure showed "Contemporaneous Footprints of Man and Dinosaur," with a legend stating that

> Geologists have rejected this evidence, however, preferring to believe that the human footprints were carved by some modern artist, while at the same time accepting the dinosaur prints as

10. Ramm, *The Christian View of Science and Scripture*, 125–26, 170 (note 12).
11. Ramm, 43–85, 149–56, 119–78.
12. Numbers, *The Creationists*, 211–17.
13. Young-age creationists use the term "created kinds," or "baramins," to refer to the types of organisms that appeared during "creation week." See Marsh, *Evolution, Creation, and Science*, 174–75.
14. Whitcomb and Morris, *The Genesis Flood*, xv.

genuine. If anything, the dinosaur prints look more 'artificial' than the human, but the genuineness of neither would be questioned at all were it not for the geologically sacrosanct evolutionary time-scale.[15]

Despite my general approval of Whitcomb and Morris' thesis, I remained skeptical of their claim. I knew that other creationists had sectioned tracks like these from the Paluxy River limestone and discovered that the sedimentary layers ended "abruptly at the edge of the track, indicating that they are not the result of a foot stepping into soft mud but are produced by carving." During the Great Depression local residents sometimes carved artificial tracks out of the limestone as a source of income.[16]

A second important development among creationists was the formation of the Creation Research Society in 1963. Ten creationists with advanced degrees in science served as founding members. After considerable haggling, a statement of belief consisting of four items was adopted. All members had to accept 1) the Bible as the historically and scientifically accurate Word of God, 2) a literal Creation week as described in Genesis, 3) the historicity of the Genesis flood, and 4) acceptance of Jesus Christ as the Savior of all mankind. Voting membership was restricted to holders of graduate degrees in science, but anyone who subscribed to the four tenets could join as a non-voting member.[17]

I found the concept of a creationist society appealing and applied for membership. My application was soon approved, and I began receiving the *Creation Research Society Quarterly*. During the two or three years I was a member, articles in the *Quarterly* reported, among other things, that all stars were created at a single time in the past and have remained virtually unchanged,[18] purportedly half billion-year-old Cambrian rocks contained sandal-shod human footprints embedded with trilobites,[19] and the second law of thermodynamics falsified the theory of evolution.[20] Even my elementary understanding of science made me question these claims.

---

15. Whitcomb and Morris, *The Genesis Flood*, 174–75.
16. Neufeld, "Dinosaur Tracks and Giant Men," 64–76.
17. Numbers, *The Creationists*, 239–67.
18. Whitcomb, "The Creation of Heavens and the Earth," 69–74.
19. Cook, "William J. Meister Discovery of Human Footprint," 97; Meister, "Discovery of Trilobite Fossils in Shod Footprint," 97–102.
20. Williams, "A Simplified Explanation of the First and Second Laws of Thermodynamics," 138–47.

I remained a staunch defender of young-age creationism and continued to believe in a worldwide flood, but I was beginning to appreciate the importance of physical evidence as a control on the limits of belief.

Two Adventist-published books appropriated from my dad's library addressed the history of earth and life. The first was George McCready Price's *Genesis Vindicated*, published in 1941. This book was a synopsis of views presented in earlier works in which Price criticized the science and philosophy of evolutionists, discussed the notion of "species," rejected uniformitarian geology, and jettisoned any thought of a former "ice age." He cast his arguments as a defense of the seventh-day Sabbath. "The Sabbath was ordained for much more than a rest day," he wrote. "It was planned by God for the express purpose of keeping ever before us the profoundly important truth that the present-day processes of nature are *not* those of the original creation." The Sabbath, he asserted, "is in its very essence a perpetual protest against any ... philosophy as that of evolution, which is the 'false science' referred to" by Ellen G. White in her book, *The Great Controversy*.[21]

The second book I appropriated from Dad was Harold W. Clark's *Genes and Genesis*, published in 1940, and selected as the "Ministerial Reading Course Selection for 1941 by the Ministerial Association of Seventh-day Adventists." Clark, one of Price's former students, was trained as a biologist and defended young-age creationism and flood geology. *Genes and Genesis* explained the basic principles of genetics as understood during the first third of the twentieth century. From these principles, Clark made a case for the acceptance of limited amounts of change in organisms. "The survival of the fittest is a real phenomenon every field naturalist must reckon with," he opined. "The theory of 'divergent evolution' ... is apparently a valid one with actually observable limits. ... A thoughtful consideration of the problems of distribution of plants and animals emphasizes the reality of the struggle for existence, the survival of the fittest, and natural selection."[22] I found Clark's *rapprochement* with limited aspects of evolutionary theory refreshing, albeit a bit surprising, given the strident tone against the theory displayed by other creationists both inside and outside of Adventism. I was so intrigued by his book that I chose to review it for my freshman composition course. It may

---

21. Price, *Genesis Vindicated*, 7–75 (science and philosophy), 159–201 (species), 202–58 (geology), 259–84 (ice age), 285–309 (Sabbath). Direct quotations taken from pages 9 and 307.

22. Clark, *Genes and Genesis*, 3, 50, 56, 58.

have been the first time I had read anything positive about natural selection and evolution from a creationist viewpoint.[23]

A third book that influenced me during this time was *Meaning in Nature* by Richard M. Ritland. He had been my dad's mammalogy teacher at Atlantic Union College, and was now director of the church's Geoscience Research Institute. When I read about the availability of his work in preliminary format, I ordered a copy. *Meaning in Nature* was especially engaging, for it provided a more positive approach to the history of earth and life than I had read from other creationists. Instead of criticizing the views of evolutionists, Ritland's book provided a cautious, philosophical approach, one that focused on evidence for design at the fundamental levels of life. The concluding sentence of the final chapter gave space for an honest search of reality, with Ritland grandly asserting that "the quest for truth is a quest for the Infinite."[24]

My reading of these and other works stimulated my thinking about the past and present. As I learned more about life, I came to appreciate both the limitations and strengths of science as an approach to truth. I also began to appreciate the considerable diversity of views among creationists about what life was like in the past and how it had changed. Price, Clark, and Ritland all agreed that life had been created, but they approached the topic from very different perspectives.

DURING THE SUMMER OF 1968, two other Southwestern Union College students and I purchased a second-hand Ford Econoline van and headed to California's Plumas National Forest to work with its Blister Rust Control program. Blister rust is a fungus that kills white pine trees, a species of primary economic importance to western loggers. Blister rust exhibits a complex life cycle involving currant and gooseberry bushes, which serve as intermediate hosts for the fungus. Each summer the Forest Service posted the locations of areas in the forest to be cleared of currants and gooseberries. We studied the postings, checked out the areas, submitted bids to the Forest Service, and hoped our bids would be competitive and selected.[25]

Our bids earned us four large lots. On each lot we established a primitive campsite from which we spread out into the surrounding forest. With

---

23. Hayward, "Genes and Genesis, by Harold W. Clark."

24. Ritland, *Meaning in Nature*, 254. The 1966 edition of Ritland's book was a preliminary version. It was republished in final form as *A Search for Meaning in Nature: A New Look at Creation and Evolution*.

25. For a description of the U.S. Forest Service control program, see Benedict, *History of White Pine Blister Rust Control—A Personal Account*.

string, we marked out lanes through the lots to organize our efforts. We used a claw mattock to pry currants and gooseberries from the ground in the same way one would use a much smaller claw hammer to pry nails from a board. At the end of each week, after crawling through the brush, we were filthy and looked forward to hot showers and a break from the routine. A kind Adventist family in the little town of Quincy allowed us to bunk at their place each weekend. We attended church with them every Sabbath, and afterward enjoyed a potluck lunch.

We students from Texas were not the only weekend visitors to Quincy. A graduate student, Leonard Brand, also benefited from the hospitality. An intelligent and serious person with a dry sense of humor, Brand was a doctoral candidate at Cornell University. His dissertation project involved a comparative study of the vocalizations and behaviors of California chipmunks.[26] I was excited to find another person interested in mammals. In addition, Leonard was a fellow creationist. Following completion of his doctorate, he would give lie to the criticism that young-age creationists never publish credible work. In addition to his creationist writings, he has authored numerous articles on his paleontological research in the peer reviewed, scientific literature.[27] He remained active in research throughout his career and has become one of the Adventism's most respected young-age creationist apologists.

MY SOPHOMORE YEAR AT Southwestern Union College, I studied general physics. I was apprehensive about the course because my math skills were pathetically inadequate—I'd taken only algebra I and geometry in high school, and freshman college algebra and trigonometry had been torture, given my inadequate background.

Our physics instructor was Samuel Myers, a Jew by heritage and an engineer by trade. Before becoming a Seventh-day Adventist, he had worked for the California aerospace industry. He was an outstanding teacher, highly organized, with lucid lectures and practical illustrations from the everyday

---

26. Brand, "Vocalizations and Behavior of the Chipmunks (Genus *Eutamias*) in California."

27. For example, see the following examples of papers in peer-reviewed journals by Brand: "Fossil Whale Preservation Implies High Diatom Accumulation Rate," 165–68; "The Vocal Repertoire of Chipmunks (Genus *Eutamias*) in California," 319–35; "Field and Laboratory Studies on the Coconino Sandstone (Permian) Vertebrate Footprints and Their Paleoecological Implications," 25–38; "Fossil Vertebrate Footprints in the Coconino Sandstone (Permian) of Northern Arizona: Evidence of Underwater Origin," 668–70; "Lithistid Sponge-Microbial Reef-building Communities Construct Laminated, Upper Cambrian (Furongian) 'Stromatolites,'" 358–70 (with first author Ken Coulson).

world. His office was as tidy as his crewcut—pen and paper were perfectly aligned on his desk. He also was one of the nicest people I knew.

Myer's lecture on oscillatory motion continues to stand out as exceptional a half century later. For me it was inspirational and transformational. The algebraic model he presented, which described the phenomenon, was a thing of beauty. It was the first time I visualized both the esthetics and utility of mathematics. Little did I know that many years later my research in behavioral ecology would attract the interest of mathematical ecologists. They would become my collaborators and use data I collected to develop elegant mathematical models which accurately predict the behavior of wild animals in time and space.

During the second semester, Myers required that we each carry out an independent research project. We wrote a formal proposal, including a tentative schedule, and provided regular, formal progress reports. I took great interest in this assignment, which gave me my first taste of research.

For my project I chose to create a physical and a mathematical model of upright floating trees. This arcane-sounding idea was motivated by an article entitled "A Preliminary Report on the Carboniferous of Nova Scotia" by Harold G. Coffin, a young-age creationist and staff scientist employed by the Adventist Church's Geoscience Research Institute.[28]

Coffin had studied multiple "forests" of upright fossil trees preserved one atop another in the Carboniferous strata of Nova Scotia. These repeated layers of upright trees were usually interpreted as evidence for the growth of successive forests over a very long period of time. Coffin, by contrast, hypothesized that the trees had floated into position during the short time interval of the Genesis flood. I was intrigued by this idea. And because Coffin had not done any modeling to show how trees could float upright, I selected this problem as the basis of my physics project.[29]

For the physical model of a tree, I used a foot-long Plexiglas tube fitted with a mass that I could slide up and down inside the tube. This model allowed me to determine the relationship between the center of gravity and upright floatation. Tick marks along the side of the tube allowed me to determine the distance the mass was from the ends of the tube. By sliding the mass up and down the tube and measuring the angle of the tilt of the "trunk" when placed in a tank of water, I was able to develop a simple algebraic equation that described the conditions necessary for upright floatation.

The introduction of my final report noted that

---

28. Coffin, "A Preliminary Report on the Carboniferous of Nova Scotia"; Coffin, "Research on the Classic Joggins Petrified Trees," 35–44, 70.

29. Coffin, "A Preliminary Report on the Carboniferous of Nova Scotia."

> No less than 85 ... stratified layers are present [in the Carboniferous strata] leading uniformitarians to believe there were at least 85 repeated rises and falls of the land. This would require eons of time. A geological time period as this cannot be accepted by creationists who believe the earth was created only several thousand years ago... [They believe] that the tidal action responsible for this sequential deposition of strata can be attributed to the alternately advancing and retreating waters of the Noachian Flood of Genesis 7 and 8.

My data and mathematical model suggested, in agreement with Coffin, that the fossil trees in Nova Scotia could have floated upright if they contained an extensive root system to which soil attached, making them bottom-heavy.[30]

Rereading my report a half century later, I see that the project was well planned, carefully executed, and thoughtfully reported. Completion of the project was an important first step in my development as a research scientist. Myers awarded me with a top grade on the project, as well as in the course. I was excited and encouraged. A young-age creationist approach to science seemed to hold promise for me.

ONE DAY DEXTER BEARY asked if I would be willing to have my picture taken for inclusion in a new version of Ellen G. White's *Steps to Christ*. This book, originally published in 1892, has come out in more editions than any other of Ellen White's many books. The new version was targeted toward young people and would feature photos of students engaged in a variety of activities. Gene Haas, secretary of the Young People's Missionary Volunteer Department of the Adventists' Southwestern Union Conference, was looking for willing subjects, and I told Beary I would help.

Haas wanted to illustrate a person's attachment to a sinful past. He thought the best way to do this would be a photograph of me sitting with a human skeleton. While I was seated, Haas placed the pelvis of an articulated skeleton on my left knee, its boney left hand in my right hand, my left arm around its back, and its right arm around my shoulders. While the skeleton and I maintained this awkward juxtaposition of flesh and bone, Haas had me stare intently into the eye sockets of the empty skull. It was a weird picture, better suited for a Halloween story than a religious publication.

When the book, *Real Happiness Is: A Guide to Discovery for the Young Who Love Life*, was published, it featured photos of several of my friends at Southwestern Union College. To this day I'm puzzled by the legend printed

---

30. Hayward, "Vertical Position of Certain Fossil Trees in Light of Flotation Principles."

beside the photo of me with the skeleton, a legend as bizarre as the photograph: "You may be chummy with this fellow in the lab. But when he represents past sins and the dead life of yesterday, then what?" I'm not sure of the intended message, but it was an eye-catching illustration.[31]

The book was envisioned as a giveaway for "witnessing" to non-Adventist kids. I never heard a report about how successful the book was in shepherding youth into the Adventist Church, but I had done my part in spreading its message.

As a junior biology major, I began to think about what I would do the following year for my senior research project. Given my interest in mammals, I toyed with the idea of doing a survey of the mammals of Johnson County, Texas, where the college was located. On the other hand, I had been thinking that a career in vertebrate paleontology would suit my interests more closely. "Vert paleo" would unite my fascination with mammals with my enthusiasm for fossils and life in the past.

In October 1969, I wrote my parents that I had obtained "Dr. Beary's permission to do a 3-credit senior project on the [Paluxy] dinosaur tracks near Glen Rose. . . I will be doing a detailed survey of the area, mapping it out, measuring and plotting all the tracks, and working out the stratigraphy." Beary was interested in seeing the project completed as a preliminary survey for his friend, Berney Neufeld, a scientist at Loma Linda University, who wanted to study firsthand the evidence for the purported "human" tracks.[32]

As the year progressed, however, things at the college did not look positive. Administrators announced that the following year Southwestern Union College would transition to a new academic system; this would disrupt my intended senior course schedule. Apparently I was not the only one who felt this way; many of SUC's best students were planning to transfer to other colleges. As I wrote my folks in April 1970, "I'd feel like the Lone Ranger if I came back next year."[33]

I had been in correspondence with Donald W. Rigby, chair of the Department of Biological Sciences at Walla Walla College, and I was impressed with his responsiveness and interest in my plans. Walla Walla College offered a far wider selection of biology courses than Southwestern, courses taught by professors actively engaged in research. Moreover, Walla Walla operated a marine station at Rosario Beach along the Washington coast, the same facility featured by Ernest Booth when he spoke to our church in

---

31. White, *Real Happiness Is*, 50.
32. JLH to parents, October 12, 1969.
33. JLH to parents, April 22, 1970.

Fort Worth six years earlier. Finally, the Walla Walla department offered a master's degree in biology. It was one of the two best biology programs in the Adventist system.

It was difficult to announce my decision to Dexter Beary. He had been very supportive of my interests over the previous three years and had become a good friend. He asked what it would take to keep me at Southwestern, but I told him I'd made my decision. Ernest Booth, who had also learned of my decision, wrote saying he didn't think I would like Walla Walla because all the biology professors there were "molecular biologists." He claimed that none of them "have a flicker of interest in field biology." In fact, the biologists at Walla Walla were quite up to date in their training, whereas Booth, for all his qualities, was still engaged in natural history activities typical of nineteenth- and early twentieth-century biology. Several of the newly-minted PhDs at Walla Walla incorporated molecular biology into their field research, but none were "molecular biologists." And as I told my parents, "a good background in cell and molecular biology would be very helpful in field work."[34] My decision to complete college at Walla Walla was firm—and turned out to be a good one.

Leaving Texas meant, of course, that I would be unable to carry out my Paluxy River footprint project. Berney Neufeld and his associates, however, carried through on their plan to evaluate the so-called "human tracks." At the completion of his project, he determined that the dinosaur tracks were real, but he found no evidence for the presence of associated human tracks:

> Except for the slight suggestion of a hominid form represented by this series, there is no verifiable evidence for the existence of bipedal man-like tracks in this layer. Were such evidence to exist, this series would at best be regarded as ambiguous data. In the absence of such other data, the most likely possibility is that these tracks are of reptilian origin.[35]

Neufeld, himself a conservative creationist, would like to have found a verifiable human trackway, but it was not to be. Another creationist, Glen J. Kuban, carried out yet another study of the trackways and came to the same conclusion.[36]

It was becoming increasingly clear that creationists like Clifford Burdick and Stanley Taylor were sensationalists with little or no evidence

---

34. JLH to parents, May 8, 1970.
35. Neufeld, "Dinosaur Tracks and Giant Men," 64–76.
36. Kuban, "A Summary of the Taylor Site Evidence," 10–18.

upon which to base their claims. I began to realize that good scientists from any persuasion are those who carefully weigh available evidence before jumping to conclusions. If a claim seems too good to be true, it probably is not true.

I also began to recognize that Christians, including members of my own faith community, were not necessarily persons of integrity, and that belief often trumped evidence. This recognition was disappointing, but it initiated a healthy level of spiritual and intellectual independence in me. "Trust, but verify" became my mantra.

4

Learning to Think

"To be a naturalist is not just an activity but an honorable state of mind."

—Edward O. Wilson[1]

The conifers greening the borders of the highway looked like a picture for a summertime Christmas card. The potential for a biologist seemed endless. I became more and more excited.

It was early September 1970. After spending the night near Boise, Idaho, I was driving the final 224-mile stretch in a trip from my parents' home in Arizona to Walla Walla College[2] in my old '54 Chevy. The drive north along I-84 through Oregon's Blue Mountains stirred my soul. I had never been in the Pacific Northwest before, and the region was all I dreamed it would be.

Dropping down from the mountains to Pendleton, I turned onto the Oregon-Washington Highway, drove past arid wheat and pea fields, through the little burgs of Adams, Athena, and Milton-Freewater, and finally arrived in College Place, Washington, my new home. Although the Walla Walla College campus seemed a bit cramped, the buildings were larger than those

---

1. Wilson. *The Creation*, 140.
2. Now Walla Walla University.

at Southwestern Union College, and they projected a more serious academic bearing.

I didn't know a soul. I had come to Walla Walla because of the biology program, not because of friends. I had been in contact with Donald Rigby, chair of the Department of Biological Sciences, so I stopped at his office first. He greeted me warmly. A man of forty-two years with sharp features and astute demeanor, he would soon occupy an important place in the pantheon of the most sagacious people I knew. I was fortunate to enjoy his wise guidance for my last two years of college.[3]

I had mentioned to Rigby that, if possible, I wanted to work as a museum assistant. At registration, he led me over to Alfred E. Perry, the mammalogist in charge of the museum. Perry was a tall, handsome man with a strong voice and, at first, an intimidating manner.

"What source would you use to key out a mammal?" asked Perry, challenging my knowledge of mammalogy.

"Well, I might start out with Booth's *How to Know the Mammals*," I responded, "but to really pin things down, I'd use Hall and Kelson." Seeing Perry's reaction when I mentioned the authors of *Mammals of North America*, the authoritative, two-volume source on this group, I knew I was hired.

Meeting Professors Perry, Rigby, and the five other members of the department quickly taught me I was dealing with professionals. These people were no mere conduits of biological information. They were personally committed—and made certain their students were committed—to direct involvement in the discovery process. That's why I had come to Walla Walla College.

The photograph in my high school biology textbook of students studying mammal specimens in the Walla Walla College collection had inspired my interest in mammals.[4] Now I was curating that same collection. Ernest Booth, author of the textbook, founded the biology department at Walla Walla in 1938, and he and his students had collected most of the specimens in the cabinets. Working with the collection was a trip through history.

Part of my job was to go through the specimens and record the species and subspecies names in pencil on the back of the attached labels. I asked Perry how I could objectively determine the subspecies name of a specimen. He responded that I should simply match the collection locality on the label with the appropriate subspecies distribution map in Hall and Kelson. I dutifully carried out this assignment, but I wondered about the value of applying

---

3. I was a two-year senior. The change in colleges meant I had to take extra coursework to fulfill Walla Walla College's requirements for general education and a biology major.

4. Booth, *Biology, the Story of Life*, 251.

a subspecies name to an animal simply because it lived in a certain area. What if the ranges had changed? Couldn't new subspecies have arisen? How well could the author of the subspecies designation be trusted? It certainly led me to question the value of subspecies designations. It turns out I was in good company. Specialists in the area of systematics, the branch of biology concerned with organizing the types of organisms according to their relationships, also have questioned the value of the subspecies designation.[5]

I had brought several of the prized specimens in my personal mammal collection—like a ringtail (*Bassariscus astutus*) from Texas and a tassel-eared squirrel (*Sciurus aberti*) from Arizona—with me from Southwestern Union College and donated them to the Walla Walla collection. A couple decades later Walla Walla no longer employed a mammalogist, and the biology department made a decision to gift the entire collection, including my contributions, to the Burke Museum at the University of Washington. I was disappointed when I learned of this, but I soon realized that the scientific value of my specimens was multiplied when housed with others at a large research institution. In 2015, I visited the Burke collection and saw the specimens I had collected and prepared nearly a half century earlier. It was a thrill to see my handwriting on the labels after all those years. The people at the Burke were pleased to have my specimens, which in some cases were their only representatives of certain species.

One of the amenities of working in the museum was getting better acquainted with Ernest Booth's son, Lowell, a fellow biology major, who also worked in the department. I had met Lowell two years earlier when visiting the Booth family at Lake Tahoe, where they were spending the summer. Lowell and I hit it off immediately. He was unfailingly friendly and kind. He had supplied his dad with mammal and bird specimens for many years, and he had done much more collecting than I ever had. As we talked, however, each of us voiced the fact we had arrived at a point in our lives where we disliked killing animals, even for scientific purposes, and that we wanted to pursue other ways to appreciate the natural world.

A GENERAL EDUCATION REQUIREMENT at Walla Walla was a course called Philosophy of Christian Education. It was listed as a freshman class, but because I had not taken a similar course at Southwestern Union College, I had to enroll. A requirement of the course was to write an essay on the quest for

---

5. See, for example, Mayr, *Systematics and the Origin of Species from the Viewpoint of a Zoologist*, 106. Ernst Mayr, one of the twentieth century's foremost biologists, stated the "limits of most subspecies are . . . subjective." See also, Wilson, *Naturalist*, 207. E. O. Wilson, equally distinguished, declared that "subspecies are arbitrary."

truth. After briefly describing four ways of knowing—experience, intuition, authority, and experimentation—and noting that to "develop proper insight into the meaning in life man must utilize all ways of gaining knowledge," I launched into a discussion of the relationship between nature and revelation. I don't think this was a requirement of the paper, but this topic seemed to be on my mind a lot. My discussion reveals, however, that by age twenty-two I was still a conservative creationist:

> The scientist who assumes the validity of Biblical history is able to interpret much of what he studies in light of what he knows about creation, the curse of sin, and the influence of the Noachian Flood. The scientist who refuses divine knowledge is at a loss to adequately explain certain geological formations, physical phenomena, and biological relationships. Fundamental universal principles such as the equivalence of mass and energy and the laws of thermodynamics become infinitely more meaningful to the scientist who makes allowance in his thinking for divine maintenance of the universe.[6]

My references to the "Noachian Flood," "physical phenomena," and "the laws of thermodynamics" suggest I was still thinking about the physics course I'd taken from Samuel Myers two years earlier at Southwestern Union College, along with the simple model I'd developed for his class on the upright floatation of trees during the flood. Little did I realize, however, that my views would shift significantly over the next several years as I learned more about rocks, fossils, Ellen G. White, the Bible, and of course, life science.

IN THE SPRING TERM of 1971, I enrolled in a required senior-level course called Philosophy of Origins and Speciation. Most Adventist biology departments offered a course with this name, or one similar to it. The term "speciation" was a euphemism for "evolution," as biologists understand the term. No Adventist biology department would have survived the consternation of its institution's constituency and governing board if the academic bulletin had listed a course on the topic of evolution.

The content of such a course varied widely, depending on the instructor. Some professors used the course to explain purported evidence for a recent creation, the Genesis flood, and limits to biological change. They also highlighted the limitations of science and analyzed the Genesis creation accounts under the assumption they were equivalent to modern scientific statements about the origins of life. Other professors presented

---

6. Hayward, "Man's Quest for Truth."

a more science-oriented course, one that would prepare students for the MCAT, GRE, and graduate school. Hot-button issues such as the age of the earth and the effects of the flood were downplayed; a course like this focused more on the nature and philosophy of science and the mechanisms of biological change. The course at Walla Walla was in the latter category.

Our professor was Dale Clayton, a young behavioral physiologist and clever experimentalist. Clayton's research interests involved circadian rhythm biology, a topic I found particularly intriguing. I was privileged to do my senior research project with him on the effects of twilight on deer mouse activity rhythms.

Clayton required us to purchase two books for his class, *Understanding Evolution*, by E. Peter Volpe, and *God, Man, and the Thinker* by Donald A. Wells. Volpe's book provided an excellent introduction to mechanisms of change. It was written in the context of the "synthetic theory of evolution," a dominant paradigm which united Darwin's theory of natural selection with understandings of biological diversity, paleontology, and population genetics. The first part of the book focused on genetic variation, mutation, natural selection, genetic drift, and other concepts related to the Hardy-Weinberg equilibrium theory. The chapters on cataclysmic evolution via polyploidy and adaptive radiation were especially intriguing; they offered a well-organized framework within which to think more broadly about biological change.

The second book, *God, Man, and the Thinker* by Donald A. Wells, was a demanding read. It was the first book I had read that challenged my personal worldview in relation to an entire smorgasbord of philosophical systems. I read about the ideas of Plato, Descartes, Aquinas, Spinoza, Calvin, Hegel, Paley, Kant, Kierkegaard, James, Feuerbach, Schleiermacher, Santayana, Freud, Otto, Jung, Tillich, and many others. The chapter entitled "Religion and Science" was of particular interest to our class. The author wrote that "of all the wars religion has waged upon infidelity and heresy, few rival the controversy between science and religion."[7] Although today's science historians might disagree with this assessment,[8] the chapter contained some important history and useful perspectives. I drew a big question mark, however, beside the statement that

> Christians must now think in terms of creation as a long process, and of the arrival of man on the earthly scene as quite recent . . . [T]he old biblical chronology has had to go. The scriptural

---

7. Wells, *God, Man, and the Thinker*, 417.
8. See, for example, Numbers, *Science and Christianity in Pulpit and Pew*, 3–4.

accounts have had to be reassessed as metaphors with a spiritual message rather than as empirical accounts with scientific status.[9]

Although I was beginning to understand the mechanisms of extensive biological change, I balked at this statement. I continued to deny the concept of deep time.

At the end of the term I submitted a paper explaining my personal philosophy of science and faith. Although I defended what I considered to be a biblically-based view of creation, I did "not question the fact that evolution has occurred in the past and that it is occurring today. . . The great diversity of living things certainly testifies to this process of adaptive evolution." This process, I opined, was necessary given tremendous environmental alterations to the world since it began:

> Certainly the earth has experienced a variety of changes since its creation. The entrance of sin, as discussed in Genesis 3, was no doubt important in this respect. The flood described in Genesis 7 and 8 . . . must have caused cataclysmic environmental changes as did the glacial period which followed the flood.[10]

Despite the fact that I continued to identify with traditional notions, I was creeping ever so cautiously out of the fundamentalist camp. My eyes were opening to a much more dynamic, expansive, and fascinating universe than I had recognized before. I was not troubled by the evidence I was encountering, but neither was I anxious to jump to conclusions. I needed a much deeper understanding of biology and the history of life before I would be comfortable distancing myself very far from my conservative roots.

EVERY PERSON WHO HAS taken education seriously has experienced a life-altering course, one that inspired greater ethical heights, encouraged new directions of thought, or stirred emotions never previously stirred. For me, General Ecology during the fall of 1971 did all these things.

The professor, Lawrence R. McCloskey, was new to campus and this was the first class he had ever taught. An experienced coral reef researcher, veteran of multiple deep sea cruises, and member of the United State Navy's SEALAB Aquanaut program, he had just been pictured in the latest issue of *National Geographic*.[11] That first day of class I found my seat and awaited a chance to size him up.

9. Wells, *God, Man, and the Thinker*, 425.
10. Hayward, "A Philosophy on God and Nature."
11. Vanderwalker, "Tektite II: Part One: Science's Window on the Sea," 256–96; McCloskey is pictured with three other aquanauts on the bottom of page 263.

He walked somberly into the classroom, all six-foot-four of him. He sported a crew cut and closely-cropped beard. He was missing fingers on his left hand, lost during an accident when he was living in an undersea habitat. I was intrigued by the peculiarities—he had clearly earned his stripes.

During one of our labs toward the beginning of the course, I walked over to McCloskey and asked a question. He was so focused on what he was doing that he completely ignored me. After the brush-off, I wasn't sure I would like him. I did admire his single-mindedness, though, and decided to give him the benefit of the doubt. Now, many years later, and recalling my own stress during my first year of teaching, I understand the intensity and anxiety he must have felt.

Before the start of the course I possessed a general-biology level of understanding of ecology. But over the next ten weeks I eagerly absorbed every detail from the lectures, text, labs, and outside readings. These were the most exciting ideas I had confronted in biology. Ecology integrated all living things and all processes in the living world—I loved the holistic approach.

Our eco-lime-green textbook, *Fundamentals of Ecology*, published in 1970, the year of the first Earth Day, was authored by prominent ecologist Eugene P. Odum. Dull-looking by comparison to today's high-priced, color-infused textbooks, Odum's writing and broad perspective captured my fancy. He perceived ecology from a systems perspective and he wrote with conviction about the need to think seriously about how humans interact with the natural world. At the end of his chapter 2, for example, I underlined the following statement:

> It is man the geological agent, not so much as man the animal, that is too much under the influence of positive feedback, and therefore, must be subjected to negative feedback. Nature, with our intelligent help, can cope with man's physiological needs and wastes, but she has no homeostatic mechanisms to cope with bulldozers, concrete, and the kind of agroindustrial air, water, and soil pollution that will be hard to contain as long as the human population itself remains out of control.[12]

At the height of the environmental movement, this and many other observations by Odum served as strong motivators for me.

I prepared well for McCloskey's first test. I was ready for anything he could throw at us. It turned out to be a tough essay exam. One by one, the other students filed out of the room until I was alone. Even McCloskey left. After several hours I walked downstairs to his office and apologized

---

12. Odum, *Fundamentals of Ecology*, 36.

for not having completed the test. He graciously told me to take the time I needed—which turned out to be six hours.

A few days later, after he had graded and returned the tests, I stood at his office door, enjoyed our first real conversation—and recognized we were kindred spirits. After congratulating me for my performance on the test, he asked if I was related to the pastor who shared my name. It turned out that he, like me, had grown up in Massachusetts. As a kid he had roomed with my dad and several other young pastors at Camp Winnekeag, the Adventist youth camp in northern Massachusetts—in those days young pastors were required to spend part of each summer helping out at camp. I discovered that he had also been responsible for inspiring my older cousin, Richard Coffen, to become a birder. Richard, in turn, had inspired me.

During the course, McCloskey recommended two books, both of which I purchased and read. The first was Aldo Leopold's, *A Sand County Almanac*, a lyrically written and remarkably insightful book. Published in 1949, it was ahead of its time in promoting an environmental ethic, and it had become a classic. The other was *Living the Good Life* by Helen and Scott Nearing, intellectuals who lived off the land in Vermont and served as models for the early environmentalist movement. These two books galvanized my commitment to live in harmony with nature. They made me realize that positive action in the world is considerably more important than doctrinal belief, a new concept to me.

Ecology is the science of how all life fits together in a world of biological and physical variables. It's a complicated topic, one that requires attention to many things. I liked the big view it afforded. It incorporated all the sciences and integrated them into a meaningful whole.

The sciences of evolutionary biology and ecology are closely related, although this point was not explicitly highlighted by McCloskey or Odum. Charles Darwin recognized this in *Origin of Species*. His chapter 3, "The Struggle for Existence," anticipates many of the fundamental principles of ecology, including population growth and decline, carrying capacity, density dependence and density independence, competition, the impact of exotic species, and of course adaptation.[13] Darwin recognized that organisms evolve within ecological systems, systems that provide the selective forces that drive adaptation. Given the close connection between the two disciplines, large universities house departments of ecology and evolutionary biology—"EEB."

Philosophy of Origins and Speciation and General Ecology were two of the most important courses I took in college. They set me up for an

---

13. Darwin, *On the Origin of Species*, 63–100.

important intellectual journey, although it would be several years before I realized the extent of their importance.

THE SUMMER BEFORE MY last year at Walla Walla, I enrolled in two courses at the Walla Walla College Marine Station, now Rosario Beach Marine Laboratory. This facility, founded by Ernest Booth in the 1940s, is situated in one of the most beautiful locations in the Pacific Northwest.[14]

The cabin to which I was assigned housed two other students, one a graduate student at Andrews University in Michigan. His major professor, John F. Stout, came for a visit. Given that we had an extra bunk available, Stout stayed in our cabin. He learned of my interest in animal behavior and offered me a position with his research group at Andrews studying communication in glaucous-winged gulls.

I had planned on staying at Walla Walla to do my master's degree. When Don Rigby, my advisor, heard I was flirting with the idea of starting graduate work at Andrews University, he told me he thought it would be in my best interest to stay put. But the research proposed by Stout sounded fascinating. Moreover, his offer included the promise of generous financial support from a National Institutes of Health grant. Once again I made a decision to respectfully disregard the advice of a trusted advisor and move to a new place. It was a decision that would completely shape my professional life, and it was one of the best decisions I have ever made.

---

14. Aamodt, *Bold Venture*, 135. Booth founded what was called the Marine Biological Station in 1947. During the first several years classes were held in a rented, unused fish cannery owned by the Fidalgo Island Packing Company, Anacortes. In 1953, a permanent facility for the Station was purchased at Rosario Beach, a few miles south of Anacortes.

PART TWO

Life Scientist

College-level biology totally captivated my interest, so I continued to study life science at the graduate level. I completed master's and doctoral degrees in zoology and became a professor and researcher. I think of my work as more a "calling" than a career. The opportunity to pass along knowledge, wisdom, and values to students and the general public is highly rewarding. Equally rewarding is the chance to remain a life-long student myself by continuing to learn directly from nature. As a consequence, life for me, both as an experience and as a subject for study, is rich, colorful, and engaging. This continued friendship with life is what has enabled me to thrive. I hardly know what it means to be bored.

5

Chasing Credentials

"At some point, you just can't proceed any further with courses and books; you have to hang around someone who is doing research well."
—Stephen Jay Gould[1]

ANDREWS UNIVERSITY IS LOCATED in the southwestern corner of Michigan, one hundred miles from Chicago and eleven miles from Lake Michigan, the fifth largest lake in the world. The eastern shore of the lake boasts the most extensive freshwater dune system on the planet. Numerous ponds and sphagnum bogs dot the glaciated topography of the state. Swells and swales add pleasing relief to the land. The rich green foliage of Michigan's extensive, although now fragmented, deciduous forest—with sugar maple, American beech, black and red oak, sassafras, and dozens of other trees and shrubs—provides cool shade from the summer sun. The mass of forest leaves becomes a palette of yellow, orange, and red in the fall. The rolling hills, quaint farms, summer greens, autumn colors, and snowy winters stirred my New Englander soul. This was a good place to begin my graduate education.

It also was a good place because my parents now lived only eighty-five miles away in Battle Creek, Michigan, where Dad had become pastor of the historic Battle Creek Tabernacle. Just across from the Tabernacle stood the pillared edifice that once housed Battle Creek Sanitarium, founded by physician, writer, inventor, and erstwhile Tabernacle member John Harvey Kellogg. During his glory days Kellogg treated capitalist tycoons, Hollywood

---

1. Gould, *Wonderful Life*, 139.

actors, and U.S. presidents at his elegant facility. The equally famous Kellogg Company, built by John Harvey's younger brother, Will Keith (W. K.), was located southeast of town. Starting with a recipe for "corn flakes" invented by John and Will, the cereal company revolutionized the world's breakfast habits and made Will a very rich man. The Kellogg brothers, their competitor C. W. Post, abolitionist Sojourner Truth, and numerous Adventist pioneers, including Ellen White, are buried in Oak Hill Cemetery at the south edge of town.[2]

Battle Creek Adventists established Battle Creek College in 1874, only eleven years after the denomination itself was established. Starting a college set the church up for conflict between those who viewed higher education as a means of exploring ideas, and those who viewed it as a training program for spreading the Adventist message. The two goals were not necessarily contradictory, but at times there was a tug-of-war between forces vying over which vision to emphasize.[3]

In 1901, Battle Creek College moved to a 1,600- acre farm site in rural Berrien Springs, where it was christened Emmanuel Missionary College. When the school began offering graduate degrees in 1959, it was renamed Andrews University in honor of J. N. Andrews, an early Adventist scholar and missionary.[4]

A PORTION OF ANDREWS University's income is supplied by Seventh-day Adventist Church headquarters, and a vice president of the world church serves as its board chair. The primary reason for this support and oversight is the presence on campus of the Seventh-day Adventist Theological Seminary. Given that it serves a world church, Andrews University attracts students from scores of countries—it houses one of the most diverse student bodies in the United States.[5]

Upon my arrival in 1972, I moved into old Burman Hall, a wooden frame dormitory that housed single male graduate students. My assigned roommate was from Malawi. I introduced myself, but the poor fellow seemed scared to death. I tried my best to be friendly and welcoming, but

---

2. For background on the Kellogg brothers and their association with the Seventh-day Adventist Church, see Powell, *The Original Has This Signature*; Schwarz, *John Harvey Kellogg*; Markell, *The Kelloggs*.

3. Vande Vere, *The Wisdom Seekers*, 18–26; Bull and Lockhart, *Seeking a Sanctuary: Seventh-day Adventism and the American Dream*, 315–32.

4. Vande Vere, *The Wisdom Seekers*, 95–103.

5. In 2018, *U.S. News & World Report* ranked Andrews University in the top three national universities in terms of Campus Ethnic Diversity (see "Campus Ethnic Diversity").

he would not utter a word. Perhaps he didn't yet understand English, or he might have been too shy to interact. Regardless, the complete lack of communication was awkward and uncomfortable in such close quarters. After a few days I explained the situation to the dormitory dean who reassigned me to a room down the hall with Montana native and fellow Walla Walla College alum, Glen Greenwalt.

Glen, along with most students living on the hall, was a master of divinity student at the theological seminary. He was a bright, serious scholar who enjoyed discussing the philosophical aspects of religion. He had already spent a year pastoring in Oregon. His bookshelves bulged with a variety of scholarly theological tomes authored by the likes of Karl Barth, Hans Küng, Paul Tillich, and Reinhold Niebuhr. He had earned a theology degree with a minor in biology at Walla Walla, loved the outdoors, possessed a strong artistic bent, and enjoyed photography. He would go on to earn a PhD in philosophical theology from Vanderbilt University, and later an MFA from the New York Academy of Art. We hit it off well and we remain good friends to this day.

Our dorm room overlooked a brick building that, for one final term, housed the Department of Biology; soon the Department would move into a new Science Complex on the east side of campus. As I glanced out the dorm window during one of my first mornings on campus, I caught a glimpse of Richard M. Ritland, briefcase in hand, ascending the outside stairs from the parking lot. He had been my dad's mammalogy instructor at Atlantic Union College in the 1950s, and he had written the book *Meaning in Nature* which I had enjoyed reading. Just the previous year he had stepped down as director of the church's Geoscience Research Institute housed at the edge of campus. I recognized him from photos but had not yet met him. I was intrigued by him, however, given his thoughtful writing and his experience as a student under Harvard's preeminent vertebrate paleontologist, Alfred Sherwood Romer. Ritland's interest in the history of the earth and life coincided with my own. I looked forward to making his acquaintance.

Another occupant of the Department of Biology was Frank Lewis Marsh, the first Seventh-day Adventist to earn a PhD in biology, and a founding member of the Creation Research Society. Marsh had been a prolific author on the topic of young-age creationism. Over the years, I had read two or three of his books and many of his articles. He was retired, but he continued to maintain an office in the department. The presence of both Marsh and Ritland in the same department was ironic—both men had been early members of Geoscience Research Institute. But strains in their relationship developed when, among other things, it became clear that Marsh was more interested in using the Bible and writings of Ellen White to reconstruct earth history, than in examining data from the earth itself. Ritland and P. Edgar Hare, another institute scientist, often found copies of Ellen White's statements on their desks, placed there by Marsh. Tensions increased until 1964, at which time Ritland arranged for Marsh's transfer out of GRI and into the Andrews' Department of Biology. To Marsh this seemed like "banishment into the farthest corner of Siberia." Seven years later, however, Ritland found himself in a similar predicament after concluding he no longer could meet the church's fundamentalist expectations and at the same time take the scientific evidence concerning earth history at face value.[6]

ONE OF MY FIRST weekends at Andrews, the university hosted a retreat for new graduate students at the Michiana Christian Service Center eight miles from campus. The purpose of the retreat was to help us forge acquaintances with other graduate students, and to set up the academic year with a positive spiritual outlook.

A short hike along an abandoned railroad bed had been planned for Saturday afternoon. Herold Habenicht, a local Adventist allergist and assistant director of the university's student health services, led the hike. Habenicht was a respected member of the local community and a kindly gentleman. As we walked along the trackway, one of the students picked up a little stone with a curious shape.

What's this?" asked the student, who handed the stone to Habenicht.

"That's a fossil," he answered, "an animal buried by the flood." His answer was reflexive, one that required no thought or consideration of other possibilities. His response seemed to satisfy the questioner, but as we continued our walk I wondered how the doctor could be so completely certain about the origin of the fossil.

Regardless, the retreat served its purpose well, and I enjoyed a pleasant time. Six or eight of us, some of whom had been acquainted before the weekend, bonded. As the retreat drew to a close, we decided to meet together on a regular basis. We called ourselves simply the "Group," and several of us remain friends to this day.

Our Group caught the attention of Raymond S. Moore, director of the Hewitt Research Center, an educational think tank located on the Andrews campus but not directly connected with the university. Moore was considered the father of the American homeschool movement. His article, "The Dangers of Early Schooling," had been published in *Harper's Magazine* in 1972 and was subsequently reprinted in the *Reader's Digest* under a different title. The article led to a book with his wife, Dorothy, titled *Better Late than*

---

6. Numbers, *The Creationists*, 320–26.

Early, which championed the view that children should not attend a formal school until they are eight or ten years of age. Moore based his beliefs on the writings of Ellen White, as well as on educational research carried out by his institute. He subsequently was interviewed numerous times by the conservative host of "Focus on the Family," James Dobson, with whom he became close friends.[7]

I first heard of Moore when I was a student at Southwestern Union College. For a year and a half he had served as a highly unpopular president of the school. Among other things, he prohibited students from engaging in competitive sports, discouraged home visits by students on weekends, and frowned upon the development of romantic relationships. During his extremely short tenure, he attempted to transform the college into a model institution operated under Ellen White's nineteenth-century social and educational ideals. In the middle of the 1963–1964 school year he was abruptly replaced by an interim president. When I came to Southwestern as a freshman three years later, the campus was still buzzing about the draconian reforms instituted by Moore.[8]

Now, after nearly a decade, Moore had not given up his attempts at reform. He invited our Group to his home for two Friday evening sessions. It soon became apparent he wanted us to serve as a nucleus for instituting Ellen White's ideals at Andrews University. We were committed Adventist students, but we quickly became uncomfortable with the pressure he exerted. We were even more put off by his boasting. He informed us, for example, that the members of his doctoral dissertation committee at the University of Southern California were completely awed when he defended his remarkable piece of research. He also mentioned that when he was young, his good looks made him very attractive to women. While these things may have been true, they were not the kinds of things most people would mention to a new group of acquaintances. We found some of his ideas appealing, but we were not ready to sell our souls to his cause, which is clearly what he wanted us to do. After our second meeting we discontinued our association with him.

A few years later, my dad and mom were traveling to church meetings in Europe. Moore, whom Dad admired for his promotion of Ellen White's

---

7. Moore and Moore, "The Dangers of Early Schooling," 58–62; "Moore Home Schooling"; "Canadian Centre for Home Education"; "About Us," Hewitt Home Schooling.

8. When I was a student at Southwestern Union College, Dexter Beary, chair of my department, told me that President Moore had prohibited students from playing competitive sports. See also "Vacation Plans Announced by Administration" [restriction of home visits], 7; "College Clinic" [romantic relationships], 10.

"standards," was traveling with them. The three of them occupied adjacent seats in the aircraft, with Mom in the middle. Flying over the Atlantic, the cabin began to get chilly, so Moore unfolded half a blanket over his lap and spread the other half over Mom's. Mom was embarrassed, sitting under a blanket with Moore while Dad was left in the cold. But what was she to do? Our family chuckled about this incident for years.

Raymond Moore was a colorful character who was impossible to ignore. His forceful personality stirred things up wherever he went. He was a true believer and a deeply committed disciple of Ellen White. He tried, but often failed, to mold those around him into true believers like himself. He died in 2007 at age 91, but his views live on in America's immensely popular home-school movement.[9]

ANDREWS UNIVERSITY, LIKE WALLA Walla College, operated on the "quarter system." For my first term, I signed up for Physiology of Behavior from John Stout, my thesis advisor. This was a tough course designed to explore the neurobiological basis of behavior. Stout had begun his career working on communication in fish and birds, but a strong reductionist bent led to a desire to get beneath behavior and down to the workings of the neurons that controlled behavior. Although he was still interested in animal communication, he was moving rapidly into the field of neurobiology. The course was a good one, although I was frustrated with the project I had selected, which involved recording the responses of auditory neurons in female crickets to male calling songs. This required immobilizing female crickets upside down, surgically opening their ventral neck region, placing the tip of a "suction electrode" on just the right bundle of neurons, and recording the changes in electrical potential while playing a recorded male song to the inverted animal. This type of work was not my cup of tea. I did not like immobilizing the female crickets and subjecting them to surgery—I had experienced growing discomfort at harming animals, regardless of how "simple"—and I have never exhibited much talent with electronic gadgetry. Although I made it through the project, it was with considerable angst. I learned lots of worthwhile biology in the process. Stout was a bright and talented professor, and he would become one of the most important scientific mentors in my experience.

I must have broken the record for the time it took for a student to take an in-class test in Stout's course. His exams were notoriously difficult, requiring extensive analysis, interpretation, and integration. One of the problems on his midterm exam involved designing a neuronal circuit that

---

9. "Raymond S. Moore," lines 1–3.

would accomplish a stated task. It took me twelve hours to complete the exam, not something for which I'm particularly proud, but afterward Stout said I had designed a better circuit than what he himself had designed. I appreciated the fact that he allowed me the time I needed to complete the exam to my satisfaction, and I have always kept that experience in mind when administering my own exams. Good students often need more time than average to reach the potential of which they are capable.

During my second fall term I enrolled in the Introduction to Paleontology course, taught by Richard Ritland. Even though animal behavior was my chosen field of study, paleontology was of more interest to me than behavioral physiology. Ritland introduced us to the geological column and the types of fossil organisms found at each level.[10] Our textbook, *Historical Geology* by Dunbar and Waage, provided an excellent overview of paleontological fundamentals. We studied the history of geology and paleontology and became acquainted with key historical figures such as Abraham Gottlob Werner, James Hutton, Baron Cuvier, Charles Lyell, Richard Owen, and John William Dawson. We read from the writings of modern paleontologists like Norman Newell, Daniel Axelrod, and George Gaylord Simpson. We enjoyed a field trip to Ohio and Indiana where we collected Paleozoic fossils. We developed a feel for stratigraphy, the study of geological layers or "strata," and for the dominant landforms of the region, the Michigan Basin and Cincinnati Dome. We visited the Falls of the Ohio, a section of the Ohio River between southern Indiana and northern Kentucky where an enormous Devonian reef is preserved. The reef showed every evidence of having been preserved in its position of growth, not floated into place during an event like the Genesis flood. We enjoyed a field trip to Chicago's Field Museum where we examined fossil animals on display.

The most important concept I learned in paleontology was that as one goes to deeper levels of the geological column, the types of fossil organisms become progressively more dissimilar in comparison with those alive today. No mammals, for example, are found in the low-lying Paleozoic rocks, and no trilobites, abundant in Paleozoic rocks, are found in the middle-level Mesozoic rocks, or in the Cenozoic rocks above those. This seemed pretty difficult to explain in terms of a flood geology model. With a flood model one would expect to find at least the occasional mammal in the lower strata and the occasional trilobite in the upper marine strata. But such is not the case, even after a couple centuries during which paleontologists scoured the planet for fossils. Ritland let the data speak for themselves, but this type of

---

10. The geological column is a theoretical classification of rocks in the earth's crust, based in part on the sequence of fossils found at the various levels.

information raised important cautionary flags in my mind about my earlier views.

Not long into Ritland's course I encountered him on the front steps of the building. I told him how interesting I found paleontology, and I mentioned that I was beginning to see problems with young-age creationist interpretations of the geological column. I said that I had recently hiked into and out of Grand Canyon and that I was impressed by the orderly layers and sequence of fossils, not something I would have expected following a worldwide flood. He agreed that we needed to be careful how evidence of the past was interpreted.

Stout, for his part, was quite dismissive of paleontology, and he exhibited concern over my association with Ritland. More than once he opined that one could not make much of paleontological evidence. He believed Ritland was more of a proselytizer about the past than a practicing scientist. Stout, by contrast, was an experimentalist, a person who sets up hypotheses that could be tested by manipulating nature. He also was a reductionist, a person who likes to get at the details of the underlying mechanisms of natural processes. He believed that observational data alone provided a weak basis upon which to form one's perspectives. I, too, valued experimentally derived data and would become an experimentalist myself under Stout's mentorship. But I also was a big-picture person who respected the wealth of data collected over the past two centuries from the earth's crust. Definite patterns were apparent in the rocks, patterns that could not be ignored or shoved under the rug. Although Ritland was not an experimentalist, he was a skilled synthesizer of information who possessed a keen eye for large-scale geological features.

From time to time I gently challenged Stout with information from paleontology and suggested that things were not as simple as we were led to believe by conservative creationists. One topic I raised concerned the "fossil forests," geological layers in several parts of the world that contain multiple levels of upright fossil trees. Ritland and his students had spent much effort studying the famous fossil forests of Yellowstone National Park and had concluded that the successive "forests" grew one atop another over long periods of time. After I spoke about this with Stout, he made arrangements for me to visit Harold G. Coffin, a staff scientist at the Geoscience Research Institute, housed at the edge of campus. With Ritland now out of GRI, the organization had taken a sharp philosophical turn to the right. Coffin, a friend and former teaching colleague of Stout's, was an invertebrate zoologist who had become interested in paleontology from a young-age creationist viewpoint. Coffin and Ritland had worked together for several years at GRI, but the two had drifted apart over philosophical differences.[11] Stout wanted me to talk with Coffin about his work on the fossil forests of Nova Scotia as a counterbalance to my discussions with Ritland.

At the agreed-upon time, I headed over to the small, brick building at the edge of campus to meet Coffin. It was a pleasure to meet him, for it was his work that led me three years earlier to carry out my General Physics project on upright tree floatation. He was a gentle soul—soft spoken, somewhat shy, and deeply sincere. His bearing was a bit like that of the taciturn, pitchfork-toting farmer in Grant Wood's famous painting, "American Gothic." We briefly talked about the fossil forests and he copied off a manuscript for me that he had written on the topic. He seemed a bit rattled during my visit, which I think may have been because he knew I was being influenced by his rival, Ritland, who held opposing views about the fossil forests.

Coffin's commitment to young-age creationism and flood geology was more than intellectual. At a 1968 conference on science and faith sponsored by the Adventist Church, and following talks by two other scholars who had questioned traditional Adventist beliefs about earth history, Coffin explained to church leaders why he believed the fossil forests had been transported, on atop another, into place just a few thousand years ago by the Genesis flood. At the completion of his talk, Robert H. Pierson, the arch-conservative president of the denomination who had been upset by two previous talks, stood up and expressed warm gratitude to Coffin for his belief-affirming presentation. "Someone has to do it!" exclaimed the emotional flood geologist.[12]

I spent considerable time comparing Coffin's manuscript with an article on the fossil forests by Ritland.[13] Each protagonist, I thought, made a convincing case for his position. Without firsthand evaluation of the evidence, however, a simple comparison of the documents made it impossible for me to take sides. I remained interested in the topic, but I decided it would be some time before the issue could be resolved objectively. As the decades unfolded and further studies were carried out, it became apparent that both Coffin's and Ritland's conceptual models were overly simplistic—both in-place forest growth and some transport of stumps may have been involved.[14] But for many years, the fossil forests were *causes célèbres* for opposing conservative and progressive forces within Adventist creationism.

11. Numbers, *The Creationists*, 324–5.

12. Lugenbeal, "The Conservative Restoration at Geoscience," 23–45.

13. Coffin, "A Preliminary Report on the Carboniferous of Nova Scotia"; Coffin, "Research on the Classic Joggins Petrified Trees," 35–44, 70; Ritland and Ritland, "The Fossil Forests of the Yellowstone Region," 19–66.

14. Fritz, "Reinterpretation of the Depositional Environment of the Yellowstone

WINTER QUARTER, 1973, FOUND our Biology Department housed in the new Science Complex. We occupied "George McCready Price Hall," the middle structure of the three-building complex. The choice of the name was unfortunate. Price, a prominent creationist with virtually no training in science, had taught at Emmanuel Missionary College, the precursor of Andrews University, for less than five years. Moreover, he had taught philosophy, not biology, and he promoted views that by 1973 had been roundly rejected, even by conservative Adventist scientists. The other two sections of the complex, Haughey Hall (mathematics and physics) and Halenz Hall (chemistry and medical lab science), were appropriately named for influential past professors of physics and chemistry, respectively.[15]

At the time of the naming, the university president was Richard Hammill, an Old Testament scholar and a former student of Price. Hammill exhibited a long-standing interest in creationism and respected Price as a mentor. Thus, Hammill's influence on the university board was the most likely reason for the name designation of our building. Following retirement, however, and much to the consternation of church administrators, Hammill became a vocal opponent of Price's young-age creationism and flood geology. Retirement had given him time to study the evidence for himself, evidence that convinced him that living things had undergone considerable change over a long period of time since the beginning.[16]

Building name aside, the new facilities were roomy, pleasant, and functional. I had my own desk in Stout's lab, a large room shared with three other graduate students. Most graduate students were teaching assistants required to oversee class labs. I was fortunate to be paid as a research assistant and was expected to carry out what I had come to graduate school to learn to do—research. I had learned bits and pieces about research as an undergraduate, but Stout gave me the priceless opportunity to practice science as a professional. Our research ventures were supported by grants from the National Institutes of Health and the United States Air Force, and they provided me with experience involving large scale, government-funded projects.

'Fossil Forests," 309–13; Yuretich, "Yellowstone Fossil Forests: New Evidence for Burial in Place," 159–62; Fritz, "Comment and Reply on 'Yellowstone Fossil Forests: New Evidence for Burial in Place,'" 638–9; Yuretich, "Comment and Reply on 'Yellowstone Fossil Forests: New Evidence for Burial in Place,'" 639.

15. Bauer, "Horn Appointed Dean of Seminary," 16 [Price Hall]; Bauer, "Three New Scholarships Endowed at Andrews," 8 [Halenz Hall]; Bauer, "Assistant Seminary Dean Approved," 16 [Haughey Hall]. See also, Young, "Andrews Dedicates Science Complex," 4–5.

16. Hammill, "Fifty Years of Adventist Creationism," 32–45; Jim Walters, "Richard Hammill: The Interview," 17–19.

Winter quarter I signed up for a second Ritland course, Biogeography. This was an excellent course to take following Introduction to Paleontology. Biogeography is concerned life with over space, whereas paleontology is concerned with life over time. Combined, they allow for development of a comprehensive view of factors influencing the history and diversity of life.

We learned about Alfred Russel Wallace, his exploration of tropical life, and his designation of six major biogeographic regions. We examined the diversity of life in each of these regions, and we learned why the degree of endemism—the restriction of species or groups of related species to restricted areas—varies greatly from region to region. For example, the Neotropical (primarily South America) and Australian (primarily Australia) regions contain the highest percentages of endemic birds and mammals, both living and fossil. This situation appears to be the result of the relative isolation of these regions from other regions. All this begged for me an important question: How did the ancestors of these isolated groups get to each region in the first place? This question ran headlong into fundamentalist assumptions about the creation, the flood, post-flood dispersion of organisms from Noah's ark. For example, if all kangaroos, except those on the ark, were destroyed by the flood and became fossils buried on the continent of Australia, how did the kangaroos on the ark get back to Australia after the flood? We also explored ecological factors involved in determining the distribution of plants and animals. Our primary textbook, *Ecological Animal Geography* by W. C. Allee and Karl P. Schmidt, was a classic and put to good use in this regard.[17]

Ritland had traveled widely, and photographs from his travels figured prominently in the course. He made available a variety of world atlases, and we were encouraged to carefully peruse the maps in relation to the distributions of organisms we were exploring. Outside reading was a significant component of the course, and we were required to turn in a reading log. Given my interest in mammals, I found the topic of the distribution and patterns of endemism in this taxonomic group enormously valuable, and a subject that raised important issues in my mind about the history of life in relation to the biblical narrative. In short, Ritland provided a solid introduction to historical biogeography, one that I thoroughly enjoyed. I think it must have been his favorite course to teach. It certainly was one of my favorite courses as a graduate student.

OTHER ANDREWS UNIVERSITY COURSES I took that were especially instructive were Parasitology and Issues in Origins and Speciation. Parasitology

17. Allee and Schmidt, *Ecological Animal Geography*.

was taught by Bill Chobotar, a specialist on internal parasites of the genus *Eimeria*. These parasites can cause a debilitating disease known as coccidiosis in fish, birds, and mammals. Chobotar would eventually become the coeditor of *Parasitology Research*, a leading international journal. During my master's program, Chobotar—"Doctor Chob," as we called him—was the graduate program director. He was a friendly, easy-going, highly knowledgeable individual we graduate students found especially approachable, kind, and helpful.

It would be difficult to take a course in parasitology and not engage with questions regarding the extent of change in organisms over time, as well as about design and the goodness of creation. In fact, one of the first things we learned was that there are more species of animal parasites than of free-living animals—virtually every animal on earth hosts more than one type of parasite, many of which are host-specific. Some parasites, in turn, have parasites of their own. Many, especially those living within their hosts, lead highly specialized lives and engage in complex life cycles involving several different hosts. The insidious ways they maximize their chances of infecting the right host at the right stage of their life cycle boggle the mind. Each one could form the basis for a Hollywood horror movie. All parasites, by definition, are dependent on their hosts for sustenance, and many have the capacity to cause tremendous harm, especially when they occur in large numbers.[18]

Issues in Origins and Speciation was coordinated by Leonard Hare, son of the well-known Adventist storyteller and missionary, Eric B. Hare. Leonard Hare was himself an entertaining raconteur who enlivened his classes with verbal, cartoon-like descriptions of biological processes. But instead of teaching the Issues course himself, he enlisted help from other faculty around campus, especially from the Department of Biology, the Geoscience Research Institute, and the Seminary. The stated purpose of the course was to provide a "comparative survey of the assumptions, attitudes, methods, and conclusions of science and religion in the handling of data . . . and their relationship to an understanding of Earth history and the present diversity of life." Indeed, that's what was accomplished. We heard lectures on topics as diverse as the meaning of Hebrew words in the Genesis account of creation, to the life and legacy of Charles Darwin.

My master's thesis involved a study of how glaucous-winged gulls, common along the Pacific Northwest coast, use communication to keep intruders out of their breeding territories. Intruding gulls take over territories,

18. Noble and Noble, *Parasitology*, 3–6.

attempt to rape female gulls when their mates are absent, eat unprotected eggs, and even kill and eat chicks. Territory owners that attack intruders risk getting injured or even killed during vicious fights. Communication is a lower intensity, less hazardous way of getting rid of an unwanted guest. I examined the influence of body orientation and sequences of behaviors during aggressive encounters by these birds.

My project was part of a comprehensive study of communication during aggressive encounters by gulls that John Stout and his students had pursued for several years. The work was funded by grants from the National Institutes of Health, under the assumption that learning fundamental principles about the process of communication in "simple" animals would enhance our understanding of how social systems are maintained among all animals, including humans. I demonstrated, both observationally and experimentally, that changes in body orientation by gulls and sequences of behavior they used influenced the outcome of their aggressive interactions. Other members of our research team found that the head and neck level of the birds conveyed important information, that movement toward and away by the territory intruder and defender was important, and that other postures and calls were influential.[19]

Based on our success, Stout obtained funding from the United States Air Force to find a way to use communication to discourage gulls from standing and sleeping on airport runways, behaviors that create serious hazards to jet aircraft. Another graduate student and I flew to Shemya Air Force Base,[20] Alaska, near the end of the Aleutian chain, where we successfully designed a behavioral technique to keep gulls off runways.[21] Unfortunately, after all our work and after the scores of thousands of dollars in grants, the Air Force decided it was easier to continue to shoot the birds than to use our benign behavioral technique. But the experience of working on Shemya Island was one of the most interesting opportunities I enjoyed as a graduate student.

As I will explain in more detail later, our research shaped the rest of my professional life—I continued to study the behavioral ecology of gulls for more than four decades. I also gained an intimate look at the intricate workings of an ecological community, which, like all communities, involves a complex network of predators, prey, and parasites, a perspective that no one can fully appreciate until they work closely with such a system. The simple explanations provided by well-meaning creationists concerning the

19. Hayward et al., "Aggressive Communication by *Larus glaucescens*," 236–76.
20. Now Eareckson Air Station.
21. Stout et al. "Aggregations of Gulls (Laridae) on aerodromes and Behavioral Techniques for Dispersal," 125-48.

effects of "The Fall," or of sin, on the original creation began to look naïve after this experience. On the other hand, the remarkable survival capabilities of these birds in the face of severe environmental perturbations, their incredible physiological and behavioral responses to changing conditions, and their astonishing twenty-eight-day development from a shell-enclosed gooey mass into a feathered chick seemed nothing short of miraculous.

My experience at Andrews University was valuable and life-changing, and it gave me much to think about. It set me up nicely for further graduate work, teaching, and research. Most importantly, it provided me with friends, colleagues, and professors who created a positive religious and intellectual climate which enabled me to develop into a productive scholar.

I was eager to pursue a PhD, and I applied to several programs, now with a focus on ecology. I accepted an offer to study at the Institute of Ecology at the University of Georgia. Unfortunately, I found myself ill-prepared to jump directly from the study of animal behavior into the more quantitative aspects of ecology featured there. Thus, in the spring of 1975, after two terms, I chose to leave Georgia. The biology faculty at Andrews University, however, asked me to come back to fill in for John Stout who was on sabbatical leave. I taught Human Physiology and Cell Physiology during the 1975–1976 academic year. I then filled a second temporary teaching position at Southwestern Union College from 1976 to the end of the fall semester 1977.

During my temporary teaching stint at Southwestern Union College, I applied to study under Don E. Miller in the PhD program at Washington State University. Miller had completed his doctoral work at the University of Wisconsin under noted animal behaviorist, John T. Emlen, and currently worked on gull communication at the gull colony at Sprague Lake in eastern Washington. My application was accepted, so in January 1977 my family and I moved to Pullman where I began coursework.

Washington State University was a good fit. Miller and I worked well together. I learned a great deal from him and from the rest of my time at WSU, an experience that positively influenced the direction of my professional life. The coursework deepened my understanding of the challenges faced by living things, and the research on the Sprague Lake gull colony held some surprises for me, the most dramatic of which was the Mount St. Helens eruption in 1980. As I will explain in chapter 7, this experience opened incredible opportunities for me to uncover unexplored aspects of the history of life.

The stress associated with graduate education prodded me to stay on top of things, although this always seemed like an impossibility. But during the summer of 1981, I successfully defended my dissertation, and my family and I moved to Union College in Lincoln, Nebraska, where I assumed the title of Assistant Professor of Biology, my first permanent position.

6

Teaching Life

"It is the supreme art of the teacher to awaken joy in creative expression and knowledge."

—Albert Einstein[1]

"Hey, you're the scientist in the video!" exclaimed a visitor at Smithsonian Institution's National Museum of Natural History. The visitor was pointing to Dr. Karen Osborn, a curator of marine invertebrates at the Museum. Karen and I were standing by a new exhibit featuring her work, and she was describing to me one of the remarkably bizarre animals she recently had discovered and named. A video in the exhibit showed her controlling a remotely operated vehicle (ROV) aboard Monterrey Bay Aquarium's research vessel *Western Flyer*. I was in Washington, DC attending the 2016 North American Ornithological Conference, and Karen had offered to give me a personal tour of the museum and behind-the-scenes collections.[2] She had taken several courses from me as an undergraduate at Andrews University,

---

1. Einstein and Calaprice, *The Ultimate Quotable Einstein*, 99-101.

2. Following graduation from Andrews University, Osborn completed a master's degree at Western Washington University, a PhD at University of California, Berkeley, and post-doctoral studies at Scripps Institute of Oceanography before joining Smithsonian in 2011. For the Smithsonian display featuring Osborn's work, see Smithsonian, "Smithsonian Exhibition 'Life in One Cubic Foot.'"

and I had mentored her honors research project. After graduating from Andrews, she had earned a PhD at Berkeley and was awarded a post-doctoral fellowship at Scripps Institution of Oceanography. Now, twenty years later, she was one of a handful of experts studying the bizarre animals that inhabit the deep, open ocean, a crucially important ecosystem.

Back at the ornithological conference, I located the meeting room where Libby Megna, another former student, was scheduled to give a talk on avian hybridization. When I entered the room I saw that all the seats were taken—I had to sit in the aisle on the floor. Libby began her talk and soon had the audience laughing and attending to her every word. Ten years earlier I had been introduced to a very shy freshman named Libby. When I asked about her interests, she timidly replied that she wanted to study animals. I hired her for our research team and assigned her to a mundane clerical task. She carried it out so amazingly well that I soon realized she was no ordinary freshman. In fact, she was a National Merit Scholar finalist, and during her junior year at Andrews University she won a Barry M. Goldwater Scholarship, the highest national undergraduate honor conferred on American STEM[3] students. She earned bachelor's and master's degrees at Andrews, all the while doing research with us on Protection Island, Washington, funded by the National Science Foundation (NSF). She was now a PhD candidate at the University of Wyoming specializing in the ecology and evolution of birds.[4]

Not long after my trip to Washington DC, I sat in the Biology amphitheater at Andrews University, eagerly anticipating a colloquium talk by Andre Moncrieff, another former student. A few months earlier when I had opened the latest issue of *The Auk*, I was excited to see Andre's name as lead author on a paper describing the newly discovered cordillera azul antbird, *Myrmoderus eowilsoni*. He and his colleagues had discovered this Peruvian species and named it after Edward O. Wilson, the renowned Harvard ecologist and conservationist. Now a PhD student at Louisiana State University, Andre was back on campus to tell us about this epic event. Ever since he was a kid, he had dreamed of describing a new species of bird, something that happens rarely these days because birds constitute such a well-studied taxonomic group. Here he was, a second-year graduate student, having done just that. Andre joined our research group when he was a high school senior and worked with us on Protection Island during four field seasons. Upon

---

3. STEM: "Science, Technology, Engineering, Mathematics."

4. At this writing, Megna is completing her doctorate in zoology at the University of Wyoming. The focus of both her master's thesis and doctoral dissertation are on avian hybridization. See, for example, Megna et al., "Equal Reproductive Success of Phenotypes in the *Larus glaucescens-occidentalis* complex," 410–16.

entering graduate school, he was awarded a Graduate Research Fellowship by NSF which funded his entire doctoral program at LSU.[5]

These and other successful scientists—along with hundreds of physicians, dentists, teachers, professors, and administrators I was honored to teach and mentor—are my "kids." I feel an almost genetic link to them. I am humbled and gratified by their accomplishments. They have taught me a great deal and given me great joy. I respect their intellectual insights and delightful personal qualities. Each one has contributed in a most satisfying way to my career as a professor of biology. This is why I love being a professor.

"ARE YOU SCARED?" SIXTY pairs of nursing student eyes homed in on me as the young lady in the front row blurted out her question. I had just stepped onto the amphitheater platform for my first lecture in Human Physiology, the first class I ever taught. It was fall 1975 and I was not quite twenty-seven years old. Andrews University needed someone to fill in for John Stout, my former master's thesis advisor, who was on research leave in Germany, and I had happily obliged. But as I stood before the class that day, I felt terribly self-conscious. I'm a shy person for whom public speaking does not come easily. Somehow I got through that first course. The next term, with a bit more confidence, I taught an upper division course in Cellular Physiology. I found that I enjoyed teaching and that I had a knack for explaining complicated concepts in ways that students could understand.

The 1975–1976 academic year at Andrews University was important to me in another way as well. Anticipation was high among the faculty about a soon-to-be-published book, *Prophetess of Health: A Study of Ellen G. White*, by Ronald L. Numbers. As a Berkeley-trained historian of science, Numbers had taught briefly at Andrews, but he soon took a position at Loma Linda University's School of Medicine to teach the history of medicine. Having grown up as a pastor's son and the grandson of a Seventh-day Adventist Church president, Numbers was surprised to discover that Ellen White, the church's prophet, had obtained much of the information for her extensive writings on diet and health from other writers rather than directly from God, as she and some of her supporters claimed.[6] She had freely copied

---

5. Moncrieff published his first peer-reviewed paper with our research group as a junior at Andrews University: Moncrieff et al., "Mating Patterns and Breeding Success in Gulls of the *Larus-glaucescens-occidentalis* complex, Protection Island, Washington, USA," 67–75. The new species of antbird was described in Moncrieff et al., "A New Species of Antbird (Passeriformes: Thamnophilidae) from the Cordillera Azul, San Martín, Peru," 114–26.

6. Numbers, Prophetess of Health, 95, 192-98.

words, concepts, and phraseology from other authors. *Prophetess of Health* was something of an historical exposé of this "borrowing." Unauthorized copies of Numbers' manuscript were already circulating, and church officials were mounting a vigorous defense. A faculty member at Andrews lent me his copy to read.[7]

I was riveted. I am typically a slow reader, but I finished the book-length manuscript in one sitting. The "Spirit of Prophecy" writings that had constrained my thoughts and behavior every day of my life, writings that informed practically every word out of my father's mouth, every morsel of food I ate, every idea I had about the past, present, and future—they were not what "Sister White" and many of her supporters claimed them to be. And if her writings on health were influenced by her contemporaries, then other parts of her writings likely had been similarly influenced.[8] Most important to me was what this meant for her numerous statements on creation, the flood, geology, and the age of the earth, statements that were at odds with so much modern physical evidence that was not available in the nineteenth century.[9] Given my background and upbringing, *Prophetess* was the most influential work I had read in terms of its impact on my religious understanding. More than any other work, *Prophetess* drew me out of my fundamentalist past.

Soon after I finished reading Numbers' manuscript, my dad came for a visit. He, along with numerous other church officials, had received

7. Unauthorized copies of Numbers' unpublished manuscript sold for five dollars each; see Butler, "The Historian as Heretic," 18.

8. See, for example, Patrick, "Author," 91-103; Fortin, "'I Have Had to Adjust My View of Things,'" 16-27. Despite her assertions to being divinely inspired, White also wrote that "In regard to infallibility, I never claimed it" (White, *Selected Messages*, Book 1, 37).

9. See, for example, White, *Spiritual Gifts*, Vol. 3, 60-96. Some of White's assertions at odds with science, but taken at face value by many believers, included the following: "[I]f there was one sin above another which called for the destruction of the race by the flood, it was the base crime of amalgamation of man and beast which defaced the image of God, and caused confusion everywhere" (64); "Since the flood there has been amalgamation of man and beast, as may be seen in the almost endless varieties of species of animals, and in certain races of men" (75); "Those who lived before the flood . . . [were] more than twice as tall as men now living upon the earth, and well proportioned" (84); "Infidel geologists claim that the world is very much older than the Bible record makes it. They reject the Bible record, because of those things which are to them evidences from the earth itself, that the world has existed tens of thousands of years" (91-2); "Because the bones of human beings and of animals found in the earth, are much larger than those of men and animals now living, or that have existed for many generations past, some conclude that the world is older than we have any scriptural record of, and was populated long before the record of creation, by a race of beings vastly superior in size to men now upon the earth" (92-93); "I have been shown that without Bible history, geology can prove nothing" (93).

unauthorized copies of the manuscript. He was sitting in our living room busily leafing through it. "This is of the devil!" he muttered. He asked if I was aware of the manuscript. I said I was, although I didn't know what to say beyond that admission. Here was a well-researched and well-written book that challenged the very foundation of Dad's life and ministry. I felt bad for him, but I don't think reading the manuscript changed his views. For the rest of his long life, he remained a loyal follower of Ellen White and defended an inerrantist view of her writings.

Prophetess of Health was published in 1976. Among other reviews, it was featured in the religion section of *Time* magazine.[10] Many Adventist Church officials were outraged. Readers of the book, they assumed, would be less likely to respond to their ecclesiastical declarations which often they backed up with statements by White. Officers of the White Estate bustled from place to place defending the words of the prophet.[11] Thinking it was money that was important to the young scholar, one of the officers, Numbers' favorite uncle, Glenn Coon, offered to pay his nephew $10,000 if he would agree not to publish.[12] When at last the book appeared in print, word circulated that Andrews faculty could order copies from the campus bookstore. I was directed downstairs to the bookstore manager's office where she handed me my copy in a brown paper sack.

After *Prophetess* was published, Numbers accepted a faculty position at the University of Wisconsin, Madison, where he pursued a long and distinguished career as the Hilldale and William Coleman Professor of the History of Science and Medicine. As fate would have it, my parents also moved to Madison where Dad became president of the Wisconsin Conference of Seventh-day Adventists. I don't think their paths ever crossed. But during a visit with my parents, my mother asked with a meaningful look, "You know who else lives in Madison, don't you?" She was, of course, referring to Numbers. In the process of researching and writing history, Numbers had achieved the reputation as the church's latest and most dangerous apostate.

ELLEN WHITE'S WRITINGS HAD always been billed by Adventists as the "lesser light," with the Bible as the "greater light."[13] I now had justification

---

10. Anonymous, "Prophet or Plagiarist?" 43.
11. Butler, "The Historian as Heretic," 29–30.
12. Butler, "The Historian as Heretic," 4.
13. See White's comment in *Colporteur Ministry*, 125: "[T]he Lord has given a lesser light to lead men and women to the greater light." Adventists generally took the words "lesser light" to mean White's own writings (see EGW Writings, "Some Hermeneutical Principles Bearing on the Ellen G. White Writings").

for questioning details concerning earth history provided by the lesser light. But how should I understand the words of the greater light? Take the biblical genealogies of Gen 5 and 11. They report very specific numbers of years lived by each of twenty patriarchs, from Adam to Abraham. The two genealogies provide the age at which each patriarch bore his firstborn son and the number of years he lived after the birth of that son. For example, Gen 11:22-23 records that "Serug lived thirty years, and begat Nabor: And Serug lived after he begat Nahor two hundred years, and begat sons and daughters." Adding up the years in the genealogies and considering other biblical and historical information, as did Archbishop James Ussher in the seventeenth century, the creation seemed to have occurred about 6,000 years ago.[14] I revered the Bible. So while I might quibble with Ellen White's comments about how earth history unfolded, it seemed that the biblical account should be taken more seriously.

Several years earlier, Lawrence Geraty, a professor of archaeology at the Andrews University Seminary, had published an article concluding that the Genesis genealogies should not be taken as chronological frameworks for history.[15] Conservative creationists, however, were of the opposite opinion.[16] So one day I sat in my office with a King James Version of the Bible, and carefully read through Genesis 5 and 11. The "begats" do not make for exciting reading. But I was a scientist trained to evaluate numbers, and the genealogies relayed forty independent numbers, two for each of the twenty patriarchs.

In addition to the numbing repetition, what stands out for any reader of the genealogies are the amazingly long lifespans of some of the patriarchs—Adam, for example, lived 930 years, and Methuselah 969 years. But as I read, I noticed something else that was most peculiar. Of the forty independent numbers, nineteen were multiples of ten. In any random set of

14. Dalrymple, *The Age of the Earth*, 19-24. Ellen White repeatedly made reference to her conviction that creation occurred about 6,000 years ago (see "Ellen G. White Statements Relating to Geology Earth Sciences"). Her statements have created tensions between Adventists who believe she was verbally inspired and those with confidence in physical data.

15. Geraty, "The Genesis Genealogies as an Index of Time," 5-18.

16. See, for example, Marsh, *Life, Man, and Time*, 67: "The Bible-believing scientist must face squarely the question, In the area of natural science which shall supersede, the clear assertions of God's inspired Book, or modern man's interpretation of what he thinks he sees in nature? When radiocarbon datings of more of more than some 6,000 years are accepted as true ages there is an immediate clash between their testimony and that of the Sacred Word." For a more recent, albeit slightly more flexible, example, see Brand and Chadwick, *Faith, Reason, & Earth History*, 112: "The creation week occurred only a few thousand years ago... although we do not know the exact time span, Scripture clearly portrays a short history of life on this earth."

forty numbers, one would expect to have only four multiples of ten. According to a chi-square statistical test, the chance of nineteen or more multiples of ten showing up in a set of forty random ages is less than one in a hundred thousand. Then I noticed another strange occurrence—eight of the forty numbers were multiples of one hundred, yet in a set of forty random ages one would expect very few, if any (four-tenths of one, to be exact) multiples of one hundred. The chance of eight or more multiples of one hundred in a random set of forty ages is also less than one in a hundred thousand. In short, it is highly unlikely these numbers represent actual ages.

I decided to run a control. I sent questionnaires to the Andrews University faculty, asking anyone who had a firstborn brother to tell me the age of the brother's father at the time the brother was born—the father's pre-generative age. I also asked the number of years the father lived after the first-born brother was born—his post-generative age. I received back thirty-eight questionnaires. Sure enough, the seventy-six numbers were randomly distributed—multiples of ten were no more common than expected.

I teamed up with a seminary student friend, Donald Casebolt, who was more familiar with Old Testament literature than I was, and together we published our study in *Origins*, one of the more responsible young-age creationist journals.[17] Our conclusion that the numbers in the genealogies could not be taken as chronological data, was hardly new, but as far as we could tell, no one previously had tested the genealogical information with formal statistical methodology. While not earth shaking, our conclusion, combined with what to me was overwhelming intra-biblical and extra-biblical evidence, led me to a similar position concerning biblical authority in matters of science and history as I had developed in regard to White's writings: Genesis was not meant to be historically or scientifically accurate in the sense that we think of historical and scientific accuracy today. It had become clear to me that the fundamental tenet of young-age creationism, based on seemingly literalist interpretations of Genesis 5 and 11, was without merit.

These realizations had little effect on my teaching. They did encourage me, however, to avoid making comments, either supportive of views I could not conscientiously hold, or of positions radically outside the religious context within which I taught. I never bent the truth to sound politically correct, but I was careful not to use terms like "evolution" and "millions of years" injudiciously. I was honest and open with students regarding evidence from the natural world, but I let them draw their own conclusions; I

---

17. Hayward and Casebolt, "The Genealogies of Genesis 5 & 11: A Statistical Study," 75–81.

had no interest in harming anyone's faith. Sometimes this felt like a tightrope walk, but most of my courses dealt with present-day processes. I remained a committed Christian and an active member of my church, and I honestly and enthusiastically supported faith in God as creator, albeit in a non-fundamentalist sense.

Toward the end of my one-year stint at Andrews University, Donald R. McAdams, president of Southwestern Union College, stopped by and asked if I would fill in at Southwestern for a year while the college awaited the arrival of a new biology faculty member. Given that my temporary job at Andrews was soon to end and a possibility of completing a doctorate in Germany had fallen through, I decided to accept McAdams' offer. This meant a move to Keene, Texas, where I had spent the first three of my college years. Southwestern was still a small college and a familiar place.

Part of my course load at Southwestern was team-teaching Science and Religion with the chair of the religion department, George Reid. At one point five members of the Geoscience Research Institute (GRI) visited campus to solicit support for a church-sponsored "Statement of Belief" on creation. Reid and I invited them to speak to our class. Although not formally stated as such, GRI's primary mission was to defend a six-literal-day creation, a short-term chronology of life on earth, and a world-wide flood responsible for major features of the earth's crust. Reid asked me to moderate the discussion.

The five panel members and I sat at the front of the classroom. I was well aware of a deep philosophical rift that divided members of the Geoscience staff. The three older scientists—Robert H. Brown, Ariel A. Roth, and Harold G. Coffin—were ardent defenders of a recent six-day creation and a world-wide flood. They considered the Bible and writings of Ellen White to be reliable sources of scientific information concerning earth history. By contrast, the two younger scientists, Harold E. James and Edward N. Lugenbeal, were fresh out of PhD programs at Princeton University and the University of Wisconsin, respectively, and their training and field experience led them to harbor serious doubts about traditional views. The two progressives sat on my left and the three traditionalists sat on my right—charged particles, it seemed, which could not occupy the same space. The traditionalists provided cautious defenses of their views, whereas the two progressives provided carefully crafted, noncommittal comments. Everyone was walking on eggshells, skirting facts and hedging perspectives. Within two years both progressives would be forced out of GRI.[18]

18. Lugenbeal, "The Conservative Restoration at Geoscience," 23–31.

Following class we ate lunch together, after which Lugenbeal and I walked back to the science building. I made some remark about the obvious differences of opinion dividing the GRI staff. Lugenbeal responded, "Some people have different gas in their tanks." Over forty years later I still think of that remark as the conflict between progressives and traditionalists continues to be played out in many arenas. Presuppositions about the nature of truth and reality lie at the root of all disagreements, whether scientific, religious, political, or personal. Most of the visible aspects of these disagreements lie with superficial information. True resolution occurs only if and when we find a way to resolve the differences in the presuppositions.

A second memorable experience during my stint at Southwestern Union College was attendance at a meeting in Dallas at which Don McAdams, SUC's president, delivered a talk to a group of Adventist historians. Knowing my interests, he invited me to join the group to hear his talk.

The title of the talk was "Ellen White and the Protestant Historians." At face value his talk was supportive of White's "prophetic gift." His research, however, clearly underscored Numbers' assertion that much of what Ellen White wrote was "borrowed" from other writers rather than channeled directly from heavenly sources. As a historian of European history, McAdams focused attention on White's book, *The Great Controversy*, which reviews the history of the Protestant Reformation from a Protestant perspective and purports to chronicle events leading up to the Second Coming. Just as Numbers had found with White's writings on health, McAdams discovered that words, phrases, concepts, and "facts"—both true and erroneous—were in large part "borrowed" from the works of other writers.[19]

By now, this conclusion was not surprising to me. Nonetheless, McAdams' findings reinforced my developing views about White's writings and those of scripture. I had come to realize that to obtain reliable historical and scientific information, I would need to depend on carefully collected data, data interpreted as objectively as possible with both caution and basic common sense.

AFTER COMPLETING MY TEMPORARY service at Southwestern Union College and finishing my PhD at Washington State University in 1981, I landed my first permanent position at Union College in Lincoln, Nebraska. Union was a fine undergraduate institution, with responsive, studious, and polite students. But it was a small college with especially heavy teaching demands on its professors. Although I liked teaching, enjoyed my colleagues, and

---

19. McAdams, "Ellen G. White and the Protestant Historians," was an unpublished manuscript circulated at the talk.

loved the prairies and wholesome people of Nebraska, I wanted to combine my teaching with research, something difficult to do at a place like Union. Preparation for up to four classes plus labs each semester, while at the same time trying to work on research and writing, pushed me toward an emotional cliff.

During my fifth year at Union, I received a letter from a search committee in the Department of Biology at Andrews University. The committee chair asked me to apply for one of two positions soon to be vacated by retirements. I was excited about the prospect. Andrews offered an outstanding undergraduate program in Biology and also administered an excellent master's program. Teaching loads were reasonable and applicants were expected to engage in research. I applied, interviewed, was offered the job, and I accepted. I would spend the next twenty-nine years at Andrews as a professor and retire as an emeritus professor.

Soon after my arrival at Andrews University, I assumed the job of graduate coordinator, a responsibility I thoroughly enjoyed. This job provided me with an opportunity to become acquainted with each graduate student, even those who were working with other thesis advisors. During the same year I inherited the graduate course, Issues in Origins and Speciation, which I had taken when I was a student at Andrews.

Given the wide spectrum of students enrolled in the course, teaching "Issues" was an interesting challenge. The description of the course in the university bulletin stated that it involved a "comparative survey of the assumptions, attitudes, methods, and conclusions of science and religion in the handling of data," and that special attention was paid "to current scientific data and its relationship to an understanding of Earth history and the present diversity of life." All enrolled students were at the graduate level, but they ranged from conservative Christians of several denominations who had grown up believing in young-age creationism, to mainland Chinese students who hadn't a clue about Christian belief and assumed completely materialistic worldviews.

As a consequence of the philosophical diversity in the class, I was careful to not come across as dogmatic about any particular viewpoint, while at the same time teaching the course within a Christian context. This meant that I affirmed a belief in divine creatorship, which I could do with complete integrity, but without providing details of what that might mean in terms of earth history. I wanted each student to understand the views of both conservative Christians and materialist evolutionists, and the variety of views in between. This was accomplished through readings, discussions, and guest lectures.

The first day of the course, I always gave students a brief synopsis of my personal background and positive religious orientation. I then asked each student to provide as much information as he or she felt comfortable about his or her own background and belief system. I always assured the students that I would be completely honest with them. I also told them that the most important thing I wanted them to gain from the course was a sense of respect for all people, regardless of one's viewpoint. I emphasized my belief that that most people are people of goodwill, despite widely divergent belief systems.

I then introduced a brief history of views about life and the earth's past. I recounted ideas of some of the early Greek philosophers, the ancient Hebrews, early Christians, classical scholars, Renaissance cosmologists, eighteenth and nineteenth century natural historians, and more recent thinkers about the natural world and its history and meaning. I also explained how different religious groups approached an understanding of nature. The bulk of the course, however, dealt with processes of nature such as genetic change at the individual and population levels, natural selection, adaptive radiation, speciation, biogeographic dispersion, plate tectonics, fossilization, and radiometric dating. Many of the students who took the course had virtually no background in the historical sciences. I wanted each student who completed the course to be prepared for related coursework she or he might take in the future.

To a large extent I believe I achieved my goals. Class meetings provided students opportunities to discuss questions and concerns regarding issues of time and process in the context of their religious views, or lack thereof. I viewed my role as a facilitator and moderator. Course evaluations suggested that students appreciated the format of the class and my approach as a teacher. Non-religious students commented that they now recognized the possibility that religious perspectives concerning the history of life might have merit, whereas fundamentalist students expressed an openness to views they previously would have dismissed out of hand. The course served as a bridge builder.

ONCE ESTABLISHED AT ANDREWS University, I began thinking about the possibility of hosting a conference on the history of creationism. Both George McCready Price and Frank Lewis Marsh, prominent creationists, had taught here, and I lectured in Price Hall, a building named after the old anti-evolutionary warrior. It was Price's extensive writings during the first half of the twentieth century that eventually led to the phenomenon of "scientific creationism" that flooded America and eventually the world.[20] In 1982 the prestigious journal *Science* had published an article by Ronald Numbers on the history of creationism in America, a modified version of an article he had published three years earlier in the independent Adventist journal *Spectrum*.[21] With all the interest in creationism and the creationism trials taking place in a variety of states, I thought a conference on the topic would be a timely event.

I knew that any conference on the history of creationism would need to feature a plenary address by Numbers, the acknowledged expert who was writing a book on the topic. So in January 1989, I wrote to him and asked if he would be willing to participate.[22] I did not hear back from him right away, but I did hear from a mutual friend, Gary Land, chair of the Andrews University Department of History. Gary told me that Numbers had contacted him and asked about me. Gary assured him that I was a serious scholar. He said Numbers was coming to visit campus a few weeks later to talk about a book project they were planning, and suggested the three of us get together for lunch.

At the appointed time I appeared at Gary's office and was introduced to Ron Numbers. He immediately impressed me as a cordial, outgoing, gracious person, very direct in manner, articulate, and bright. Gary asked where we should eat, and Ron responded "What I'd really like is a vegeburger!" So we walked over to The Gazebo, the university's fast-vegetarian-food restaurant. Over sandwiches we talked about the possibility of a conference, and we discussed names of other historians who might be interested in participating.

For several reasons the conference never materialized, but considering it as a possibility gave me an opportunity to become acquainted with Ron. Since that time, we have corresponded about issues of common interest and become friends. Like me, he is the son of an Adventist pastor who earned an undergraduate STEM degree from an Adventist college.[23] We both find the history of science and its intersection with religion fascinating and important. Hardly the demon-possessed heretic he had been caricatured, he is an engaging conversationalist, an honest scholar, and a sensitive human being who continues to value aspects of his Adventist heritage, even though

---

20. Numbers, *The Creationists*, 399–431.

21. Numbers, "Creationism in 20th-Century America," 538–44; Numbers, "'Sciences of Satanic Origin,'" 17–30.

22. JLH to Ronald L. Numbers, January 31, 1989.

23. Numbers earned BA degree in mathematics and physics from Southern Missionary College (now Southern Adventist University) in 1963. https://medhist.wisc.edu/faculty/numbers/cv.pdf.

he has distanced himself from organized religion. His highly-respected studies on the history of Ellen White, John Harvey Kellogg, and creationism have put Seventh-day Adventism on the map with scholars outside the denomination.[24]

"DINOSAURS ARE UGLY, AND my God didn't make anything ugly!" An elderly lady in the audience was peeved with my suggestion that perhaps God was responsible for creating dinosaurs. Her comment was made during the question-and-answer period following a talk I gave about these iconic creatures at the Battle Creek Tabernacle. The movie "Jurassic Park" had recently been released creating an enormous cultural sensation. In response, an editor for the *Adventist Review* asked me to write a feature article on dinosaurs. The appearance of the article had led to an invitation to speak at my father's former parish.

The *Adventist Review* is the Seventh-day Adventist Church's general magazine. Writing an article about dinosaurs for distribution to over 100,000 readers, most of whom were young-age creationists who lacked scientific training, was an intriguing challenge. Many Adventists still believed that dinosaurs never existed, or if they did exist they were inventions of the devil. I decided the best way to frame the topic would be in the context of seven questions commonly asked by conservative Christians: 1) Did dinosaurs really exist? 2) What do inspired writings say about dinosaurs? 3) What were dinosaurs like? 4) Did God create dinosaurs? 5) Did dinosaurs and humans live together? 6) How and when did dinosaurs go extinct? 7) What should I teach my children about dinosaurs? Framing the article in the context of questions allowed me to gently lay to rest some of the distorted views Christians have held about dinosaurs.

The article appeared in the August 12, 1993 edition of the *Review*,[25] and my first glimpse of the issue left me dumbfounded. Both the front and back covers featured a colorful cavalcade of dinosaurs and other prehistoric creatures, splendid artwork so overpowering that the name of the magazine was barely visible. Never before had the *Review* featured such a stunning cover.

Responses to the article were both fascinating and varied. In a letter to the editor, one pastor opined, "I had to write to express appreciation for James L. Hayward's 'Dinosuars" . . . His candor and commitment to the facts ought to set new standards for denominational essays on topics of this

---

24. Butler, "Seventh-day Adventist Historiography," 149–66. Butler noted that "Numbers still looms as the Papa Hemingway of the new SDA scholarship . . ."

25. Hayward, "Dinosuars," 12–14.

nature." Another wrote, "Dinomania has hit the *Adventist Review*! And why not, if you can deal with it in such a forthright and balanced manner? Congratulations!" A third pastor, however, was less sanguine: "I have had my fill of dinosaurs this summer! With media blitze for the worldly and murderous movie Jurassic Park at record levels . . . I don't care to see more."[26]

Despite occasional expressions of ire, I contributed a second, more detailed piece on dinosaurs to the independent Adventist journal *Spectrum*, and I wrote another cover story about these animals for the *Journal of Adventist Education*.[27] Adventist editors and readers seemed eager for reliable information on these animals.

I have written many other non-technical articles about science and life for both the religious and secular press. I have always believed it is my responsibility to find ways to give back to the public in gratitude for its support of science. One way I can do so is to provide scientifically credible writing about the natural world written in a way that non-scientists find accessible and interesting. The most important thing I've learned about writing has been the value of maintaining an attitude of generosity and respect for those who may disagree with my perspectives. We all arrive at the conclusions we do because of our genetic heritage, our environment, our education, and our experiences. These are different for every person. Therefore it is not surprising there are many different opinions about every topic. I believe people of good will come to their different views honestly. I may disagree with their views and may do so even vigorously, but I strive to do so with respect.

A second thing I have learned is the value of recounting history as a way of helping people recognize the complexity of issues about nature. History allows an examination of various ways of looking at things in the past tense. This takes consideration of a controversial topic out of the emotionally charged atmosphere of the present. It allows for an objective evaluation of the consequences of various perspectives when examined through the lens of time, and provides an opportunity to avoid making the mistakes of the past.

ONE TIME I WAS asked to give a guest lecture in an Andrews University Seminary course which introduced future pastors to issues concerning science and faith. I began by affirming faith in God's creatorship, but also addressed some of the scientific problems facing a literalistic interpretation of Genesis. One of our brightest pre-med biology majors was sitting in on the course.

---

26. Hoenes, "Letters: Dino and Other Saurs (cont.)," 2: Marks, "Letters: Dino and Other Saurs (cont.), 2; Widmer, "Letters: Dino and Other Saurs (cont.)," 2.

27. Hayward, "Noah's Ark or 'Jurassic Park'?, 6-14; Hayward, "A Closer Look at Dinosaurs," 29-36.

After my lecture she cornered me in the hall and said she was disturbed by my perspectives. She told me that she recognized there might be more than one way to look at the data, but that she was compelled to take as conservative a view as possible. During my lecture I had remarked that we should be more concerned about caring for the creation than figuring out how or when it occurred. This statement especially agitated her. "If God didn't create life, I don't care anything about taking care of the planet, nor do I care about how I treat you!" I was taken aback by her harsh words. For one thing she apparently misinterpreted my cautionary remarks concerning strict literalism as indicating disbelief in creation. For another, I was stunned by her relegation of ethics to a position lower than her chosen hermeneutic.[28]

She was a young person, maturing and growing, and I do not know how she would respond today. Her response back then, however, helped me to realize the fragility of faith among many fundamentalist Christians, along with how self-centered it can be. It's ironic to me that many agnostics and atheists are more concerned about the quality of life on our planet than people who believe God is responsible for the existence of every blade of grass. To people like our student, it is more important to be right than to be caring—or perhaps it would be more accurate to say they will be caring only if they know they're right. Considering how difficult it is to know for sure that one is right, these priorities seem backward to me.

Carl Jung diagnosed fanaticism as "overcompensated doubt."[29] It is not uncommon for people with an overly fragile "faith" to completely reverse course when they face an undeniable challenge to a cherished belief. Pastors, teachers, and parents reinforce this tendency by telling young people that unless you believe thus-and-so, you may as well have no beliefs at all. I have heard people say that unless you believe in a six-literal-day creation or in a worldwide flood, you might just as well give up on religion. Fanatical belief trumps both reasonable faith and ethical practice.

DESPITE THE USUAL CHALLENGES that come with any occupation, I thoroughly enjoyed my teaching career. I have no regrets about my decision to become a biology professor. I particularly valued my three decades of teaching at Andrews University, where I was blessed with congenial colleagues, bright students, and the time and incentive to do research. Sharing information through teaching, guiding students in research, and developing a research track record was for me a winning and satisfying combination.

---

28. JLH diary entry, May 11, 1991.
29. Jung, *Letters [of] C. G. Jung*, 30.

Time for learning, sharing, and creative activity—what more could a curious person wish for in a profession?

7

Learning Firsthand

"The known is finite, the unknown infinite; intellectually we stand on an islet in the midst of an illimitable ocean of inexplicability. Our business in every generation is to reclaim a little more land."

—Thomas Henry Huxley[1]

CHARLIE AMLANER AND I landed our boat at the south edge of Harper Island on Sprague Lake. We scrambled out, climbed the volcanic ash-covered slope, and hiked the short distance to the gull colony. I had not set foot here since the previous year when Mount St. Helens emptied its fury on the colony. The eruption had buried nests and eggs and sent my research into a tailspin.

As we made our way to the nesting area, anxious gulls flew up and circled about. Hundreds of nests, most containing from one to three eggs, punctuated the pale, dusty colony surface. But we were not here to observe living birds—there would be plenty of time for that later. We were here to look for last year's nests and eggs buried beneath the ash.

I recently had talked with a geologist friend who told me that a fossilized dinosaur nesting colony had been discovered in northern Montana. Nests, eggs, and baby dinosaurs had been buried by sediments eroded from

---

1. Huxley, "On the Reception of the 'Origin of Species,'" 557.

the Rocky Mountains which were then rising to the west. Volcanic ash deposits were also present in the region.[2] I wondered if my study site could serve as a modern-day analog to the Montana dinosaur colony. That's what Charlie and I were here to find out.

We walked over to where there had been a high concentration of ring-billed gull nests the year before. I got down on my knees and carefully scraped away the layer of volcanic ash. Charlie was poised to capture any finds on film. Within minutes my spade struck an ash-coated, brownish green structure with a convex surface—an eggshell! Then another and another! Soon I had uncovered an entire buried nest with three eggs. As I continued to dig, more nests with eggs were uncovered. We had hit pay dirt.

The eggs were not fossilized, but they had been protected by the overlying ash. Had they not been completely covered, they would have been eaten by predators. The year-old insides contained a smelly paste of decomposing fats and proteins. Despite the fact that these gull eggs were not yet fossils, they would teach us important things about events that lead to egg fossilization, as well as about the process of fossilization itself. And because bird and dinosaur eggs are very similar, preservation of the gull eggs would help us understand processes leading to dinosaur egg fossilization.[3]

As it turned out, our dusty find opened up an entirely new research arena in paleontology, and it connected me with some of the top people in dinosaur research. Like most scientific discoveries, ours was the result of curiosity, initiative, knowledge, and plain old good luck converted to action.

This chapter is about scientific discovery of physical reality, which has played a crucial role in my journey from fundamentalism to faith. For me, nothing is more satisfying than uncovering a hitherto unknown corner of the universe and then sharing that corner with the rest of the world. To illustrate the excitement and joy of discovery, I share several of my own long-term research projects that have opened new areas of inquiry in paleontology and ecology. But first I will mention a few reflections on the nature and value of scientific research.

First of all, I think physical reality should serve as a control on the contours of belief and faith. People who undervalue physical reality are vulnerable to all sorts of spurious ideas—that the earth is flat, that flying saucers

---

2. Horner and Gorman, *Digging Dinosaurs*, 21–63; Horner and Makela, "Nest of Juveniles Provides Evidence of Family Structure Among Dinosaurs," 296–98; Gavin, "A Paleoenvironmental Reconstruction of the Cretaceous Willow Creek Anticline Dinosaur Nesting Locality: North Central Montana," 7.

3. Hayward, "Breath of Vulcan," 4–8.

bring aliens to earth, that water filtered through lava cures cancer, that prayer cloths perform miracles, that vaccinations cause autism, that global warming is a myth, that dinosaurs and humans walked together. Faith does not involve believing in things falsified by evidence from the physical world. This is not to say that science provides a foolproof basis for understanding; in fact, science does not employ the idea of proof. Scientific perspectives shift over time, but generally our understanding of the universe shifts closer to reality as evidence accumulates. Advances in technology and medicine, practical applications of scientific understanding, provide powerful support for the idea that the scientific method is an effective way to progressively illuminate physical reality.

Scientific research forces investigators to become intimately familiar with the systems they study. My research on the fossilization of eggs and on the behavioral ecology of gulls has provided me with insights about life in the past and present that I never could have obtained from reading or classroom work. Intimate and longterm connection with nature, especially in association with the rough and tumble of the scientific peer-review process, is a prerequisite for anyone hoping to speak intelligently about the complexities of life and its history. Research involves the combined skills and drama of Curious George, Indiana Jones, and Sherlock Holmes, but scientific research also involves tedium, innumerable trips down blind alleys, and countless failures. Patience, and lots of it, is required for the successful researcher. The folly of attempting to be seen as an expert in matters of science without an active research program is illustrated by the life and work of George McCready Price. Price disliked of fieldwork, set himself up as an armchair critic of geology and evolutionary biology, wrote extensively on these topics—and has been thoroughly discredited, even by other creationists.[4] But lest we become overconfidant about our knowledge, we need to keep in mind the cautionary remark by Scottish biologist, D'Arcy Thompson, that we can "never know all, about the smallest, humblest thing."[5]

We must also recognize that every scientist has bias. But scientific methodology, carefully applied, helps us minimize, as much as possible, the effects of bias on scientific conclusions. In science, the philosophical

---

4. Numbers, *The Creationists*, 88–119. One of Price's former students reported that "Often in class, while showing us pictures of some geological feature high on a mountainside, he would remark, 'Why should I risk my neck trying to climb up there when the picture show it very clearly'" (Hammill, "Fifty Years of Creationism," 33). About Price's derisive comments, young-age creationist Leonard Brand wrote that "Creationists, perhaps beginning with George McCready Price, have developed some bad habits when speaking on the subject of evolution" (Brand, *Faith, Reason, and Earth History*, 149).

5. Thompson, *On Growth and Form*, 19.

assumptions behind a hypothesis should be relatively unimportant; what is crucial is that the scientific method is applied rigorously as one tests that hypothesis. In fact, philosophical background and interests can be an important creative force in shaping one's research hypotheses, and indeed career. In an earlier chapter I described the first research project I tackled as a student—development of a simple mathematical model to define factors necessary for the upright floatation of trees. The motivation for this project was the belief that the Genesis flood ripped trees from the ground, floated them about, and eventually left them in an upright position once the flood waters receded. I no longer consider a worldwide flood to be a viable explanation for the data, but that does not negate my conclusions about the factors necessary for the upright floatation of trees. In the same way, my more recent work in experimental paleontology has been motivated by curiosity about the past, curiosity inspired by my fundamentalist roots, even though my perspectives on what that past was like have shifted since my youth.

Field research, my specialty, combines white-collar cognition with blue-collar grunt work. I enjoy physical labor—assembling an elevated observation blind, pounding nest stakes into the ground, building camera platforms. It's fun to figure out ways to use limited resources in creative ways. For nearly all my career I have worked on remote islands, places where you have to make do or lose opportunities to obtain important data. Learning to use what is at hand—scrap lumber, driftwood, an old piece of umbrella or tripod, a clothespin—to do what needs to be done is an important skill to develop.

These days good research almost always involves collaboration. Scientific research generally requires the knowledge, ideas, and skills of a variety of experts. Collaboration has been a crucial aspect of my research career. I cannot overstate the advantages I have enjoyed as a result of collaboration. In most cases my collaborators became good friends and introduced me to other helpful people.

Good research also involves good storytelling. Humans love stories and scientists are no exception. The scientist who makes ripples on the pond of knowledge needs to be able to communicate effectively. Narratives in science need to be presented, not only factually and with integrity, but also in ways that motivate continued listening or reading. I work hard on both my technical and popular writing. Good writing happens in concert with good reading, so each day I try to read well-written literature.

MOUNT ST. HELENS' ASHFALL happened the year before I began teaching at Union College. As much as I enjoyed working at Union, my teaching load was so intense that it was difficult to think about research. I did, however, manage to publish a report on the effects of the ashfall on the nesting gulls. Don Miller, my dissertation advisor at Washington State, and Calvin Hill, the friend who was with me when the ashfall occurred, were coauthors. Our paper appeared as the lead article in the October 1982 issue of *The Auk*, a prominant ornithological journal.[6] In 1989, Charlie Amlaner and I published the results of our discovery of ash-buried eggs and nests in the *Journal of Vertebrate Paleontology*.[7]

These two papers formed the basis for a productive research tangent—a tangent, because most of my research would continue to focus on the behavior and ecology of living animals. Yet this foray into historical biology and paleontology would remain a point of interest during the remainder of my career and provide many students with research projects. It would also give me firsthand experience and insights into the geologic column and history of life as I continued to shape my philosophical perspectives.

WHEN I SEARCHED FOR someone who knew something about eggshell fossilization, I came up with only one name—Karl Hirsch. He was connected with the University of Colorado Museum of Natural History. In late summer 1983, I wrote to him and described my experience with Mount St. Helens ashfall. I mentioned that I was a novice in paleontology, included a copy of our *Auk* article, and asked for any information he might be able to provide on eggshell fossilization. He quickly responded, saying that as far as he knew, he was the only person in North America working on fossil eggs. Moreover, no one anywhere was working on egghell taphonomy.[8] He was delighted to find someone else with an interest in fossil eggs. The following year he called saying he would soon be visiting Lincoln, Nebraska, where I was living at the time, and he wanted to get together.[9]

Karl was a strong extrovert, smoked tobacco, loved cognac, and spoke with a thick German accent. By contrast, I'm a strongly introverted, non-smoking, teetotaling, monolingual American, yet we hit it off immediately. As a young man, Karl was conscripted as a Nazi soldier. During Hitler's invasion of Russia he suffered three wounds, one which nearly cost him a leg. "Out of two hundred twenty men in my unit," he said, "only ten were

---

6. Hayward et al., "Volcanic Ash Fallout: Its Impact on Breeding Ring-billed and California Gulls," 623–31.

7. Hayward et al., "Turning Eggs to Fossils: A Natural Experiment in Taphonomy," 196–200.

8. Taphonomy, a branch of paleontology, is the study of how things become fossils.

9. JLH to Karl Hirsch, August 30, 1983; JLH to Karl Hirsch,

left after the war was over." In 1945 he was captured by the Russians and spent the next two and a half years as a starving prisoner of war at a Siberian labor camp. After his release, he and his wife, Hildegard, immigrated to the United States where they became rock hounds. In 1973 they found a fossil bird egg in the Nebraska badlands, and this got Karl interested in these ancient relics. No one seemed to know anything about fossil eggs, so he decided to learn about them himself.

Except for two courses at the University of Colorado, Karl had no formal training in geology or paleontology. In Germany he had been trained in accounting and management, but here in the States he worked as a maintenance technician at Rocky Flats Weapons Plant in Denver.[10] He had taught himself what he needed to know about geology and paleontology, and he even learned scanning electron microscopy for the purpose of imaging and describing eggshell microstructure. He eventually published thirty-three technical papers on fossil eggs, including one in the prestigious journal *Science*, thus establishing himself as the world's expert on the topic. In 1990 the University of Colorado awarded him an honorary doctorate in recognition of his groundbreaking work, and in the same year The Paleontological Society honored him with its prestigious Strimple Award.[11] When I met him, Hildegard had recently died, leaving him depressed and lonely. His fossils and his friends were all he had left.

Karl was anxious for someone to maintain an interest in fossil eggs after he was gone. He was most interested in eggshell microstructure, and we published a paper together on the microstructural changes in gull eggshells buried by Mount St. Helens ash.[12] I was more intrigued, however, by the taphonomy of whole eggs and large-scale taphonomic features such as fracture patterns and fragment orientation, which could tell us important things about ancient environments and dinosaur behavior. Following Karl's death in 1996, several younger paleontologists continued to pursue his eggshell microstructure studies, and I continued with my studies on the taphonomy of whole eggs and eggshell fragments.

Karl and I enjoyed two extended trips together during which we visited fossil egg sites and consulted with various paleontologists. In August 1992,

---

10. Anonymous, "Karl Hirsch: Anything but Ordinary," 2–3.

11. Finley, "'Addition' Hatched from Dinosaur Egg," 1B–2B; Harris, "Presentation of the Harrell L. Strimple Award of the Paleontological Society to Karl F. Hirsch," 527–28; Hirsch, "Response by Karl F. Hirsch," 528–29; "Karl Hirsch and the Hirsch Eggshell Collection"; Harris, "Presentation of the Harrell L. Strimple Award of the the Paleontological Society to Karl F. Hirsch," 527–28.

12. Hayward et al., "Rapid Dissolution of Avian Eggshells Buried by Mount St. Helens Ash," 174–78.

we visited the Museum of the Rockies at Montana State University. There Jack Horner showed me the museum's extensive dinosaur nest and egg collection, all cataloged and neatly stowed on heavy-duty metal shelves. We then traveled to Egg Mountain—really only a large mound—near Choteau, Montana, where fourteen years earlier Horner had discovered the first evidence of nesting dinosaurs in North Amerca. Karl took me to several sites in the vicinity of Egg Mountain where dinosaur nests with eggs had been uncovered.

In 1993, Karl and I once again traveled to Egg Mountain. When we arrived, the site was bustling with paleontologists instructing volunteers who had paid for a chance to dig up dinosaur remains. An extensive dinosaur bone bed had been found, and enthusiastic volunteers were exposing the bones. Other volunteers were marking locations where concentrations of eggshell fragments had weathered out at the ground surface. All personnel were housed in large teepees—the site looked like a nineteenth-century Native American village.

The next morning we drove to Dinosaur Provincial Park, Alberta, where we enjoyed a tour of the dinosaur-infested badlands. From Dinosaur Provincial Park we traveled southwest the next day to Devil's Coulee, near the little town of Warner, Alberta. Here in 1987 a high school student and fossil enthusiast, Wendy Sloboda, found some pieces of dinosaur eggshell exposed in the eroding badlands. This led to further exploration which revealed the presence not only of duck-billed dinosaur eggs, but also bones of juvenile duck-bills. Sloboda, it turned out, had discovered a dinosaur nesting site similar to the one at Egg Mountain further south.[13]

These two trips networked me into the paleontological community. Karl knew just about everyone working in the area of dinosaur paleontology. During our trips to field sites, museums, and professional meetings, he introduced me to many of the top people in the field, some of whom ended up as collaborators. Now that he is gone, I miss his friendship, his thickly accented phone calls ("Hi Chim! This is Karl!"), his cheerful enthusiasm, and his professional guidance.

Karl's pioneering work in eggshell microstructure and Jack Horner's discovery of the dinosaur nesting ground at Egg Mountain stimulated great interest among paleontologists. This interest led to the first book on the topic, *Dinosaur Eggs and Babies*, edited by Kenneth Carpenter, Hirsch, and Horner. The introductory chapter referenced the two papers on taphonomy my colleagues and I had published to that point and predicted the results

---

13. Carpenter, *Eggs, Nests, and Baby Dinosaurs: A Look at Dinosaur Reproduction*, 21.

of our work would "shed light on dinosaur nesting sites,"[14] which is indeed what happened.

LOTS OF THINGS CAN happen to an egg laid at a nesting site before it becomes a fossil. Burial by volcanic ash is an important one, but there are many others. Eggs, for example, can be predated, burned, crushed, attacked by bacteria, dissolved by acidic soil, or get washed into the sea. Eggshell fragments can be trampled at the nest site or transported by water, wind, or rising tides. None of these possibilities had been rigorously examined. Knowing how these factors affect eggs and eggshell fragments could provide "forensic evidence" about the behavior of dinosaurs and the types of environments in which they lived. Given the tremendous interest in dinosaurs, I decided this would be a fruitful area of research.

My students, colleagues, and I carried out an extensive series of experiments to find out what happens to eggs under various circumstances. We used modern chicken, ostrich, and emu eggs for our experiments. These eggs served as excellent proxies for ancient eggs, both bird and dinosaur, because bird and dinosaur eggs share such similar physical properties. We lowered chicken eggs into the Pacific Ocean to a depth of about 2,000 feet from the oceanographic research vessel *New Horizon*, and demonstrated that eggs at those intense pressures don't crack. We found that when gulls build nests and lay eggs too low along the beach, high tides cause nests and eggs to float away from shore; eventually the eggs drop from the disintegrating nest to the ocean floor. We found that chicken eggs placed on the ocean bottom are not eaten, but gradually serve as substrates for the growth of bacteria and other microorganisms. We discovered that eggshell buried in soil laced with various species of soil bacteria, or placed in solution of different levels of acidity, develop characteristic patterns of pitting on the eggshell surface. We crushed whole eggs under sediment loads and found that the fracture patterns differ depending on whether the eggshell is hollow, freshly laid, or filled with plaster to mimic eggs that have fossilized. We heated ostrich and emu eggshell fragments at different temperatures for varying lengths of time, and showed that during a forest fire eggshells turn various colors—some quite beautiful—depending on the type of egg and the amount of heat. Each of these experiments helped with the interpretation of the taphonomic histories of fossil eggs described from around the world.[15]

14. Carpenter et al., "Introduction," 1–11.
15. For a summary of our work in eggshell taphonomy, see Hayward et al., "Eggshell Taphonomy: Environmental Effects on Fragment Orientation," 5–13.

Our taphonomic work that attracted the most interest, however, were experiments on eggshell fragment orientation. We found that the ratios of eggshell fragments oriented concave-surface up versus concave-surface down vary depending on their transport histories. Fragments transported by wind or water tend to exhibit a concave-surface down orientation. By contrast, if transport has not occurred, the predominant orientation is concave-surface up. This simple test allowed us to infer that dinosaur eggshell fragments found at a site in northern Montana, and at another site at Devil's Coulee, Alberta, were in the locations of the ancient nest sites and had not been transported from other locations.[16]

Finding dinosaur eggshell fragments predominantly concave-surface up implied, among other things, that these sites had not been inundated by flowing water. Had these eggshell fragments been pushed around, for example, by the Genesis flood, they likely would have assumed predominantly concave-down orientations. Moreover, eggshell at some dinosaur sites occur at multiple levels separated by one or more sediment layers. This suggests the sites were used for more than one nesting season, not just a single season in the year purported for Noah's flood.[17]

Our eggshell taphonomy work provided paleontologists with useful tools and concepts for reconstructing the original environmental conditions at dinosaur nest sites. It has been heartening to see our ideas and techniques adopted by other scientists. Moreover, research in taphonomy has taught me a great deal about the fossil record, and has supplied ample reason for me to reject the notions of flood geologists.

MOST OF MY RESEARCH has focused on the behavior and ecology of living animals, including gulls, harbor seals, marine iguanas, and bald eagles. As I mentioned earlier, I studied gull reproductive behavior for my PhD dissertation, and this was the reason I was on a gull colony in eastern Washington when Mount St. Helens erupted in 1980. I had already spent three field seasons working on another colony studying gull communication for my master's degree, so I was well acquainted with these birds. Gulls make excellent subjects for animal behavior studies: they nest in large, open colonies with hundreds or even thousands of individuals; they are active during the day; they exhibit interesting and relatively complex behavior and

---

16. Hayward et al., "Eggshell Taphonomy: Environmental Effects on Fragment Orientation," 5–13.

17. Horner, "Ecologic and Behavioral Implications Derived from a Dinosaur Nesting Site," 51–63; Chiappe et al., "Sauropod Eggs and Embryos From the Late Cretaceous of Patagonia," 23–29.

communication patterns; they walk, run, fly, and swim with equal ease; and more than four dozen species of gulls make comparative studies interesting and feasible.

For my master's thesis research project I determined how gulls use *sequences* of behavioral units and *body orientations* to communicate messages. From motion picture film and video recordings, I transcribed the sequences of behaviors and body orientations used during territorial disputes. I found that body orientation plays a significant role during aggressive encounters by these birds. For example, body orientation toward an intruder by a territory defender conveys a higher level of threat than orientation away from the intruder. Moreover, the communicative function of a behavior may be altered by the behaviors that precede it in sequence. Just as humans use body postures, orientation, and syntax when we communicate with one another, so do gulls.[18]

The philosophical implication of this to me is profound. Gulls use the same elements of communication—vocalizations, postures, orientations—as we do, albeit with considerably less complexity. Both gulls and humans modulate communicative signals by changes in vocalization amplitude and pitch, along with changes in the rate of movement. Especially fascinating to me is that communicative signals cross species boundaries. If I orient my body toward a gull, stare directly at it, or raise my arm toward it, I communicate more threat than if I stand still and look the other way. Similarly if a gull orients toward me, raises the feathers on top of its head, and vocalizes an attack call, I know that I had better watch my head! Common rules of communication bond us together as social creatures. Although we humans may be more complex than gulls, each of us exists as part of the remarkable, interacting fabric of nature.

IN 1987, THE SUMMER after I moved to Andrews University, Joseph Galusha invited me to participate at the research site he had established on the Protection Island gull colony, the largest seabird colony in Washington State's inland wanters. I had become acquainted with Joe during the summer of 1971 when I was a senior biology major taking summer coursework at the Rosario Beach Marine Laboratory. Joe was completing his master's degree research on gull behavior under John Stout who, in turn, became my master's thesis advisor. Upon completion of his master's degree, Joe earned a doctorate at Oxford University with Niko Tinbergen, the "father" of gull studies. During the time Joe was his student, Tinbergen, Konrad Lorenz,

---

18. Hayward et al., "Aggressive Communication by *Larus glaucescens*. Part V. Orientation and Sequences of Behavior," 236–76.

and Karl von Frisch won the 1973 Nobel Prize in Physiology or Medicine for their pioneering work in animal behavior. When Joe returned to the States with a newly minted Oxford doctorate, he was hired to teach biology at Walla Walla College.

Joe understood gull behavior better than anyone I knew, and he had developed an excellent research setup on Protection Island, home to thousands of nesting glaucous-winged gulls. It was a generous offer to share his field site with me—many researchers are protective of their productive research sites. Little did I know that I would spend the next thirty-two field seasons working on Protection Island where gulls, bald eagles, harbor seals, vegetation, and even geology would attract my focus. I would come to know and love this island better than any place on earth. Joe not only shared this outstanding research site with me, he also taught me much about gull behavior, research techniques, and how to mentor students.

Protection Island is located in the Salish Sea at the southeast corner of the Strait of Juan de Fuca, Washington. The island is about a mile and a half long and a half mile wide, and is shaped a bit like a plump, reclining comma with long, gravel spits forming its tips. The main part of the island consists of a grassy plateau, 100 to 200 feet above sea level. Two wooded areas also occur on the plateau. The northern edge of the plateau—the convex hump of the comma—forms a nearly vertical cliff along which the island's geologic history is vividly exposed by the sediment layers. From a single location at the top of the island, the San Juan Islands to the north, Vancouver Island to the northwest, the Olympic Mountains to the south and west, Mount Rainer to the southeast, and the North Cascades to the east and northeast are all visible. I could not have asked for a more asthetically pleasing site at which to do research.

Western Washington is famous for its lush, evergreen forests and abundant rainfall, but because of its position in the rain shadow created by the Olympic Mountains, much of Protection Island is a dry, tallgrass prairie. The temperatures are mild and mosquitoes, which plague denizens of the surrounding mainland forest, are mostly absent; a lack of standing freshwater and frequent seabreezes keep the pesky critters away. A research site on an island within an inland sea, surrounded by scenes of other islands and snow-covered peaks, and blessed with pleasing temperatures and a paucity of mosquitoes, is a rarity for field biologists. I had always dreamed of studying animals on an isolated island like my boyhood hero Sam Campbell, and that's what I was privileged to do on Protection Island for more than three decades.

FROM 1987 TO 2001, I spent the field seasons getting acquainted with Protection Isand. I engaged in a variety of disconnected projects—collecting gull chick carcasses for a gull bone development project, timing the duration of various gull behaviors, collecting and analyzing the contents of great-horned owl pellets, assessing bald eagle activity patterns, characterizing the diversity and distribution patterns of vegetation, and quantifying the taphonomic characteristics of eggs and eggshell. In the process I learned a great deal about the island and its tenants. Much of my time was spent perched atop a bluff overlooking Violet Point, the eastern gravel spit, and each hour for fifteen-hour days I counted the number of birds of each species in various habitats on the spit below. By 2001 I had accumulated a large data set which nicely showed contoured fluctuations of numbers of each species in the various habitats. When I plotted these fluctuations, I saw that they varied in complex ways with environmental variables such as time of day, tide height, wind speed, and day of the year. My modest analytical skills, however, did not extend to understanding how to evaluate these complex relations. I needed something more than basic statistics to figure out the meaning of the fluctuating trends in the data.

In the fall of 2001, Shandelle Henson, a new professor in Andrews University's Department of Mathematics, gave a seminar in which she described how she analyzed fluctuations in lab populations of flour beetles. She was a member of the well-known "Beetle Team," an interdisciplinary group of mathematicians, statisticians, and biologists from Rhode Island, Arizona, California, Idaho, and now Michigan, that provided the first demonstration of the mathematical phenomenon of "chaos" in an animal population—a big deal theoretically and one that captured the attention of ecologists worldwide.[19] I didn't understand the mathematics she used, but I did understand that she possessed the mathematical tools to analyze fluctuations in animal numbers. After the seminar I went up to her and briefly explained that I had an extensive data set that described rising and falling numbers of marine birds and mammals. I asked if she would be willing to take a look to see if her methodologies could be used to analyze these data. To my surprise, she agreed.

I sent my data to her, and after a few days she responded that she thought they were something with which she could work. Our first meeting, however, turned out to be a clash of "two cultures"—mathematics and biology. After I described the gull system, we agreed that fluctuations in the number of gulls "loafing" on the marina pier would work best for a first try at analysis. But when I began to list important environmental factors—time of

---

19. Cushing et al., *Chaos in Ecology: Experimental Nonlinear Dynamics*.

day, windspeed, barometric pressure, air temperature, solar radiation, tide height, day of the year, and so on—she protested. "No, no, just give me the *two* most important factors!" Thinking she was terribly naïve, I said it would be impossible to list only two factors—ecosystems are complex, and any model worth thinking about would need to incorporate many factors. After a good natured argument during which I continued to view her perspective as that of a hopelessly clueless mathematician, I skeptically compromised with a list of *three* factors: tide height, time of day, and day of the year. She said she would try to work with these three variables.[20]

Two weeks later she announced she had developed a mathematical model that described the rises and falls of my loafing gull counts. When I saw the graph that showed how beautifully her model described the number of gulls on the pier, I was astonished. I discovered that I was the one who was clueless and Shandelle was right: you don't need, or even want, to include all the environmental factors impinging on a system to model it effectively. She explained that the purpose of a mathematical model is to find the *main* factors that drive the system. If all the factors were included it would no longer be a model, it would be the system itself. In this case the main factors appeared to be tide height, time of day, and day of the year.

Shandelle then explained that the real test of model effectiveness is whether it can *predict* the behavior of a system in the future. Now a believer in her technique, I constructed a spreadsheet listing the tide height forecast, available from the National Oceanographic and Atmospheric Administration (NOAA) website, for every hour of the day for each day we planned to work on Protection Island the following spring. Shandelle used her differential equation model to generate predictions of rises and falls of counts of gulls on the pier. All we had to do now was wait for the next field season and hire a couple students to collect help collect the data needed to test the predictions.

SHANDELLE, TWO STUDENTS, AND I arrived on Protection Island on May 8, 2002, got set up, and began our counts the next day. From atop a bluff overlooking the colony, we counted gulls on the pier every hour, from 5:00 am until 8:00 pm for twenty-nine consecutive days. Each count was a time-consuming process, frustrated occasionally by fog, eagle disturbances, or caretakers cleaning the pier.

At one point Shandelle had to travel to Rhode Island for a meeting with the Beetle Team, leaving the students and me to do the counts. During her absence a seasonal island resident, Warren Odegard, whom I knew

---

20. Henson and Hayward, "The Mathematics of Animal Behavior: An Interdisciplinary Dialogue," 1249–58.

from previous visits, appeared with his Thor, a forty-plus-foot landing craft which he tied up to the pier. That in itself would not have posed a problem for us; short gaps in our counts would not create difficulties for our analysis. The problem was that Warren decided it was a good time to make extensive repairs on the outside of his boat. His activity would seriously interfere with our counts. I called Shandelle and told her what was happening.

"You've *got* to find a way to keep him off the pier!" she exclaimed. I agreed, but this would be tricky—he had as much right to be on the pier as we did. So I decided to offer him a bribe.

"Hi Warren!" I said, as I approached him on the pier. "We're doing some research which requires us to count gulls on the pier at the top of each hour every day. I'll pay you one hundred dollars if you'll agree stay off the pier while you're here on the island." Warren thought a moment about my strange offer and then said, yes, he would be willing to stay off in exchange for my bribe. I reached into my pocket, pulled out five twenties, and handed him the cash. He kept his word and our counts continued unimpeded by repairs to the Thor.

At the end of the twenty-nine days, Shandelle compared our counts to her model predictions. The model accounted for 61 percent of the variability in the data.[21] Sixty-one percent may not sound spectacular, but for ecological and behavioral data from a wild population, this level of predictability is spectacular. Based on these results, we applied for a National Science Foundation (NSF) grant to extend our work to other parts of the gull colony system. Our proposal was successful, and we were awarded funds to support travel, salaries, equipment, and supplies for continued work. All those tiresome counts were paying off. Our work was novel—no one had ever made successful predictions like these for vertebrate animals in a natural population. Over the next nineteen years NSF granted us 1.25 million dollars to support research on the mathematical prediction of animal behavior in relation to environmental variables, including climate change.

With help over the years from more than sixty students, colleagues, and volunteers, we have used Shandelle's mathematical approaches to assess the behavioral dynamics of harbor seals, bald eagles, and four species of gulls in the United States, and of marine iguanas on Isla Fernandina in the Galápagos Islands. Her approach has worked well in every case. Since 2004 we have published more than thirty scientific papers on our joint work.[22]

21. Henson et al., "Predicting Dynamics of Aggregate Loafing Behavior in Glaucous-winged Gulls (*Larus glaucescens*) at a Washington Colony." 380–90.

22. A summary of much of our work can be found in Henson et al., "Modeling Animal Behavior in a Changing Environment," 3–12.

OUR MOST EXCITING PROJECT involved a complex interaction between gull egg cannibalism and egg-laying synchrony. We began this project unknowingly in 2006. In 2005, we documented a dramatic failure of gull reproductive success on Protection Island. By the end of the breeding season, fewer than a dozen gull chicks had survived—there should have been thousands. In 2006, we decided to determine what factors were important to the reproductive success of these birds. We established five study plots, each containing thirty or more breeding territories. A numbered, wooden stake was placed by each nest when the first egg was laid. The first egg was marked "A," and subsequent eggs, if laid, were marked "B" and "C." Every day we checked each egg in each sample nest until hatching, or until some other fate such as predation eliminated the egg. We knew of only two species of egg predators on Protection Island—bald eagles and the gulls themselves. When bald eagles preyed on a nest, all the eggs were destroyed. When only a single egg was lost, it was usually because a gull had cannibalized it.

Over six field seasons, egg cannibalism by gulls accounted for 55 percent of the eggs lost. We had known that egg cannibalism played a role in the colony, but we were surprised at how large a role. Cannibalism turned out to be the most important factor determining the degree reproductive success, or lack thereof, in the colony as a whole. The rate of cannibalism each year varied from about 14 percent of the eggs laid, to over 40 percent. What could cause such large year-to-year differences?

We considered a variety of environmental factors which might fluctuate with the rate of cannibalism. The only factor that stood out was sea surface temperature. When sea surface temperature is high—even by only a fraction of a degree—forage fish move to deeper water. In contrast with other seabirds such as puffins and cormorants, gulls can't dive. So if fish go to deeper water, gulls go hungry. Hungry gulls look around for other food, and eggs are the most nutritious non-fish foods available. An adult gull can obtain nearly all the calories it needs in a day if it devours only two of its neighbors' eggs. Some gulls do just that—and more.[23]

Sea surface temperatures are on the rise in most of the world's oceans. Will gull egg cannibalism rise as the seas get warmer? Our research suggests it might. What will this mean for populations of gulls and other seabirds? We don't know, because our unintentional climate change experiment is still ongoing. But though we don't know the ultimate fate of ocean warming on gull reproduction, we think we do know how female gulls combat the effects of cannibalism on their reproductive success.

23. Hayward et al., "Egg Cannibalism in a Gull Colony Increases with Sea Surface Temperature," 62–73.

When we began monitoring reproductive success in 2006, we noticed something very strange. We would check nests in our study plots one day, and there would be lots of new eggs; the next day, however, there would be just a few new eggs, but the day after that there would again be lots of new eggs. We thought, that's funny—it seems as though female gulls in our sample areas tend to lay their eggs together on alternate days. We graphed our data and sure enough, a distinct up-and-down, every-other-day, zig-zag pattern emerged. The graphs seemed to confirm our perception of what was happening: the females, which individually lay an egg every other day until they completed their clutch, were synchronizing their egg-laying. What looked like egg-laying synchrony only occurred in some but not in other years. It seemed to happen in years when both the sea surface temperatures and egg cannibalism rates were high.

We knew, however, how easy it is to see patterns in data when patterns don't really exist. This is because the human mind wants to see patterns everywhere—just think how the ancients saw constellations of stars in the night sky, which in reality have no intrinsic meaning. We had to come up with a way to determine if the up-and-down fluctuations were random—like constellations—or if they were nonrandom and held intrinsic meaning. It took us quite some time to come up with an objective way to do this, but we finally determined an effective method. In the end our perceptions were supported: statistically significant egg-laying synchrony occurred in years with high rates of cannibalism and when sea surface temperatures were high.[24] Why would this be?

The mathematicians on our team—Shandelle Henson and Jim Cushing from the University of Arizona—developed a series of models which provided an answer. The models showed that cannibalism confers an advantage to cannibals in the short term—it serves as a "lifeboat" mechanism to carry them through bad years when the food supply is poor. When good times return, they can resume noncannibalistic behavior. At the same time, by engaging in egg-laying synchrony during years of high cannibalism, the females in the colony lower the chance their eggs will be cannibalized. This is because cannibals can eat only so many eggs on a given day; if most eggs are laid on one day, the chance that a particular egg will be eaten is reduced. Natural selection appears to have favored behavioral flexibility which allows gulls to switch between synchronous and non-synchronous egg-laying, depending on the rate of egg cannibalism in a given year.

---

24. Henson et al., "Socially-Induced Synchronization of Every-Other-Day Egg-Laying in a Seabird Colony," 571–80.

What are the long-term effects of cannibalism on the population? The mathematicians developed other models demonstrating that in the long run, this ability to switch between high levels of cannibalism plus synchrony in bad years, and low levels of cannibalism and no synchrony in good years, allows the population to persist over the long haul. If, however, the string of bad years is too long, the population could experience a "tipping point" and completely collapse.[25]

One final question needed to be answered to complete our story about cannibalism, egg-laying synchrony, and climate change: What signal enables the female gulls to synchronize their behavior? Is it chemical, visual, auditory, or something else?

If you hang several identical pendulum clocks on a wall, with their pendulums swinging out of sync, after a while all the pendulums will swing synchronously. Slight vibrations generated by the clocks travel through the wall and function as synchronizing signals. Every synchronous system requires a synchronizing signal such as these vibrations.

Gordon Atkins, a physiologist on our team with extensive experience in the analysis of auditory signals in insects and birds, has worked hard to identify the signal that synchronizes egg-laying in our gulls. Through a clever series of experiments and observations, he may have discovered it. He noted that the copulation call emitted by males during the act of mating is loud and distinct. This call, emitted by a single male, can be heard throughout the entire colony. By playing recorded copulation calls back to a small group of nesting gulls isolated from the rest of the colony, he was able to stimulate courtship and copulation at will. He showed that the call alone, separate from the dramatic wing-flapping that occurs during the call, was a sufficient stimulus to elicit courtship and copulation.[26]

Atkins then mounted a series of automated cameras on posts in dense parts of the colony. Each camera was programmed to take a digital photo of a small area of the colony every five minutes. Each nest within view of the camera was monitored daily for the presence of new eggs. With this technique, Atkins demonstrated a strong, negative relationship between the occurrence of copulation and egg laying. On days when a female gull lays an egg, she seemed to exhibit no urge to copulate. Instead, she waited for the *next* day to copulate. Hormonal cycles account for the every-other-day egg-laying pattern in individual gulls, but the copulation call seems to

---

25. Henson et al., "Socially Induced Ovulation Synchrony and Its Effect on Seabird Population Dynamics," 495–516.

26. Atkins et al., "Copulation Song Coordinates Timing of Head-tossing and Mounting Behaviors in Neighboring Glaucous-winged Gulls," 560–67.

synchronize the laying patterns of densely-nesting females during years of high cannibalism.[27]

So how do these research experiences relate to my journey out of fundamentalism into a more open view of reality? Participation in research demonstrates that natural patterns can be described, quantified, and predicted. Natural patterns tell us important things about reality. To deny the existence of patterns in, for example, the fossil record, or to ignore their existence because of so-called "faith commitments," amounts to an absurd and gross trivialization of the notion of faith. Serious and mature faith development requires careful attention to physical reality. Faith should be consistent with physical reality, not contradictory to it. Research offers firsthand glimpses into reality, which for me provide a meaningful and joyful context for real faith.

---

27. Atkins et al., "How Do Gulls Synchronize Their Ovipositions?" in preparation.

PART THREE

Evidence

The evidence on which we base our perspectives is crucially important for understanding life's journey. But all evidence must be interpreted, and our interpretations are inevitably colored by our worldviews. It is impossible to be completely objective. The capacity for objectivity, however, increases as more and more evidence is brought to bear on reality, especially when that evidence derives from multiple, independent sources. If increasing evidence from independent sources consistently points to a particular conclusion, our interpretation may be on the right track. It is important, however, to remain open to the possibility that new evidence may alter our interpretations and conclusions. In the following chapters, I present converging lines of evidence that led me to my current inferences about the nature and history of earth and life.

8

Parsing the Word

"One of the ironies of biblical literalism is that it . . . is modernistic, and it sells its symbolic birthright for a mess of tangible pottage."

—Conrad Hyers[1]

"Jesus loves me this I know, for the Bible tells me so." So I sang and so I believed.

Anything that told me Jesus loved me deserved complete respect. Indeed, the Bible held ultimate significance for me as a youngster. I never placed another object atop "God's Word." I learned the names of all sixty-six of its books. I underlined special texts. I competed in Bible sword drills.

I wore out several Bibles. One or two had dark blue, zippered, faux-leather covers with Jesus' words in red. In my late teens I received a crisp, new King James Version. It contained soft, ultra-thin pages and featured my name embossed in gold type on the cover. I loved the smell of its black, genuine leather binding.

It seemed almost sacrilegious when Bibles appeared in non-Elizabethan English and sported cheap green, red, or multi-colored paper covers.

---

1. Hyers, "Biblical Literalism," 823.

It was great to know that Jesus loved me, but there was also a frightening motivation for studying the Bible. In *Messages to Young People*, Sister White told us that

> You know not where you may be called upon to give your witness of truth. Many will have to stand in the legislative courts; some will have to stand before kings and before the learned of the earth, to answer for their faith. Those who have only a superficial understanding of truth will not be able clearly to expound the Scriptures, and give definite reasons for their faith. They will become confused, and will not be workmen that need not to be ashamed.[2]

That message drilled into my young consciousness. I was a shy kid and slow of speech. The prospect of standing before courts and kings petrified me. Yet it galvanized my determination. I did not want to be confused or ashamed—or to face even more dire consequences.

There was another problem: memorization and I did not get along. My first letter home as a high school junior at Ozark Academy complained that we had to "learn one memory verse every day" for Bible Doctrines class, and that for the final test we would need to spit them back word-for-word *and* provide the exact chapters and verses.[3] After years of familiarity, I knew Bible facts pretty well. But word-for-word memorization was not my forte.

I figured I would have to wing it during the impending inquisition. Perhaps I could just paraphrase things. But if I was asked to regurgitate chapter and verse, I would flunk and be hauled off to be tortured.

Thankfully, I made it through adolescence without experiencing torture, or even having to defend my faith. Legislators, kings, and learned scholars showed no interest whatsoever. Nor did anyone else.

One of the assumptions made by conservative Adventists and other fundamentalists was that the Bible existed as a seamless whole with every verse complementing every other verse. It was God's Perfect Word—a divine acrostic that could be read forward, backward, diagonally, and every other possible way.[4]

---

2. White, *Messages to Young People*, 186.

3. JLH to parents, September 1, 1965.

4. For example, see Chapter 23, "Christ's Ministry in the Heavenly Sanctuary," in Anonymous, *Seventh-day Adventists Believe . . . A Biblical Exposition of Fundamental Doctrines* (Washington, DC: Ministerial Association, General Conference of Seventh-day Adventists, 1988), 312–331, where texts used to defend this uniquely Adventist doctrine are drawn from Genesis, Exodus, Leviticus, Psalms, Daniel, Micah, Matthew,

My nineteenth-century Adventist forebears used this "proof-text" method to come up with their distinctive Adventist beliefs. Mix-and-match. That was the approach. "Bible studies" designed to convince potential converts continue to use this approach, as do so-called "Bible marking programs" in which a text in one part of the Bible is linked to a text somewhere else in the sixty-six books. Proof-texting is a convenient approach for argumentative types, fervent denominationalists, and evangelists who can defend pretty much any doctrinal position with carefully selected texts, forceful presentations, and just the right spin.[5]

This state of affairs led to endless questions and disputes among would-be biblical interpreters. Who was the "king of the north" (Dan 11:40–45)? What is the meaning of the "daily" (Dan 8:11–13)? Was Jesus all God or all man—or both? Was there a time gap between Gen 1:1 and 1:2? What is the relation between law and grace? Can humans reach perfection? Who wrote the book of Hebrews? These and innumerable other esoteric questions created major stirs within Adventism while I was growing up. Answers to these queries, however, never made any difference in how we treated our neighbors.

As a college junior, I enrolled in a religion class called Ancestry of the Bible. The class was intriguing and informative. It provided my first glimpse into the complex and convoluted history that led to the making of the collection of books we call the Holy Bible.

The course textbook was a classic: *The Ancestry of Our English Bible* by Ira Maurice Price, Professor of Semitic Languages and Literature at the University of Chicago, and a founding member of the faculty there. Although his text was originally published in 1907, we used the third edition, updated in 1956 by two more recent University of Chicago scholars.

From Price's book and from our professor, George Reid, I learned about the Jewish scribes who created handwritten reproductions of the Hebrew texts which survived the Jewish diaspora, the order by Antiochus Epiphanes in 167 BC to destroy all copies of the Jewish law, and the destruction of Jerusalem in AD 70. I learned also that many Jewish books—at least twenty-four mentioned in the Old Testament alone—were lost forever to civilization.[6]

Mark, Luke, John, Romans, 1 Corinthians, 2 Corinthians, Galatians, Ephesians, Philippians, Hebrews, 2 Peter, 1 John, and Revelation.

    5. Downing, "The Art and Practice of Biblical Proof-texting."

    6. Price et al., *The Ancestry of Our English Bible*, 19–20.

The well-intentioned scribes were not always objective; at times they added words "to maintain propriety or reverence." These additions may not have been numerous, but they nonetheless have influenced the understanding of the text by Christians.[7]

By far, the most common changes introduced by the scribes were unintentional. Sometimes, for example, they failed to perceive the sense of a passage because the original Hebrew writers did not use vowels. As a result it was impossible at times to tell if a particular consonant belonged to a preceding or a following word. Other times the scribes inadvertently repeated or omitted words, or transposed letters within words which gave them different meanings. These errors tended to multiply as copying was repeated over and over through the centuries. This is not to say the stories and messages were drastically altered, but it would be unwise to put stock in a literal reading of every word of every text, especially after translation into a modern language.[8]

A bewildering array of oral traditions and documents eventually led to such Old Testament texts as the Samaritan Pentateuch, the Greek Septuagint, rival Greek texts, the Latin and Syriac Bibles, and the Targums. And as if this wasn't confusing enough, there were the Apocrypha and the Pseudepigrapha, which some scholars considered to be authoritative, but others did not.[9]

Canonization, the choice of which books to include in scripture, occurred over a period several hundred years during formation of the Old Testament. The Pentateuch—Genesis, Exodus, Leviticus, Numbers, and Deuteronomy—was formed during the fourth century BCE. The fifteen books of the Prophets were canonized about 200 BCE, and the Writings, which include the remaining eleven books of the Old Testament, were finally recognized during the second century CE.[10]

Elements of the New Testament, originally penned in Greek, survived in more numerous texts than the books of the Old Testament. In copying and translating the New Testament from Greek, similar problems arose as with the Old Testament texts, leading to alternate readings in our modern Bibles. Canonization of the New Testament books took several hundred years, with inclusion of the book of Revelation taking the longest.[11]

ANCESTRY OF THE BIBLE class also taught me the difference between "textual criticism" and "historical criticism." Textual criticism is an attempt to

---

7. Price et al., *The Ancestry of Our English Bible*, 21.
8. Price et al., *The Ancestry of Our English Bible*, 21–23.
9. Price et al., *The Ancestry of Our English Bible*, 40–149.
10. Price et al., *The Ancestry of Our English Bible*, 16–17.
11. Price et al., *The Ancestry of Our English Bible*, 146–47.

establish the original reading of the text by collation, or a comparison of existing manuscripts. The ultimate goal of textual criticism is to produce a text as close to the original as possible. Reid referred to this type of analysis as "lower criticism," a term no longer in vogue today.[12]

Historical criticism, by contrast, involves exploring the historical context of the biblical text with other texts written about the same time and in the same region to better understand what the text meant to people when it was written. Historical critics attempt to 1) identify the original sources of the text, whether they be oral traditions or other texts ("source criticism"); 2) classify each text as to the type of literature it represents, be it poetry, stories, history, laws, prose, etc. ("form criticism"); and 3) establish how the author assembled the text from prior sources in an effort to present a particular theological or philosophical perspective ("redaction criticism"). Reid referred to this type of analysis as "higher criticism," a term also no longer in common use today.[13]

With all this complex history involving oral traditions, written documents, fragments of documents, mistakes by copyists, and intentional alterations in the text by scribes for more than a millennium and a half, wouldn't my understanding and appreciation of the Bible be enhanced by knowing as much as possible about the text *and* its historical context? Strangely enough, this is not the view of fundamentalists who view the Bible, at least in the form of its "original autographs," as the inerrant "Word of God," untainted by historical contingencies.[14]

MUCH OF THE CONFLICT between modern science and a biblical inerrantist interpretation of reality centers on Gen 1 to 11. Genesis 1 and 2 contain the creation stories, and Gen 5 and 11 feature genealogical frameworks that connect the Israelites with Adam at creation. Genesis 6 to 9 recounts the flood story. Under the assumption that these and other Old Testament texts were meant to convey facts about history and science, belief in a young earth, acceptance of flood geology, and denial of evolutionary change seem reasonable to a twenty-first-century western reader who is not a biblical scholar. I have discovered, however, there are good reasons to doubt this assumption. Careful consideration of the biblical text itself provides what is perhaps the most compelling reason.

---

12. Wegner, *A Student's Guide to Textual Criticism of the Bible*, 23–43.

13. Gladson, "Taming Historical Criticism," 19–34; Tate, *Handbook for Biblical Interpretation*, 197–98.

14. Geisler, ed., *Inerrancy*; Preus, "The Inerrancy of Scripture," 47–60.

Take, for example, God's words in the Ten Commandments. As a child, I had always been taught the Exod 20 version. But reading the Pentateuch one day, I came across another rendering in Deut 5. My Seventh-day Adventist forebears and teachers focused on the Exod 20 version for good reason—it was this version that was used to support the belief that the Sabbath was a memorial of a literal six-day creation week, an important component of Adventist doctrine.[15] The Exod 20 version, which I had committed to memory as a child, states:

> Remember the sabbath day, to keep it holy. . . *For in six days the Lord made heaven and earth, the sea, and all that in them is, and rested the seventh day: wherefore the* LORD *blessed the sabbath day, and hallowed it* (Exod 20:8–11, italics supplied).

When I discovered Deut 5, I found quite a different rendering of the same command:

> Keep the sabbath day to sanctify it, as the LORD thy God hath commanded thee. . . *And remember that thou wast a servant in the land of Egypt, and that the* LORD *thy God brought thee out thence through a mighty hand and by a stretched out arm: therefore the* LORD *thy God commanded thee to keep the sabbath day.* (Deut 5:12–15, italics supplied).

Both versions refer to the same thing—a statement of the Sabbath commandment spoken into existence by God himself. But the second version is about deliverance of the Israelites from Egyptian bondage, not about creation week. Both sets of words are attributed to directly to God at the same event. For someone who insists on interpreting the Bible as God's literal word, this is a problem. Not only is the wording different, but so is the purpose for keeping the Sabbath holy.

Other Old Testament texts make some pretty horrific claims that could lead to serious questions about divine goodness: God destroys "every living substance . . . upon the face of the ground, both man, and cattle, and the creeping things, and the fowl of the heaven," except those saved in the ark (Gen 7:23); God rains "brimstone and fire" on two cities, burning all the inhabitants to death (Gen 19:24–25); God commands the Levites to "slay every man his brother, and every man his companion, and every man his neighbor" for idolatry (Exod 32:27); God commands the slaughter of couples caught in adultery (Lev 20:10); God declares the rule of an "eye for eye, tooth for tooth" (Lev 24:20); God stipulates that a man caught collecting

---

15. White, *Spiritual Gifts, Volume III*, 90–92; Anonymous, *Seventh-day Adventists Believe*, 68–77. 248–66.

sticks on the Sabbath must be stoned to death (Num 15:32–36); God sends poisonous snakes to bite the Israelites for complaining they had neither food nor water (Num 21:5–6); God commands that the Israelites to kill all Midianite men and boys (Num 31:7). God is depicted as a pretty scary tyrant. Texts like these are common in the early books of the Old Testament.

Then there are some real mind benders. Take Lev 14:33–54. Here God talks matter-of-factly about striking "the plague of leprosy in a house of the land of your possession . . ." Why would God do this? No reason is given. He just does it! But read on—and things get weirder. God immediately provides detailed, step-by-step instructions on how to *cleanse* the house of the very disease he's just inflicted! This makes absolutely no sense to my twenty-first-century mindset. What's going on here?

A RECENTLY PUBLISHED TRILOGY by Brian Bull, a scientist, and his colleague Fritz Guy, a theologian, has aided my understanding of these puzzling texts. Their trilogy provides a non-biblical scholar like myself with insights into what the Genesis text would have meant to someone when Genesis was written. The first book in the trio examines the creation story in Gen 1, the second book explores the flood story in Gen 6 to 9, and the third book provides a general guide on how to a twenty-first-century reader should interpret Genesis.[16] The insights provided did not originate with Bull and Guy, but their innovative presentation makes the original meaning of Genesis easily accessible to someone like me who does not read ancient Hebrew and who is unacquainted with ancient Near Eastern culture.

Bull and Guy note that twenty-first-century readers are ill-equipped to understand parts of the ancient text. One problem is a major difference in the way we and the ancient Hebrews categorized events. The Hebrews possessed only two explanatory categories for everything that happened. An event happened because either God did it or humans did it. There was no other option. If there was rain, hail, an earthquake, famine, a windstorm, lightening, sickness, or anything else that humans could not cause, God was responsible. By contrast, today we would place these events in a third explanatory category, natural regularities. Science has taught us how weather systems work, how tectonic plates cause earthquakes, how genes control traits, and how microorganisms cause disease.[17]

Thanks to Bull and Guy and the writings of other biblical scholars, the puzzling text about leprosy in Lev 14, along with many other Old Testament

---

16. Bull and Guy, *God, Sky & Land*; Bull and Guy, *God, Land, and the Great Flood*; Bull and Guy, *God, the Misreading of Genesis, and the Surprisingly Good News*.

17. Bull and Guy, *God, Sky & Land*, 97–104.

passages, now make sense to me. Because humans could not be the cause of leprosy, God had to be the cause. God was the source of both the bad and the good, and he was both the cause and the cure. The ancient Hebrews were not stupid. But they had only two explanatory categories within which to work. We now have a third, natural phenomena, where we pigeonhole many events, like the appearance of an infection or the onslaught of a hurricane.

A second problem highlighted by Bull and Guy is that most of us do not understand ancient Hebrew. Understanding the nuances of specific words of an original language—the function of textual criticism—is particularly important for perceiving the intended meaning of a word within particular contexts.[18]

I have a good friend, Abraham Terian, a gentle Armenian scholar whose ancestors lived for nine hundred years in the Old City of Jerusalem, a place where he too was raised. Abraham is one of the few people who can read ancient Armenian. Over many years he has translated ancient Armenian texts into modern languages.[19] He and I have spent many hours together, he the sagacious literary scholar, me the eager novice. He is steeped in Middle Eastern culture, both ancient and modern, and he possesses a thorough understanding of scripture in its original languages. He understands the text, because he grew up within the culture from which the text originated. On multiple occasions he has commented to me that "you always heard this Bible text meant such-and-such, but it really means thus-and-so."

For example, when I read the first verse of Genesis, "In the beginning, God created the heavens and the earth," my mind automatically pictures the vastness of the universe as we perceive it, and the extent and shape of our planet. But the Hebrews and their neighbors had no concept of limitless space, the nature of the sun, moon and stars, or of the earth as a relatively tiny sphere revolving around a much larger sun. For them the earth was a flat disc. If they were to travel to the edges of the disc, they imagined they would drop off into the unknowable abyss. The sun, moon, and stars were smaller than the earth and revolved around it. The sun rose progressively higher in the sky during the morning, and then dropped below the horizon in the evening, passing below the earth and emerging on the other side once again the next morning. The stars did the same thing, except they were visible in the sky at night and migrated below the earth during the day. The sky, or "firmament," was a hardened dome with "windows"—perhaps

---

18. Bull and Guy, *God, Sky & Land*, 18–29.

19. For example, Terian, *The Armenian Gospel of the Infancy, with Three Early Versions of the Protevangelium of James*; Terian, *Macarius of Jerusalem: Letter to the Armenians, AD 335*; Terian, *The Festal Works of St. Gregory of Narek: Annotated Translation of Odes, Litanies, and Encomia*.

like venetian blinds—that allowed the passage of rain, snow, and hail from cisterns above the dome. Heaven, the abode of God and the angels, was above the firmament, and hell was somewhere deep below the earth. These were not foolish concepts. They were based in the limited, common-sense observations that ancient, prescientific peoples were capable of making.[20]

A SPECIAL CONCERN AMONG modern fundamentalists deals with the extent of the earth covered by the Genesis flood. The flood story doesn't mention a thing about geological formations, but to fundamentalists the flood is the only biblical event capable of accounting for the complexities of geology. Fundamentalists have become skilled at speculating how the flood squeezed earth history into a few thousand years. They support their position with a seemingly literal reading of scripture which states that "the waters prevailed exceedingly upon the earth; and all the high hills that were under the whole heaven, were covered. Fifteen cubits upward did the waters prevail; and the mountains were covered" (Gen 7:19–20).[21]

The geological evidence, however, when evaluated honestly and viewed as an integrated whole, fails to support the concept of a recent creation or a worldwide flood. Vast quantities of physical evidence have piled up against fundamentalist interpretations of Gen 1 to 11.[22] I'll highlight some of this evidence in chapters 9 to 13.

Leonard Brand, a bright, knowledgeable, well-published scientist who nonetheless has staked his belief in a recent creation and a worldwide flood, once asked if it would "be easier just to accept the long geological time scale and fit creation into that scenario." His candid reply to his own question was "Probably."[23] But as Bull and Guy point out, the good news for Brand and others with similar views is there is no need to conclude from the biblical text that the flood covered the entire planet and foreshortened the geological time scale. And that is true even if the text is interpreted literally as Brand prefers.

Bull and Guy's conclusion is based on internal evidence from the Bible itself, especially translations of the Hebrew word *'erets*, the word translated *earth* in the flood story. This word also can be translated as *land, world, soil,*

20. Horowitz, *Mesopotamian Cosmic Geography*; Walton, *Ancient Near Eastern Thought and the Old Testament*, 165–78.

21. The best known example of this genre is Whitcomb and Morris, *The Genesis Flood*; a recent example is Brand and Chadwick, *Faith, Reason, & Earth History*. This latter work is scientifically better informed and more forthright about some of the problems associated with "flood geology" than *The Genesis Flood* and most other young-age publications.

22. See, for example, Young and Stearley, *The Bible, Rocks and Time*; Montgomery, *The Rocks Don't Lie*.

23. Brand, *Faith, Reason, and Earth History*, 267.

ground, or *country*. *'Erets* is used 2,504 times in the King James Version; 1,553 times it is translated land, 712 as earth, 140 as country, and four times as world. Bull and Guy found that the proportion of times *'erets* is translated as *earth* in Gen 1 to 11 is much higher than in the rest of Genesis. When we read "earth," our minds automatically envision a planet, whereas when we read "land," we commonly think of a more restricted area. When the writer of Genesis 1 to 11 used the word *'erets*, he was referring to the land with which he was familiar. He had no concept like we do of the world as a spherical planet.[24]

Others, such as John Walton, an Old Testament scholar at Wheaton College, take the same approach. Walton begins his book, *The Lost World of Genesis One*, by reminding us that although the Old Testament was "written for us . . . it was not written *to* us. It was written to Israel."[25] He notes that the culture of surrounding the Jewish people during Old Testament times was very different from today's culture, and this fact must be taken into account as we translate and try to understand the text. In a passage consistent with Bull, Guy, and Terian's perspective, Walton writes:

> Deity pervaded the ancient world. Nothing happened independently of deity. The gods did not "intervene" because that would assume that there was a world of events outside of them that they could step into and out of. The Israelites, along with everyone else in the ancient world, believed instead that every event was the act of deity—that every plant that grew, every baby born, every drop of rain and every climatic disaster was an act of God. No "natural" laws governed the cosmos; deity ran the cosmos or was inherent in it.[26]

In his concluding chapter Walton states that "the most careful, responsible reading of the text will proceed with the understanding that it is ancient literature, not modern science."[27]

The Jewish philosopher Philo, the rabbis of the Talmudic era, and the twelfth-century Jewish scholar Maimonides all rejected literal understandings of the creation and the flood in favor of metaphorical or allegorical interpretations. Yet each of these respected Jewish scholars considered Genesis a God-inspired text. Moreover, they lived long before the concepts of modern science could have tainted their views.[28]

---

24. KJV Old Testament Hebrew Lexicon, "*'erets*"; Bull and Guy, *God, Land, and the Great Flood*, 85–96.

25. Walton, *The Lost World of Genesis One*, 9.

26. Walton, *The Lost World of Genesis One*, 20.

27. Walton, *The Lost World of Genesis One*, 162.

28. Colson and Whitaker (translators). *Philo, Volume I*, xiii; Tigay, "Genesis,

MANY PEOPLE HAVE DIFFICULTY thinking metaphorically and symbolically. My dear father was one such person. I've already mentioned that when he was in high school he would not read his literature assignments because "they were not true." Indeed, throughout his ministry he disapproved of English teachers as "liberals." His Bible was heavily underlined and annotated, but he missed much of what scripture has to offer because of his restrictive window of interpretation.

As a kid, I assumed Dad's view of things. College, however, opened my eyes to a wider and richer world. As a sophomore I enrolled in American Literature. Wilma McClarty, a young, wild-eyed, frizzy-haired, totally inspiring professor was our guide. We read the prose and poetry of Jonathan Edwards, William Cullen Bryant, Nathaniel Hawthorne, Edgar Allan Poe, Ralph Waldo Emerson, John Greenleaf Whittier, James Russell Lowell, Walt Whitman, Emily Dickinson, Joel Chandler Harris, Willa Cather, Robert Frost, and many others. I recall how intrigued I was by symbolism and metaphor in Hawthorne's *The Scarlet Letter*, in Poe's "The Masque of the Red Death," in Frost's "Stopping by Woods on a Snowy Evening." I still leaf through *The American Tradition in Literature*, our two-volume text, to discover new stories or poems and to renew old acquaintances. Since completing McClarty's course a half century ago, I have read many other literary classics, including Dostoevsky's *The Brothers Karamazov*, Hemingway's *The Old Man and the Sea*, Steinbeck's *The Grapes of Wrath*, and Fitzgerald's *The Great Gatsby*. The use of metaphor and symbolism in these fictional works affords them enduring voice. McClarty was one of several great mentors who awakened in me a sense of truth and beauty in language.

Enlightened by courses like American Literature, I began to appreciate interesting facets of biblical literature. I learned, for example, that numbers in scripture were often used by the writers as symbols to make a point. The number seven represented completion, achievement, and perfection. The patriarch Enoch, who "walked with God," was the seventh generation from Adam (Gen 5:24); God completed his "good" creation on the seventh day (Gen 2:2); the Sabbath occurred on the seventh day of the week (Gen 2:3); seven pairs of "clean" animals were taken into the ark (Gen 7:2–3); Naaman was told to bathe seven times in the Jordon River to be healed of leprosy (2 Kgs 5:10); seven letters were sent to seven churches in Revelation (Rev 2, 3); etc. Likewise, the number forty was often used to depict lengthy time periods: rain fell for forty days and forty nights during the flood (Gen 7:4); Hebrew spies sent to check out the Promised Land by Moses spent forty

---

Science, and 'Scientific Creationism,'" 20–27; Twersky, ed., *A Maimonides Reader*, 44–45; Minkin, *The Teachings of Maimonides*, 192.

days on their trip; the Israelites spent forty years wandering in the wilderness (Num 32:13); Moses spent forty days and forty nights on Mount Sinai (Deut 9, 10); Jesus fasted for forty days and forty nights in the desert (Matt 4:2); etc. A literalist approach to scripture would take these numbers as historic realities, and in so doing completely overlook the symbolism involved.

CHIASTIC STRUCTURE IS ANOTHER feature built into many of the biblical texts by the Hebrews. A chiasm consists of a series of statements followed by a similar series, but presented in reverse order to the first. A very simple example is represented by Jesus' words in Mark 2:27: "The sabbath was made for man, and not man for the sabbath." Thus:

    A Sabbath
     B Man
     B' Man
    A' Sabbath

Chiasms usually are considerably more complex, however, and contain many more elements. A middle element, or apex, of the chiasm often contains the main point of the text. Consider, for example, the well-known chiasm found in the story of the flood (Gen 6:1–8:22), as interpreted by Princeton University's Bernhard W. Anderson:

A Introduction (6:9–10)
  B Violence in God's creation (6:11–12)
    C God resolves to destroy what he has made (6:13–22)
      D God's command to enter the ark (7:1–10)
        E Beginning of the flood (7:11–16)
          F The rising flood waters (7:17–24)
            G GOD REMEMBERS NOAH
          F' Flood waters recede (8:1–5)
        E' Drying of the earth (8:6–14)
      D' God's command to leave the ark (8:15–19)
    C' God resolves to not to ever destroy again (8:20–22)
  B' Covenant of peace and blessing (9:1–17)
A' Conclusion (9:18–19)

As Anderson notes, the "first part of the story represents a movement toward chaos, with the hero Noah and the remnant with him as survivors of the catastrophe. The second part represents a movement toward the new creation, with Noah and his sons as representatives of the new humankind who were to inherit the earth." The apex and central message of the story is that, from beginning to end, God remembers Noah.[29]

Anderson's interpretation of chiastic structure within the flood story represents only one of many such interpretations related to the flood narrative. Details differ but the general chiastic structure of the biblical text seems obvious. As Gordon J. Wenham points out, by constructing a text in the form of a chiasm, the author uses "literary form . . . to underline a theological point." Moreover, chiastic structure was a commonly used technique by authors of other Mesopotamian literature, including of the Gilgamesh Epic, an earlier story that in many ways parallels the Genesis flood story.[30]

Using numbers, chiasms, repetition, poetry, and other creative devices, biblical writers, in common with other writers of the time, drove home their messages—not scientific or historical messages, but messages about God and his relation to people and the rest of creation.

I REVERE THE BIBLE. It gives me much to ponder and makes me a better person. Reading and hearing the text day in and day out, year in and year out, washes through me, inspires me, changes me.

Genesis 1 faces me with the mighty, see-all divinity, Elohim (translated "God" in the King James Version of the Old Testament), whose word alone is powerful enough to create. I feel the miracle of organization emerging out of the topsy-turvy void, the greening of our world with every seed-bearing plant, every fish in the sea, bird in the air, every creeping thing on land. In Gen 2 I visualize a sculptor, YHWH (translated "Lord God" in the King James Version of the Old Testament), who leans in close to the earth and shapes things from clay, who relishes an intimate connection with his creation. Genesis 1 and 2 provide meaning to my life, they convey the reality of a genetic connection with the enigmatic, transcendent, yet ironically immanent divine source of the universe.

Job asks the same questions I ask—"why" questions. Why do bad things happen to good people? Why are there parasites and predators? Why is there pain and suffering? Why do children die? Why does anyone die? Why doesn't God answer my questions? God answers Job with more questions, just like he does with me. I learn that I have not been singled out. This has been God's message for millennia—Don't try to make sense

---

29. Anderson, "From Analysis to Synthesis," 23–39.
30. Wenham, "The Coherence of the Flood Narrative," 336–48.

out of everything. You don't know the end from the beginning. Be patient. I'm in charge.

The Psalms show me I can be brutally honest with God. I can ponder why things are the way they are. I can tell God how angry I am. I can shake my fist. I can scream, shout, yell, and cry. I can express joy when good things happen. I can sing and dance when things are great. I can express my doubts, my failings, my loves, my hates. I can express awe and wonder. I can declare both my failings and my achievements. I can enjoy the cadence of the words, be elevated by the sentiments voiced.

My favorite Old Testament book is Ecclesiastes—brutally honest, tell-it-like-it-is reality. "I have seen all the works that are done under the sun; and, behold, all is vanity and vexation of spirit" (Eccl 1:14). "For in much wisdom is much grief" (Eccl 1:18). "All go unto one place; all are of the dust, and all turn to dust again" (Eccl 3:20). I love the rhythm of text: "To everything there is a season; a time for love and a time for hate. A time for every purpose under the heaven" (Eccl 3:1). Pete Seeger loved the words as well, and set them to music—music sung by him, as well as by Judy Collins, The Seekers, The Byrds, Bruce Springsteen, and others.

Stories of Jesus in Matthew, Mark, and Luke move me. The incarnation of God in a manger. The star in the sky that shown on all peoples. Rough-hewn shepherds paying homage. Aristocrats bringing rich gifts. Jesus, a person for all people, low and high. Jesus, healing the sick. Jesus, feeding the hungry. Jesus, teaching about the Kingdom of Heaven. Why wouldn't everyone want to be a member of his Kingdom? To be comforted, to be filled, to obtain mercy, to be called God's child, to see God. The pathos of the crucifixion. The forgiving spirit of Jesus. The betrayal by Judas. The scene in the Garden. The death. The resurrection.

The Gospel of Saint John—rich in metaphor, full of mystery. It starts with a creation story more enigmatic than the Genesis accounts—inscrutable, just like the universe. "In the beginning was the Word, and the Word was with God, and the Word was God. The same was in the beginning with God. All things were made by him; and without him was not any thing made that was made. In him was life; and the life was the light of men" (John 1:1–4). Also, "Ye must be born again" (John 3:7). "I am the bread of life" (John 6:48). "I am the way, the truth, and the life" (John 14:6). "And ye shall know the truth, and the truth shall make you free" (John 8:32).

I GREW UP HEARING the Bible referred to as "God's Word." I now understand that the Bible consists of writings by people who, like me, were searching for meaning and a better understanding of reality and the sacred. They were dedicated—chroniclers, poets, narrators, philosophers, preachers, prophets, raconteurs—with a compulsion to share their understanding, their art, their philosophy, their warnings, their stories, and their relationship with God, in whatever way they conceived of the divine. It is in this sense the Bible is a "sacred text," one to be revered and held in highest esteem, the work of faulty humans who were inspired in their musings about their encounters with the divine.

I still make sure the Bible sits atop of any stack of books. But I do not believe it contains history or science in the way we think about these disciplines today. I would do grave injustice to the Bible if I forced it to read as if it were modern history or modern science. If I did, I would overlook so much of what *is* important in the text—subtleties, illusions, elegant structure, passion, metaphor, beauty, and yes, a rich understanding of ancient views of reality which are different than those of ours today. All of this contributes to my perception of truth, insofar as I am capable of perceiving it. All of this brings me closer to the divine.

I see no reason to ignore the messages of the Bible because of scientific evidence. I see no reason to ignore a scientific understanding of the reality because of the Bible. For me, both science and the Bible inspire me to seek God and place high value on the universe of which I am part.

9

Dividing the Earth

"Whenever a true theory appears, it will be its own evidence. Its test is, that it will explain all phenomena."

—Ralph Waldo Emerson[1]

"Time to get the hell out of here!" someone shouted. A small group of people had gathered at a roadblock on State Highway 504 leading to Mount St. Helens, trying to get a better look at the temperamental peak which, over the past eight weeks, had been threatening to erupt. Suddenly, on this beautiful May 18, 1980 morning, jets of gray ash shot from the peak and the entire north side of the mountain collapsed into the valley below.

It *was* time to get out. A heavy-set couple from California jumped into their Ford Torino station wagon and sped away. Kathie O'Keefe and Gil Baker threw photo gear into their green Oldsmobile and peeled away as well. Soon Gil and Kathie were exceeding 100 miles per hour down the narrow road, a low cloud of searing ash following close behind.

When they caught up with the Torino, Gil shouted "He's only doing 80. What'll I do?"

"Pass him!" exclaimed Kathie.

---

1. Emerson, *Nature*, 1065.

They careened around the Torino on a blind curve. Kathie looked back just as the cloud enveloped the station wagon they had passed. They charged on, the high, leading edge of the cloud curling over the top of their car like a gigantic wave breaking over the shore.

After several minutes, but what must have seemed like hours, they outran the deadly shroud. They turned north onto Highway 505, and never stopped until they reached the I-5 interstate.[2]

While this drama was unfolding, Calvin Hill and I continued to collect data on the gull colony at Sprague Lake, Washington, two hundred miles to the east. We remained clueless about what was happening to the west, other than taking note of the sound of an explosion. Even four hours later, as the encroaching cloud of ash made it difficult to read our instruments, we remained ignorant as to the source of the darkness.[3]

While we considered our options in the gathering gloom at Sprague Lake, a rescue helicopter hovered over the Torino stopped along State Highway 504. Ash stirred up by the rotor prohibited landing, so the pilot veered over to the nearby Toutle River. Pararescuers leapt from the low-hovering copter into the shallow water. They slogged ashore, plodded through hot ash, and thirty minutes later reached the station wagon. The driver was lying, motionless, just outside the car, and the ash-covered lips of the woman in the passenger seat were still moist. When the rescuers touched her, skin sloughed away from her form. The dead couple were Fred and Margery Rollins, retirees from Hawthorne, California. They had driven to Washington to see the mountain.[4]

The 1980 eruption of Mount St. Helens changed my life and the lives of countless others. Depending on one's location—or dumb luck—some of us were fortunate, others not. Yet despite the death and carnage, this eruption was a mere blip on the screen of earth history compared with earlier volcanic events—Mazama, Vesuvius, Krakatoa, and Katmai, to name just four of the really big ones. And today, more than five hundred volcanoes are classified as active, and countless quakes shake and rattle the planet.[5] Stories like those of Kathie, Gil, Fred, and Margery could be multiplied millions of times.

All this destruction derives from the endless jostling of tectonic plates, the twenty-five or so jigsaw pieces forming the earth's crust. The jolting, colliding, rubbing, and shuddering of these pieces release enormous quantities

---

2. Waitt, *In the Path of Destruction*, 160–61.
3. Hayward, "Breath of Vulcan," *The Living Bird Quarterly*, 4–8.
4. Olson, *Eruption*, 175.
5. Bullard, *Volcanoes of the Earth*, Revised edition, 443, 445–49. A volcano is considered "active" if it has erupted during historic times.

of energy, energy that powers volcanoes, earthquakes, and tsunamis.[6] Like most cosmic phenomena, this unimaginable power not only devastates but creates. Mountains take shape, islands emerge, habitats open, soils rejuvenate, scenic beauties materialize, and new species appear.[7]

I DON'T KNOW WHEN I first learned about continental drift and plate tectonics. Volpe's *Understanding Evolution*, one of my college textbooks at Walla Walla College, devoted a single paragraph to the topic. Volpe noted that continental drift theory, "earlier ridiculed, has been revived and has gained a measure of scientific respectability in several quarters."[8] Unlike other parts of the book, however, this statement impressed me little. Perhaps I even discounted the idea, subconsciously thinking of the biblical texts that appear to speak of a stable earth: "The world also shall be stable, that it be not moved (1 Chr 16:30); "The world also is stablished, that it cannot be moved" (Ps 93:1); and "Who laid the foundations of the earth, that it should not be removed forever" (Ps 104:5).

Recently I scanned through my class notes from when I was a graduate student at Andrews University for any mention of continental drift. I found only one brief comment. During his lecture on October 16, 1972, Richard Ritland, my Introduction to Paleontology professor, briefly mentioned continental drift during a lecture on the geologic column. In my notes I scribbled, "Continental drift—Has not apparently affected Cenozoic, therefore occurred prior to." That was it. The next semester I took Biogeography from Ritland, but nothing in my notes or in the class handouts indicates the slightest reference to continental drift. Continental drift would soon play a major role in biogeographic theory, but when I took Biogeography, continental drift had not yet been integrated into the topic on a broad scale.[9]

Early in 1976, a lecture entitled "Should We Drift with the Drifting Continents?" by Harold James piqued my interest. I had completed my master's degree, and I was enjoying my temporary teaching stint at Andrews

---

6. Press and Siever, "Earth," 420, 498–524; DeMets et al., "Geologically Current Plate Motions," 3.

7. The statement that "new species appear" deserves explanation. Tectonic activity creates new habitats—mountains, valleys, islands, rivers, etc.—often isolated from other habitats. This isolation allows for the occurrence of a common type of species formation called "allopatric speciation." For further explanation and examples, see Herron and Freeman, *Evolutionary Analysis*, 616–23.

8. Volpe, *Understanding Evolution*, 108–9.

9. All this has changed. See, for example, Briggs, *Biogeography and Plate Tectonics*, 9 who noted, "The plate tectonic revolution in earth science had a gradual but decisive effect on biogeography."

University. I was sitting in on Issues in Origins and Speciation, the graduate course I had taken as a student three years earlier, and James was giving a guest lecture. He was fresh out of a PhD program in geology at Princeton, an epicenter of plate tectonic theory. There he had rubbed shoulders with Harry Hess, a founding father of the theory.

After reviewing some of the early data leading geologists to embrace the once discounted idea of continental drift, James noted:

> Predictions and confirmations appeared to make drifters the geological prophets of the present and at least the immediate future. If the continents were once joined it should be possible to reassemble them, in theory that is. Join them the scientists did and that with no less than the sophistication of computers. The fit was amazingly good. On the basis of this fit it should be possible to predict where changes in rock type from one continent would be matched by changes in rock type on the "adjacent" continent. The match was gratifying.[10]

James's lecture sparked my interest in the topic and proved pivotal to my developing perspectives on earth history.

The theory of plate tectonics and continental drift turned earth science on its head. The paradigm shift was similar in scope to the Copernican revolution. Time-worn interpretations of earth features had to be reinterpreted, research protocols had to be revised, and geology textbooks had to be rewritten. In 1973, Oxford geologist Anthony Hallam commented on this stunning and fundamental shift of viewpoints:

> So strong was the feeling against continental drift until quite recently that in some institutions an open adherence to this doctrine would have put at serious risk the attainment of tenure by junior faculty members, while their more secure senior colleagues would have been all but drummed out of their invisible college. At the present time, only a few years later, almost the reverse situation holds.[11]

What type of evidence, collected and evaluated within the course of just a few years, would lead a group of scientists to completely reconstruct the fundamental principles of their science? Fortunately for me, this evidence was elegantly explained in *The New View of the Earth* by Seiya Uyeda, a professor of geophysics at the University of Tokyo. He also served as a research fellow at Scripps Institution of Oceanography and as a visiting

---

10. James, "Should We Drift with the Drifting Continents?"
11. Hallam, *A Revolution in the Earth Sciences*, 105.

professor at Stanford, MIT, Columbia, and Caltec. Not only was he a key participant in plate tectonics research, he was an excellent writer. I had just completed my PhD, and this remarkable book, written for earth-science laymen like myself, completely captured my interest and convinced me of the reality of a dynamic earth.

WHEN KIDS FIRST STUDY the globe, one of the first things they notice is how the east coast of the New World matches so closely the west coast of the Old World. They especially note the large bulge extending from the west side of the African continent, with the countries of Western Sahara, Mauritania, Gambia, Guinea, Sierra Leone, and Liberia now populating the western edge. That western edge would tuck neatly into the curved, eastern margin of North and Central America. At the same time, the Brazilian bulge, along the east coast of South America, would nestle comfortably against the western coast of southern Africa. If the Old and New Worlds were two puzzle pieces, they would be the first selections for a match. Why would this be?

This question has been asked countless times by people, ever since the first world maps appeared. The best known of these queries was by thirty-year-old German astronomer and meteorologist, Alfred Wegener (1880–1930), considered the father of continental drift theory. The "concept of continental drift first came to me as far back as 1910," he recalled, "when considering the map of the world, under the direct impression produced by the congruence of the coastlines on either side of the Atlantic."[12] This observation led him on a quixotic quest for geodetic, geophysical, geological, paleontological, biological, and paleoclimatic data consistent with the hypothesis that the Old and New Worlds had literally slid east and west, respectively, after splitting apart.[13]

Based on the fact that closely-related organisms lived on either side of the Atlantic, scientists had long postulated the existence of a land bridge between the Old and New Worlds. They believed this bridge had subsequently disappeared through geological subsidence—land sinking. Wegener, however, saw no geological evidence for such a bridge; he considered the circumstantial evidence for one-time continental unification much stronger. He noted, for example, that rock sequences on the east coast of South America and the west coast of Africa matched one another precisely, as did the sequence and species of fossils contained in the rocks. Moreover, he highlighted the common occurrence of various fossils, including those of

12. Wegener, *The Origin of Continents and Oceans*, 1.
13. Greene, *Alfred Wegener: Science, Exploration, and the Theory of Continental Drift*.

tongue ferns, genus *Glossopteris*, in South America, Africa, Australia, New Zealand, and India, as evidence pointing to an ancient, conjoined supercontinent he called Gondwanaland.[14]

On January 6, 1912, Wegener presented a lecture on his views at Senckenberg-Museum in Frankfurt am Main, followed by articles in a German professional journal and his 1915 book, *Die Entstehung der Kontinente und Ozeane*.[15] Despite the impressive evidence marshalled by Wegener, he did not come up with a convincing mechanism for his theory. To most people it seemed preposterous that entire continents could move around over the surface of the globe. Where would the energy come from to perform such a feat? By the time Wegener died in 1930, his theory enjoyed little support.[16] As for biogeographers, they fell back on the land bridge theory to account for related organisms on either side of the Atlantic.[17]

THE CONGRUENT SHAPES AND similar rocks of the east and west coasts, respectively, of the New World and the Old World are certainly impressive. The first piece of evidence, however, that made me really sit up and take note of the possibility of continental drift involved polar wandering.

The earth functions as if a giant bar magnet extends through its center, from north to south magnetic poles. Molecules of magma, while still liquid, behave like tiny compass needles; as they cool and solidify to become volcanic rocks, the molecules line up with the polarity of the giant bar magnet. The orientations of the molecules within the volcanic rocks can be measured with an instrument called a magnetometer. Magnetometer measurements have been carried out over many parts of the world in volcanic rocks of many different ages. The molecules in volcanic rocks that form today all point in the direction of today's magnetic north. Geophysicists, however, discovered that molecules in ancient volcanic rocks point to positions different from today's magnetic north. Moreover, old rocks in Europe and in other regions point to different positions of magnetic north than rocks of the same age in North America. And here is the intriguing part: The "north pole" positions, indicated by progressively younger rocks on

14. Wegener, *The Origin of Continents and Oceans*, 5, 61–80, 97–120, 142.

15. Wegener, "Die Herausbildung der Grossformen der Erdrinde (Kontinente und Ozeane)auf geophysikalische Grundlage"; Wegener, "Die Entstehung der Kontinente," *Dr. A. Petermanns Mitteilungen aus Justus Perthes' Geographischer Anstalt*, 185–195, 253–6, 305–9; Wegener, "Die Entstehung der Kontinente," 276–92; Wegener, *Die Entstehung der Kontinente und Ozeane*; the much expanded fourth edition of this latter book was translated into English and is cited in Note 11 above.

16. Hallam, *A Revolution in the Earth Sciences*, 22–36.

17. Hallam, *A Revolution in the Earth Sciences*, 111–12.

different continents, converge and move closer and closer to today's magnetic north pole. When the positions of the now separated continents are corrected for their positions during progressive stages of continental drift, the magnetic molecules no longer point in different directions—they line up almost perfectly.[18]

It was this evidence that inspired a resurgence of Wegener's continental drift theory during the 1950s and 1960s. Additional evidence would make Wegener's theory even more compelling.

By the 1920s, scientists recognized the existence of an enormous underwater mountain range now called the Mid-Atlantic Ridge. This ridge extends for nearly the entire north-south extent of the Atlantic Ocean. Further exploration revealed the existence of similar ridges in the other oceans. What was the origin of these enormous rises along the ocean floor?[19]

A series of sensitive instruments was developed that allowed shipboard measurements of ocean floor features, such as the mid-ocean ridges. One instrument was the sonic depth recorder, a device that sent sound waves from ship to seafloor and measured the length of time it took for the echo to return to the ship. Using this technology, the topography of the ocean floor was determined with an accuracy of about three feet. Precise, topographic maps of the seafloor were generated. Topographic features provided important clues as to the types of processes influencing the ocean bottom. For example, it was discovered that the mid-ocean ridges were huge—a bit less than two miles high and more than twelve hundred miles wide. Another discovery was the existence of deep valleys along the tops and running the lengths of the ridges, suggesting the ridges were under tension.[20]

A second instrument was a thermal probe which could be lowered from a ship and forced into soft ocean floor sediments. Thermometers positioned along the length of the probe allowed for measurement of heat flow through the ocean sediments. Intriguingly, heat flow was three or four times higher along the mid-ocean ridges than at other points along the ocean bottom, and heat flow reached its highest intensity on either side of the deep valleys that bisect the ridges.[21]

A third instrument was the proton-precession magnetometer. This device, towed at a distance behind ocean-going vessels, measured minute changes in the magnetic fields of the ocean floor. Magnetometer readings

---

18. Hallam, *A Revolution in the Earth Sciences*, 37–43.
19. Uyeda, *The New View of the Earth*, 51.
20. Uyeda, *The New View of the Earth*, 44–53.
21. Uyeda, *The New View of the Earth*, 50.

revealed something very peculiar—the existence of series of magnetic stripes paralleling and extending out laterally from the mid-ocean ridges. The stripes consisted of volcanic rocks, with molecules in successive stripes exhibiting reversed polarity—the magnetic molecules in one stripe pointed north, the molecules in the next stripe pointed south, those in the next one pointed north, and so on. Not only that, but the striping sequence exhibited mirror-imaging on either side of the ridges. Why this was the case soon became apparent.[22]

In 1968, during my sophomore year of college, the United States instituted the Deep Sea Drilling Project. This project and its successors involved the construction of ships capable of drilling and recovering core samples of the soft sediments and basaltic rocks that make up the ocean floor. Analysis of the cores revealed that samples taken progressively further away from the mid-ocean ridges were progressively older. The basalt forming the ridges themselves, by contrast, was young—and warm. The implication from these samples and from the magnetometers was clear: the seafloor is spreading away from the ridges, ridges from which new seafloor is generated. The alternating orientations of magnetic stripes suggested that the giant bar magnet extending through the earth periodically flips polarity. As new ocean floor forms at the mid-ocean ridges and pushes out laterally, its molecules of basalt take on the current orientation of the magnet. When the magnet reverses polarity, the new ocean floor being manufactured and pushed away from the ridge acquires the new polarity. The pattern of magnetic stripes on either side of the ridge thus form mirror images of one another. Moreover, this horizontally-oriented process is precisely consistent with the magnetic orientations of basalt layers stacked vertically on land—both in terms of ages and magnetic orientations. The vertically-stacked, terrestrial layers flip-flop in the same way, with the ages and magnetic polarities of the layers matching the ages and magnetic polarities of the stripes on the seafloor. No one knows why the flip-flops in the magnetic poles occur, but the evidence for them is clear.[23]

When I learned about all this, I became convinced of the reality of seafloor spreading. Few complex processes in nature are supported by evidence this clear-cut. But serious questions remained. Where do the continents fit in? Where does the old seafloor go as it get pushed farther away from the ridges? Where does the energy for all this movement come from? What is the rate of seafloor spreading? I kept learning.

---

22. Uyeda, *The New View of the Earth*, 48–50.
23. Uyeda, *The New View of the Earth*, 62–92.

IT SOON BECAME EVIDENT that the earth's crust is divided unevenly into tectonic plates, the jigsaw-puzzle pieces mentioned earlier. These plates quite literally float on the earth's mantle, a semisolid layer of higher-density rock beneath the lower-density crust. The crust, with its continents and oceans, rides atop the plates. New seafloor manufactured along a mid-ocean ridge forms new plate material, and the entire plate moves laterally away from the ridge.[24]

The earth is not expanding, so what happens to the old plate edge which is getting pushed further and further away from the mid-ocean ridge? One thing it can do is collide head-on with another plate and cause it to buckle. As the collision proceeds, the buckle becomes a mountain chain. The Himalayas represents one such chain. The Himalayan Range continues to form during a collision between the Indian Plate and the larger Eurasian Plate. The collision is ongoing, and ancient sediments, once the floor of a shallow sea, form the summit of Mount Everest, the tallest peak in the world, which continues to rise. The old seafloor at the summit, nearly six miles above current sea level, contains fossil crinoids and trilobites, marine animals that once lived in a shallow sea.[25]

The other, more common, plate-to-plate boundary involves the old leading edge of a growing plate diving beneath the edge of the second plate. The boundary along which they meet forms a subduction zone. In Japan, for example, there is a subduction zone where the Pacific Plate dives beneath the eastern edge of the Eurasian Plate. Subduction zones form deep trenches, in this case an extension of the famous Marianas Trench. Amazingly, the subducting plates, once theoretical inferences, can now be imaged using seismic tomography.[26]

When a plate slides beneath another plate, tremendous heat is generated by the intense friction. This heat builds up and is released in the form of volcanic eruptions. The slippage also generates earthquakes. Subduction zones occur along much of the perimeter of the Pacific Ocean forming the "Ring of Fire," a moniker based on the existence of hundreds of lively

---

24. Plummer and Carlson, *Physical Geology*, 492–512.

25. Allégre, *The Behavior of the Earth*, 185–86; Odell, "The Highest Fossils in the World," 73–74; Sakai et al., "Geology of the Summit Limestone of Mount Qomolangma (Everest) and Cooling History of the Yellow Band under the Qomolangma detachment," 297–310; Myrow et al., "Stratigraphic correlation of Cambrian–Ordovician deposits along the Himalaya: Implications for the age and nature of rocks in the Mount Everest region," 329.

26. Uyeda, *The New View of the Earth*, 125–32; Liu and Zhao, "P and S Wave Tomography of Japan Subduction Zone from Joint Inversions of Local and Teleseismic Travel Times and Surface-Wave Data," 1–22.

volcanoes, including Mount St. Helens, along it perimeter.[27] This geologically active region is beautiful and attracts large human populations which are vulnerable to the havoc created by the earthquakes and erupting peaks. Indonesia, Japan, California, and Chile are only four such regions.

ANOTHER FASCINATING PIECE OF evidence involving plate movement concerns "hotspots." Hotspots are point locations at which searing heat burns through the earth's crust. Hotspots do not move with the tectonic plates, but the plates move over the hotspots. Geoscientists are not sure why hotspots occur, but they seem to be generated deep within the mantle.

Every so often heat builds up to a point at which a hotspot erupts through the crust and forms a volcano. The volcano eventually dies out, but the plate with its crust continues to move, taking the old volcanic cone with it. Soon heat builds up again and another volcano bursts through, this time at a new position along the plate. In this way a line of volcanic cones develops, oriented in the direction of plate movement. As predicted, the rocks that form these volcanoes are progressively older and more eroded in the direction of plate movement.[28]

A classic example of hotspot activity involves the Hawaiian Islands, really just a long chain of volcanic cones. The Pacific Plate is currently moving in a northwesterly direction, the direction of the vector formed by the Hawaiian Islands. The rocks of each island get progressively older and more eroded the further they are from the Big Island of Hawaii at the southeastern end of the chain. The Big Island is the most volcanically active of the Hawaiian Islands. A new island, named Loihi, is forming southeast of the Big Island, but it has yet to breach the water's surface.[29]

If we were traveling in a submarine in a northwesterly direction, past the westernmost Hawaiian Island of Niihau, we would begin encounter a series of highly eroded, underwater volcanic structures called the Emperor Seamounts, remnants of ancient islands that have since disappeared. Continuing in the same direction we would pass the Colahan Seamount, but soon have to make a sharp turn to the north in order to follow the long line of remaining seamounts. The rocks that compose these underwater peaks are progressively older in the direction of our travel than those of the Hawaiian Islands. They were formed by the same hotspot that formed the

---

27. Ludman and Coch, *Physical Geology*, 99
28. Uyeda, *The New View of the Earth*, 195.
29. Uyeda, *The New View of the Earth*, 196; Malahoff, "Geology of the Summit of the Loihi Submarine Volcano," 133–44.

Hawaiian Islands, but as they were being formed, the Pacific Plate rotated somewhat and took a more northerly trajectory.[30]

Yet another example of hotspot activity involves the Yellowstone region in Wyoming. Yellowstone Valley is in the position of an old volcanic mountain that collapsed on itself following several enormous eruptions. The occurrence of these eruptions is indicated by the presence of the widespread distribution of tephra,[31] and by the caldera (basin) formed by the collapses. Yellowstone National Park's geysers are an indication that the region continues to reside over an active hotspot. To the west of Yellowstone and on into Idaho, northern Nevada, and Oregon, a series of progressively older volcanic structures reflect the movement to the southwest by the North American Plate over the hotspot. It's likely this hotspot will erupt again, a catastrophic event that will dwarf the 1980 eruption of Mount St. Helens and impact the lives of many more people over a huge area of North America and around the world.[32]

ALL THIS EVIDENCE ABOUT polar wondering, mid-ocean ridges, continental drift, seafloor spreading, subduction zones, and hot spots made complete sense to me. But I still wanted to understand what kind of processes would be responsible for moving these enormous tectonic plates around the surface of the earth.

As I noted earlier, Alfred Wegner's theory did not go very far during his lifetime because he failed to provide an adequate mechanism for continental drift. What forces could possibly account for movement at this scale? Paleomagnetism, seafloor spreading, and hot spots had convinced geophysicists that continental drift was real. But they needed a mechanism. So they set to work trying to uncover the forces involved.

One of the first ideas to emerge was that convection currents at the top portion of the mantle—the asthenosphere—were responsible for plate movement. Convection currents are what we see at the surface of hot oatmeal when it begins to boil—hot mush from the bottom of the pan moves upward; when it reaches the surface, it moves to the sides of the pan as more hot mush rises to takes its place. Similarly, convection currents in the mantle are driven by heat rising from deeper regions of the earth and from radioactive decomposition. But when scientists estimated the forces involved, they

30. Clague and Dalrymple, "The Hawaiian-Emperor Volcanic Chain," 5–54.
31. Tephra: any type of particle ejected from a volcano during an eruption.
32. Pierce and Morgan, "The Track of the Yellowstone Hot Spot," 1–52; Alt and Hyndman, *Northwest Exposures*, 279–80; Fritz and Thomas, *Roadside Geology of Yellowstone Country*, 62–76.

realized that convection currents alone were inadequate to move something as massive as an overlying plate. The forces created by convection currents, even though they probably play some role in the overall dynamics of plate movement, would be too small to overcome the friction created by the plate sliding over the mantle. Moreover, the currents do not necessarily flow in the same direction the continents are moving.[33]

A second hypothesis has to do with the fact that new plate material emerges at the tops of mid-ocean ridges, which are thousands of feet above the ocean floor. Gravity pulls down on this new plate material causing it to slide down the side of the ridge, push against the somewhat older ocean floor, forcing it to move away from the ridge. This seems like a reasonable idea, and this mechanism probably does play a role in plate movement. But once again, the calculations indicated this so-called "ridge-push" force could not account for very much of the plate movement.[34]

Other forces have been invoked, including suction along subduction zones, tidal forces by the sun and moon, and centrifugal force as a result of the earth's spin on its axis. The last two of these forces had originally been postulated by Wegener, but were discarded by later scientists as inadequate.[35]

Each proposed force probably plays at least a minor role in plate dynamics. But only one force has received widespread acceptance over the past few decades—"slab-pull" force. Slab-pull force is the force of gravity pulling on a relatively cool, subducting plate as it dives beneath the edge of another plate into softer and warmer mantle rock. As it does so, it pulls the rest of the plate along with it, like gravity pulling a coat off a table. Geophysicists measured all manner of factors associated with each tectonic plate and its velocity—plate area, circumference, above-water continental area, length of the ridge, length of the trench created by subducting plate. They examined various combinations of these factors and found that plate velocity was greatest when the ratio of trench length to plate circumference was high. In other words, the higher the percentage of plate circumference involved in subduction, the higher its plate velocity.[36]

Slab-pull force is modulated by the size of the continents atop the plate. This makes sense because the thick continental area of a plate is more

---

33. Forsyth and Uyeda, "On the Relative Importance of the Driving Forces of Plate Motion," 163–200; Uyeda, *The New View of the Earth*, 176–78.
34. Uyeda, *The New View of the Earth*, 192.
35. Uyeda, *The New View of the Earth*, 192–93.
36. Uyeda, *The New View of the Earth*, 192, 197–201.

massive than the thin oceanic area forming the rest of the plate; consequently larger continents create more drag.

There are many details still to be worked out with this so-called sinking-slab model, but it seems to account for much of what we see.[37]

How fast do the plates move? Clearly not fast enough to feel movement, except during earthquakes! But is it rapid enough to perceive with sensitive instrumentation? The answer is yes, the movement is readily detectable.

Recently I spoke with a cartographer who creates maps for the United States Geological Survey (USGS). She told me that map-making technology has developed to such precision that when creating maps, she and her colleagues must take into account the movement of the continents, measured by a network of Global Positioning System (GPS) units. It's often said that the continents move at about the same rate as one's fingernails grow—an eighth of an inch or so per month. At this rate, since I was born in 1948, North America would have shifted away from Europe more than eight feet; since the time of Christ it would have moved over 230 feet, three-quarters of the distance across a football field. But these estimates overlook the variability in plate velocities—a ten-fold difference occurs between the velocities of the slowest and fastest plates. Plates with the lowest velocity move less than half an inch per year, whereas those with the highest velocity move about three and a half inches per year.[38]

In science, a "theory" is a well-substantiated statement about nature, one that unifies what previously appeared to be disparate lines of evidence into a coherent way of looking at reality. The theory of plate tectonics is an outstanding example of this type of unification. The theory has revolutionized the way we think about the earth, its continental shapes, landforms, and dynamics. So many features of the earth—volcanos, earthquakes, mid-ocean ridges, valleys, mountain ranges, etc.—once unconnected phenomena in the minds of geologists, are now seen as linked components within an enormous and very active earth machine. The general acceptance of this theory constitutes a dramatic example of a major paradigm shift in science, comparable in significance to the Copernican revolution when humans discovered they were not at the center of the universe. Plate tectonic theory does not yet explain all geological phenomena, but it comes much closer to doing so than any other theory.

---

37. Uyeda, *The New View of the Earth*, 197–99.
38. DeMets, et al., "Geologically Current Plate Motions," 1–80.

Many creationists now accept the theory of plate tectonics and continental drift. Indeed, the evidence is too compelling for knowledgeable people to deny. But, despite their acceptance of much of the theory, young-age creationists balk at the long periods of time thought to be involved. In their minds the rate of movement had to have been more rapid in the past than at present. Here's what young-age creationist Leonard Brand wrote:

> The significant amount of continental movement that must be included in our catastrophic theory requires more rapid movement than neocatastrophic [standard] concepts of geology accept. If this process took 1,000 years, a continental movement of 2,000 miles would require an average speed of 1.2 feet/hour. The process seems to have begun near the end of the flood and continued for a while afterwards.[39]

We see what devastation occurs at plate boundaries in response to movements of a few inches a year—violent earthquakes, volcanic eruptions, and plate deformation. To compress the history of continental drift into a few thousand years would require the release of unimaginable quantities of heat and kinetic energy over a short period of time. As Brand truthfully pointed out, "The greatest difficulty with this hypothesis is posed by the physical effects of moving continent-sized plates that fast."[40] Indeed, the difficulty is not only great but insurmountable. As one Christian oceanographer, critical of rapid continental drift, pointed out, "The excess crustal heat [generated by moving plates this fast would be] sufficient to boil away all the water of the earth's surface 2.8 times."[41] In short, young-age creationists find themselves in an unenviable situation—acceptance of the processes of plate tectonics, but unwilling to accept the necessary time involved.

IN HIS LECTURE BACK in 1976, Harold James asked "Should we drift with the drifting continents?" The answer, of course—as he well knew—is yes, we have no choice. The earth, like everything in the universe, is in constant motion. The implications of plate tectonics for our understanding of the earth, its history, and the history of life are profound.

39. Brand, *Faith, Reason, and Earth History*, 295. An updated version of the book omits the "average speed of 1.2 feet/hour" estimate, but candidly admits that a proposed model "for rapid plate tectonics during the flood . . . has not yet explained how to deal with the heat generated by such rapid continental motion" (Brand and Chadwick, *Faith, Reason, & Earth History*, 425).

40. Brand, *Faith, Reason, and Earth History*, 295.

41. Barnes, "Thermal Consequences of a Short Time Scale for Sea-Floor Spreading," 123–25.

As we work toward a more comprehensive understanding of our planet, we must realize, like my USGS mapmaker colleague, that we need to pay close attention to this motion—not just for making maps but for understanding reality.

10

Gauging Time

"Deep time is so alien that we can really only comprehend it as metaphor."

—Stephen Jay Gould[1]

"That looks like a mollusk layer!" I exclaimed. I scrambled sixty feet up the steep embankment to the stratum of interest, and to my delight the light-colored objects were indeed fossil mollusk shells. They were embedded in a ten-foot thick layer of sand, pebbles, and cobbles several yards below the cliff summit. I took pictures, recorded the GPS location, and placed the specimens in sample bags. Mollusk shells may not sound like exciting finds, but these fossils would provide important information about the identity of the rock layer within which they had been preserved.

My colleagues and I were studying the deposits of silt, sand, and gravel that make up the 75- to 200-foot cliffs surrounding Protection Island, Washington. Previously these cliffs had yielded mammoth teeth and tusks, a giant beaver skull, ancient bison teeth, and an abundance of compressed plant fossils embedded in thick peat deposits. We were interested in what the fossils and sediments surrounding them could tell us about the history of this remarkable island. Protection Island today hosts tens of thousands of

---

1. Gould, *Time's Arrow, Time's Cycle*, 3.

breeding marine birds and mammals; in the past it was home to an alternating series of marine, freshwater, and terrestrial inhabitants. We wanted to uncover the details of this history.

The mollusk shells could provide us with a time marker—they were well-preserved and still contained most of their original calcium carbonate. The carbon in the carbonate could reveal their age. Descendants of these mollusks live in Washington's intertidal zone today, and the animals that occupied these fossil shells lived when this layer was submerged within an ancient intertidal zone. Here they were now, six stories above the tide and covered, in turn, by many feet of non-marine sediment.

We predicted these shells were preserved in sediments of the Everson Formation, a mollusk-laden sedimentary layer approximately 13,000 years old, a commonly exposed formation in the surrounding region.[2] Until we had the shells age-dated, however, we would be unable to make this assertion with complete confidence.

Once back in Michigan, I selected the best preserved shell and shipped it to Beta Analytic, Inc., Miami, Florida. Beta Analytic specializes in accelerator mass spectrometry (AMS) carbon-14 dating. Lab personnel pride themselves in a dedication to accuracy. Results from this sophisticated lab have aided in the temporal reconstruction of archaeological and paleontological sites around the globe.

A few weeks and several hundred dollars later—high quality radiometric dating is not cheap—I received an email from Darden Hood, Beta Analytic's president, informing me that the specimen "provided plenty of carbon for an accurate measurement and the analysis proceeded normally." Good news. The shell was determined to be 13,080 years old, plus or minus 50 years—smack-dab in the Everson. Prediction confirmed![3]

We now had a radiometric age for one of the many sediment layers forming the island. It would not possible to date every layer, because not every layer has the right kind of material for dating. But now that we had an age for this layer, we knew that any lower deposits were older and any higher deposits were younger.

We were not so lucky with our second sample. From the base of the north cliff, I noticed an enormous block of sediment had slumped away from a section about half way up the bluff and slid partway down the cliff face. I spotted a long, yellowish cream-colored object exposed along the front of

---

2. Dethier et al., "Late Wisconsinan Glaciomarine Deposition and Isostatic rebound, Northern Puget Lowland, Washington," 1288–1303.
3. Darden Hood to JLH, November 26, 2013.

this slumped section. Through binoculars, I saw that the object was an intact mammoth tusk. There was just enough of a slope to allow us to scramble up to the tusk and remove a small sample.

As with the shell deposit, we determined the GPS location of the tusk, recorded other pertinent information, and shipped the sample off to Beta Analytic. We knew there was a good chance there would be too little carbon-14 left in the specimen for accurate age determination—the layer in which it was found appeared to be part of the very old Whidbey Formation, which formed well before the range of carbon-14 dating.[4] The people at Beta Analytic are confident of dates only up to 43,500 years old; after that point so much carbon-14 has decayed away that it is nearly unmeasurable.

Sure enough, the report noted that "The ^{14}C [carbon-14] activity was extremely low and almost identical to the background signal. In such cases, indeterminate errors associated with the background add non-measurable uncertainty to the result."[5] We had struck out—but not entirely. At the very least we had established that everything below the sediment layer containing the tusk was older than 43,500 radiometric years. This was a valuable piece of evidence, even though we wished the results could have been more specific. We now had two time markers: the layer with the shells and the layer with the tusk. These time markers would help us place the various layers and fossils that make up the island in proper historical perspective.

IN PRINCIPLE, RADIOMETRIC DATING is not difficult to understand. Ernest Rutherford and Frederick Soddy of McGill University discovered the all-important "half-life" principle in the early twentieth century.[6] Radioactive atoms decay so that over a given period of time, half the atoms in a sample break down to form different kinds of atoms, or daughter products. Then, over the next period of time of the same length, half of the remaining atoms break apart—until essentially all the radioactive atoms have broken apart, or decayed. The decay is thus exponential—a half to a fourth, a fourth to an eighth, an eighth to a sixteenth, and so on.[7]

Each radioactive element has its own unique half-life. The half-lives of some radioactive atoms are only milliseconds in length, whereas the

---

4. Easterbrook, "Stratigraphy and Chronology of Quaternary Deposits of the Puget Lowland," 155.

5. Beta Analytic Laboratory to JLH, "Report of Radiocarbon Dating Analyses," email, April 14, 2014.

6. Dalrymple, *The Age of the Earth*, 70–71.

7. A simple explanation of the mathematical formulas used in determining radiometric dates is found in Dalrymple, *The Age of the Earth*, 84–85.

half-lives of other atoms are on the order of days, centuries, or even billions of years. The half-life of potassium-40, for example, is 1.25 billion years, whereas the half-life of uranium-238 is 4.47 billion years. By measuring the ratio of radioactive atoms to their daughter products in a specimen, the radiometric age can be determined. Environmental factors have little or no effect on the decay rates of non-carbon atoms.[8]

There are scores of types of radioactive atoms with different half-lives, so depending on the material, more than one type of "atomic clock" can often be used for dating. Results from one type of clock can be checked against the results from other types of clocks. The consistency is remarkable. As with any analytic process, measurements incur some experimental error and spurious results are sometimes obtained. All scientific techniques are subject to error, but it is not the exceptions that overly concern us—although they can sometimes teach us something important as well—it is the overall trends.[9]

Carbon-14 dating has been carefully calibrated using materials of known ages, including historically-dated objects, tree rings, coral layers, and lake sediments. These have allowed geochronologists to apply corrections to measured C-14 dates up to about 26,000 years before present. Older dates, which cannot be calibrated using materials of known age, must be viewed with somewhat less confidence.[10]

BACK IN THE 1950S, claims about the ages of fossils led young-age creationist chemist Peter Edgar (Ed) Hare to develop a technique designed to disprove the results of carbon-14 dating. Hare had completed a degree in chemistry at Pacific Union College, a small Seventh-day Adventist institution sixty miles north of San Francisco, and he had earned a master's degree at Berkeley. After he finished at Berkeley, Pacific Union College hired him back to teach chemistry. While there he read an article in *Scientific American* entitled "Paleobiochemistry" by Philip H. Abelson. Abelson claimed that 300-million-year-old fossils contained amino acids, the building blocks of proteins.[11]

Hare was intrigued. He didn't believe amino acids could survive for 300 million years. He believed that life was only a few thousand years old

---

8. Dalrymple, *The Age of the Earth*, 80–90.

9. Dalrymple, *The Age of the Earth*, 122–24; Bottomley, "Age Dating of Rocks," 44–47.

10. Reimer et al., "Intcal13 and Marine13 Radiocarbon Age Calibration Curves 0–50,000 Years Cal BP," 1874, 1878.

11. Abelson, "Paleobiochemistry," 83–92.

and that the Genesis flood was responsible for burying the organisms now found as fossils. He knew that the twenty or so different types of amino acids exhibit different levels of stability over time, with some amino acids disappearing before others. He hypothesized that if the mollusks had become fossils at different times, the ratios of amino acids in shells of different ages would be different. Conversely, if these same fossils had been destroyed by the flood, they would all display the same amino acid ratios. He decided to test this hypothesis for his PhD dissertation at the California Institute of Technology.

Hare found a sequence of marine terraces along the California coast, each of which contained fossil mollusk shells of the genus *Mytilus*. He analyzed the amino acid content of shells in the different terraces, believing they would all exhibit the same ratios of amino acids. To his surprise, shells from different levels exhibited different mixtures of amino acids—just as one would expect if they were deposited at different times. In fact, the carbon-14 dates for the shells and the pattern of amino acid mixtures he found correlated nicely.[12]

Philip Abelson, author of the *Scientific American* article that captured Hare's attention years before, learned of Hare's research and was intrigued. He offered Hare a job at the renowned Geophysical Laboratory at Carnegie Institution, where Hare spent the rest of his highly productive career. Based on Hare's study of *Mytilus*, Hare and Abelson developed the amino acid racemization dating technique for estimating the ages of organic materials. In 1969, when the Apollo 11 astronauts brought back samples of moon rock, it was Hare who analyzed the samples for the presence of amino acids.[13]

I first met Ed Hare in 1985 at a conference in West Yellowstone, and in 1988 I roomed with him while attending another conference in Los Angeles. In 1994, I showed him around Egg Mountain, Montana, famed for the presence of dinosaur eggs and nests. Dinosaur eggs and eggshell fragments abound around Egg Mountain, an important dinosaur nesting locality during the Cretaceous Period. Hare, who had worked on characterizing the amino acids in eggshells, was intrigued. Dinosaur eggshells are known to contain amino acids, and he proposed that after his retirement the two of us would travel to North American dinosaur nesting sites with his portable amino acid analyzer and do onsite tests for amino acids in eggshell specimens. Sadly, before this plan could become reality, Ed fell ill and died in 2006. The scientific community lost not only a brilliant instrumentalist

---

12. Hare, "Amino Acid Dating of Fossils," 104–9.

13. Benton, "Odyssey of an Adventist Creationist," 46–53; Hare et al., "Analyses for Amino Acids in Lunar Fines," 1799–1803.

and the acknowledged father of amino acid geochemistry, but a wonderfully kind and thoughtful gentleman.[14]

Ed Hare served in various leadership positions in his local church and remained a committed Christian throughout his life. As a result of his discoveries, however, he became convinced that life has existed on Planet Earth for a very long time, and that radiometric dating, if carefully performed, is a trustworthy source of information.[15]

As I NOTED ABOVE, many types of radiometric dating techniques are used to determine the age of rocks and fossils. Each one is based on the "half-life" principle. Robert Brown, an otherwise conservative creationist, led the way to a view among more progressive creationists that Planet Earth itself is billions of years old, just like scientists said it was. He was adamant, however, that life itself was only a few thousand years old.[16] How did he come up with such a seemingly self-contradictory position?

Brown was a physicist with a PhD from the University of Washington.[17] He could find no way to discount the principles of inorganic radiometric dating. As he wrote, "the rates of radioactive disintegration might logically be expected to be as constant and dependable as the basic characteristics of the physical universe, and, therefore, reliable as units of time measurement." He argued that statements in the Bible "refer only to a modification of the planet's surface and its adornment with plant and animal life." He believed the material of the planet was created billions of years ago, but that life was created only a few thousand years ago during creation week depicted in Genesis.[18]

The problem with his approach, of course, was that fossils, the traces of once living things, were preserved smack-dab in middle of those very old rocks. Young-age creationists like biologist Frank Lewis Marsh immediately recognized this problem and took issue with Brown. Marsh accused Brown and other physicists of falling "on their faces before the god of radioactive time clock dating of inorganic materials"—he discounted the entire enterprise.[19] Brown, on the other hand, argued that the fossils were preserved in

---

14. Taylor, "Peter Edgar Hare (1933–2006)," 16; Miller, "Obituary. Peter Edgar Hare (1933–2006)," 87–88.

15. Benton, "Odyssey of an Adventist Creationist"; Taylor, "Peter Edgar Hare (1933–2006): American Scientist and Committed Adventist Layman."

16. Numbers, *The Creationists*, 326.

17. Brown, "Ion Formation and Decay in a Mercury Resonance Cell as Evidenced by Electrical Image Forces."

18. Brown, "Radioactive Time Clocks," 295–96.

19. Brown, "R. H. Brown Comments on Radioactive Age Panel," 22–24. The quotation by Marsh is included within Brown's comments.

the rocks without affecting the ancient ages of the rocks. His argument was impossible to maintain from a scientific perspective; instead, it was based on his confidence in "a straightforward acceptance of the book of Genesis," tempered with the view that "an understanding of radioisotope dating can assist one in avoiding unwarranted interpretation of inspired testimony."[20]

So how did Brown square his view with the results of carbon-14 dating of once-living things, given the fact that the fundamental "half-life" principle works the same way for carbin-14 and inorganic radiometric dating? He spent much of his career arguing that the processes leading to the production of carbon-14 were different in the past than they are today. He was willing to accept carbon-14 dates up to about 4,000 years, but on the basis of his understanding of the Bible he argued that carbon-14 production before the flood had to have been lower than it is today leading to older apparent ages.[21] In short, he accepted science when it agreed with his religious presuppositions, but he rejected science when it conflicted.

More recently, young-age creationists such as Leonard Brand and Arthur Chadwick, uncomfortable with this scientifically inconsistent position, took Marsh's approach by questioning the entire enterprise of radiometric dating. They admitted with Brown that "The most serious problem faced by the short-age theory is radiometric dating . . ." But unlike Brown, at least with respect to inorganic matter, they predicted "that we will discover more reasons why radiometric dating . . . does not give correct time in years."[22]

Prediction in science is a time-honored practice, one that leads to confidence that a process is well understood if the prediction holds up under close scrutiny. Scientific predictions, however, are made because physical evidence is pointing in the direction of the prediction. This is not the case for Brand and Chadwick's prediction. Accumulating data from numerous independent lines of evidence point ever more convincingly to the view that radiometric dating provides reasonable ages for ancient rocks and fossils.[23] For me, to believe otherwise would be wishful thinking, and to suggest otherwise would be irresponsible.

20. Brown, "Radioactive Time Clocks," 289, 295.

21. Brown, "Can Tree Rings Be Used to Calibrate Radiocarbon Dates?" 47–52; Brown, "Correlation of C-14 Age with the Biblical Time Scale," 56–65. See also Brown, "Radiocarbon Dating," 299–316; Brown, "Scientific Creationism?" 57–58.

22. Brand and Chadwick, *Faith, Reason, & Earth History*, 406, 463.

23. Abelson, "Creationism and the Age of the Earth," 119; Giberson, *Saving Darwin*, 204–6.

THE RESULTS OF CARBON-14, uranium-lead, potassium-argon, and a variety of other types of radiometric dating techniques are only a few of the evidences convincing geologists—and me—that both earth and life are very old. I have already mentioned amino acid racemization dating and tree ring dating. But one of the most intriguing evidences for ages much older than those championed by young-age creationists involves layers of ice in the icecaps of Greenland, Antarctica, and elsewhere.

When snow falls in a place where yearlong freezing temperatures dominate, it accumulates, consolidates, and forms layers, one layer per year. The sun never sets over Greenland and Antarctica during their summers, so snow that has fallen warms to form "hoarfrost," a coarse-grained, low density form of snow. In winter, by contrast, the sun never shines and newly-fallen snow remains dense and appears relatively dark. As the years roll on, the weight of the upper layers of snow compresses the lower layers to form "firn," a well-compacted snow. After about 200 years the spaces within the firn in which air bubbles are trapped are sealed off and the firn becomes ice. The light and dark appearances of the summer and winter snow remain intact. After about 8,000 years the ice reaches a little less than one mile deep. At this point the pressure is so great that the air dissolves into the ice, but the summer and winter layers remain visually distinct.[24]

Visual distinctiveness is only one of many ways by which the ice scientists count years. For example, windblown dust from the world's deserts is most abundant in the late winter sublayers. Hydrogen peroxide, formed when sunlight interacts with air, is found only in the summer sublayers. The amount of carbon dioxide and sulfur dioxide in the air changes by season, and when these compounds are mixed with falling snow to form acids, changes in the seasonal concentration of these acids are reflected in the electrical conductivity of the ice. Changes in these and other factors are assessed using a variety of measurement devices to determine where one layer ends and another layer begins.[25]

How do scientists get at these ice layers, seeing that they extend to a depth of about two miles in places? Consecutively deeper, 5.2-inch-diameter ice cores, each several feet long, are removed from the icecap down to the bedrock using drill rigs. When the cores are brought to the surface they are photographed and sliced into horizontal and vertical sections. The sections are then subjected to a battery of tests to assess environmental conditions when particular layers of snow formed. Cores from Greenland, Antarctica,

---

24. Alley, *The Two-Mile Time Machine*, 48–51.
25. Alley, *The Two-Mile Time Machine*, 51–58.

and other locations are maintained at a temperature of -36°C at the National Science Foundation Ice Core Facility in Lakewood, Colorado.[26]

The most interesting and important data from these ice cores yield insights into climate history and provide crucial bits of information which help climate scientists make predictions about how the climate will change in the future. The predications allow for the development of plans for mitigation on behalf of human well-being. The number of years ago that a particular ice layer formed is, of course, one of the more basic pieces of information of interest to scientists researching the cores.[27]

Due to intense pressure in the lowest layers, the distinct bands of ice that are so evident in the upper layers begin to merge. It gets more difficult to distinguish these very deep layers. As Richard Alley, one of the scientists who worked on this project, wrote:

> [D]espite heroic efforts, the quality of the ice cores was not always perfect, so measurements were difficult in some places. Even so, the various methods we tried for counting layers agreed with each other within a few years in one hundred over the most recent 50,000 years, and we could count well over 100,000 years, although with errors increasing, probably as much as ten years in one hundred in the oldest ice.[28]

Although some uncertainty is associated with counting layers at the deeper levels, it's clear to nearly everyone that the ice layers go back for a very long time, much longer than the few thousand years hoped for by young-age creationists. It is difficult to imagine that counting uncertainties, which certainly exist, could result in errors of 100,000 years or more, although that is what young-agers claim.[29]

FURTHER EVIDENCE FOR THE integrity of temporal information derived from ice cores concerns profiles of ancient temperatures and comparisons of these profiles with those from other data sources. Temperature profiles in ice cores are estimated by oxygen isotope ratios in frozen water that makes up the ice cores. The frozen water, of course, came from atmospheric water vapor deposited as snow. The water vapor, in turn, had earlier evaporated from the ocean surface.

---

26. Alley, *The Two-Mile Time Machine*, 17–30, 23–25.
27. Alley, *The Two-Mile Time Machine*, 83–192.
28. Alley, *The Two-Mile Time*, 57.
29. Vardiman, "Ice Cores and the Age of the Earth."

Although most water molecules contain oxygen-16 isotopes (^{16}O—oxygen atoms with eight protons and eight neutrons in their nuclei), some water molecules contain oxygen-18 isotopes (^{18}O—oxygen atoms with eight protons and ten neutrons in their nuclei). Water with these rare ^{18}O isotopes is heavier than water with ^{16}O isotopes, and is thus less likely to evaporate from the ocean surface. Because of this, these heavy water molecules are less likely to evaporate during cool weather than during warm weather. Thus, during cool weather, there is less ^{18}O in the atmosphere than during warm weather. So the ratio of ^{18}O to ^{16}O isotopes in ice layers formed from snow (from water vapor evaporated from the ocean) under cool conditions is lower than in ice layers formed under warm conditions. The relationship between oxygen ratios and temperature is so tight that temperatures when the ice levels were formed can be quite precisely determined.[30]

As already noted, climate scientists are confident their multiple counting techniques allow them to determine yearly patterns back to about 100,000 years with only small margins of error. Not only does the ice extend much deeper, albeit with less distinguishable layers, but polar ice was deposited only during the latter part of the Cenozoic Era. The history of earth and life extends back much, much earlier. In other words, the ice cores represent only the tip of the proverbial iceberg of earth history.

Additional evidence reinforcing the view that climate scientists know what they are talking about comes from deep sea sediments. Seafloor ooze, which accumulates at a rate of a few fractions of an inch per year and exceeds a depth of more than a half mile in places, contains the remains of trillions of foraminiferans, coccolithophores, diatoms, and radiolarians, tiny, mineral-secreting, planktonic organisms which are abundant in seawater. The shells of foraminiferans and scales of coccolithophores consist of calcium carbonate ($CaCO_3$), whereas beautifully sculpted skeletons of diatoms and radiolarians are formed from silicon dioxide (SiO_2). When these microorganisms die, they drop out of the water column and accumulate at the seafloor surface.[31]

Both $CaCO_3$ and SiO_2 contain oxygen, which is absorbed by the living planktonic organisms from seawater. Because ^{18}O is less likely to evaporate from cool seawater than from warm seawater, cool seawater contains a higher ^{18}O to ^{16}O ratio than warm water. The shells of planktonic organisms reflect the ratio of ^{18}O to ^{16}O dissolved in the water when they were alive; in other words, they function as tiny paleo-thermometers. By determining the

---

30. Benn and Evans, *Glaciers & Glaciation*, 90–91.

31. Bond et al., "Correlations between Climate Records from North Atlantic Sediments and Greenland Ice," 143–47.

^{18}O to ^{16}O ratios in the shells of progressively younger seafloor sediments in core samples taken from the seafloor, scientists can quite accurately estimate changes in sea temperatures over time. And here is what is important for my understanding: The temperature profiles of the sediment cores beautifully match those inferred from the ice cores. They also match temperature profiles from pollen deposits in lake sediments and rings in the wood of trees, both of which can be carbon dated.[32]

The above explanation is complicated, but in a nutshell here are the main points: Climate scientists, people who have devoted years to this research, have developed a number of ways to count years, in both the polar ice caps and in the seafloor sediments. They are confident in the accuracy of their counts back to about 100,000 years, although the ice extends to much deeper levels. Ancient temperature signals inferred from the ice and from the seafloor match up nicely, as do the temperature signals from Greenland and Antarctic ice. They also match up nicely with pollen deposits and tree rings. Finally, these temperature records account for only the relatively recent history of the earth and life.

In short, impressive evidence strongly favors the interpretations of the climate scientists who are confident they can count back in time over many thousands of years. Given the nature and strength of the evidence described above, I am convinced they can do this with the levels of accuracy they have reported.

TIME AND SPACE ARE among the fundamental realities of physical existence. Five hundred years ago, Christians were scandalized when Copernicus and Galileo suggested the earth was not the center of the universe. Galileo was sentenced to house arrest for the rest of his life by the Catholic Church for promoting this heresy.[33] It was shocking for Christians to think that the earth and humans were not at the center of space.

Eventually, however, Christians accommodated to the fact that the earth was not at the center of space, despite theological arguments by Catholic and Protestant prelates to the contrary. Martin Luther, for example, according to one witness, charged his contemporary, Nicolaus Copernicus, with attempting to "turn the whole of astronomy upside down" with his sun-centered view of the solar system, piously stating that "Even in these

---

32. Taylor, "Rapid Climate Change," 320-7; Gross and Gross, *DataStreme Ocean*, 246-47.

33. Sobel, *Galileo's Daughter*; Finocchiaro, "That Galileo Was Imprisoned and Tortured for Advocating Copernicanism," 68-78.

things that are thrown into disorder [by Copernicus] I believe in the Holy Scriptures, for Joshua commanded the sun to stand still, and not the earth."[34]

I know of no Christian today, Protestant, Catholic, or Orthodox, who believes the earth is at the center of the universe. Indeed, in 1992 the Catholic Church publically acknowledged its error in condemning Galileo.[35] Christians have come to embrace the physical realities of *space*. Few educated Christians even quibble with the notion of an expanding universe in which our world is mere speck. Now the challenge for many conservative Christians is *time*, the other fundamental dimension of physical reality.

Having grown up with the view that creation occurred only a few thousand years ago, I understand the reluctance of many folks to embrace long ages. At least five factors are involved in this reluctance: 1) a seemingly straightforward reading of the Bible, especially the genealogies of Genesis 5 and 11, makes the notion of a young earth seem like the only option; 2) our parents, grandparents, aunts, uncles, pastors, friends—pretty much everyone we knew growing up—assumed the earth was young; 3) many evolutionists who believe in long ages are also agnostics or atheists, so belief in long ages must be wrong; 4) a long horizon of suffering by myriads of creatures is troubling; and 5) a short history for the earth makes intuitive sense—we lose our bearings and our control of history when millions and billions of years are involved. A young earth stretches back only a few scores of human generations, whereas an old earth involves unimaginable lengths of time, time before which humans were purported even to be around.

After struggling for years with the concept of long ages, I came to a point at which I recognized the real problem was not long ages but my need for control—control over time, control over the universe, even control over God. How could I allow history to take so long to unfold that I could not conceive of the amount of time involved? How could I allow for a universe in which organisms have the freedom to change and evolve over such long periods of time? How could I allow God to create a world in a way different than my interpretation of what the biblical writers wrote?

Once I gave up trying to control time, the universe, and God—control I never had in the first place—physical reality became much more meaningful and enjoyable. Science and discovery became exciting. I no longer had to make excuses, ignore information, or twist evidence. I was comfortable with the universe and comfortable with the idea of an ineffable God. My view of God expanded to embrace the mystery associated with deep time.

---

34. Luther, *Luther's Works. Vol 54. Table Talk*, 358–59.
35. Holden (ed.), "Vindication for Galileo," 1303.

11

History Writ Large

"My album is the earth, and the pictures in it are faded and badly torn and have to be pieced together by detective work."

—LOREN EISELEY[1]

I NEARLY STEPPED ON the black, serrated object glistening against the pale sediments of Dinosaur Provincial Park, Alberta. I picked up the shiny thing and showed it to Philip Curry, our lanky guide and one of the world's foremost dinosaur experts. "That's the tooth of an *Albertosaurus*," he said as I handed him the fossil. "It's a nice specimen. It will go into the collection with your name as collector." *Albertosaurus*, a smaller cousin of the more famous *Tyrannosaurus rex*, was an important top predator in this region.[2]

I had spent the last day and a half with Currie, a founder of the Royal Tyrell Museum of Paleontology. With us were dinosaur egg expert Karl Hirsch, Boulder geologist Emily Bray, and undergraduate paleontology student Darla Zelenitsky who later would become another of Canada's top dinosaur paleontologists. We had met the previous day at Devil's Coulee, 180 miles to the south, where aggregations of dinosaur eggs, most likely nest remains, were eroding out of the badlands. The aggregations were

---

1. Eiseley, *The Night Country*, 161.
2. Hutchinson and Padian, "Carnosauria," 94–97; Erickson et al., "Giantism and Comparative Life-History Parameters of Tyrannosaurid Dinosaurs," 772–75.

instrumental in helping paleontologists fill in important details regarding dinosaur life and reproduction. During this trip, I set up an experiment at Devil's Coulee to determine the effects of weathering on the preservation of eggshell. Years later, Darla and I would characterize the distribution of dinosaur eggshell within one of Devil's Coulee's presumed fossil nest sites.[3]

Dinosaur Provincial Park is a UNESCO World Heritage Site, and Phil wanted to show us a couple of the most impressive dino treasures in the back country of this remarkable place. He led us to a spot where a shelter covered a nearly complete, articulated skeleton of a hadrosaur, or duck-billed dinosaur, partially excavated, but still firmly embedded in the sediment. The specimen was well preserved. Even ligaments attaching bones to bones were intact.

Phil then led us across the badlands to a second site, this one a massive bone bed of ceratopsians, horned and beaked dinosaurs. The well-preserved bones were so densely packed, it would have been impossible to walk among them without treading on them. Ceratopsian bones were so common in the park, Phil said, there were no plans to excavate these magnificent fossils. They would simply weather away into the surrounding sediments.

EVER SINCE DISCOVERING MY first fossil in Tennessee as a youngster, I have been fascinated by life in the past. Although most of my research has focused on the behavior and ecology of living organisms, my students, colleagues, and I have published a dozen or so papers in the paleontological literature. I don't consider myself an expert in paleontology, but I maintain a strong interest in all things prehistoric. I believe it is only by understanding the past that we can understand the present.

The general picture of the history of life depicted by fossils has been remarkably stable over the past century and a half. This is not to say paleontology is a dead science, or that most of the bugs have been worked out of paleontological theories. Paleontology is a vibrant enterprise conducted by well-trained scientists using the latest technological advances. In the past, fossils were dug up and displayed with little attention to burial conditions, arrangement within the sediment, and presence of associated remains. All that has changed. Today, when a paleontologist excavates a fossil, careful records are kept of contextual information. Fossils are no longer simply relics to put on display, they are treasure troves of information about past climates, behaviors, and ecological interactions. Healthy squabbles over the meaning of fossil discoveries continue to enliven the field. Yet with some

---

3. Hayward et al., "Eggshell Taphonomy at Modern Gull Colonies and a Dinosaur Clutch Site," 343–55.

notable exceptions, the big picture of the pageant of life, from the earliest fossiliferous deposits to more recent deposits, has remained quite constant for many years.

AMONG THE FIRST THINGS I learned when I began to study fossils were the dominant characteristics of the geologic column. The geologic column is a theoretical construct of the vertical sequence of rocks and associated fossils that make up the earth's crust, pieced together from numerous locations that contain overlapping segments. No location on earth contains the complete column, but there are places in the American West and other localities where large portions of the column are represented.

The geologic column is divided into numerous subsections, but for purposes of this discussion I will refer only to the three main sections: 1) Paleozoic rocks are the deepest of these three subdivisions, and according to radiometric dating are the oldest. Rocks in this section contain many marine fossils but some terrestrial life forms as well, including many non-flowering plants. 2) Mesozoic rocks, the middle subdivision, famous for the dinosaur fossils they contain, also contain the first evidence of flowering plants, birds, and mammals. 3) Cenozoic rocks, the top section of the column, contain a tremendous diversity of plant, bird, and mammal fossils, including evidence of human-like primates and modern humans.[4]

George McCready Price, the most famous and most influential creationist during the early twentieth century, rejected the notion that the geological column represented an orderly temporal sequence. He built an extensive writing career around the view that the supposed order in the geologic column was nonexistent; he believed it was an imaginary construct invented by evolutionists to account for fictional changes in life over time. Price's self-styled "great law of conformable stratigraphic sequences . . . by all odds the most important law ever formulated with reference to the order in which the strata occur," asserted that "Any kind of fossiliferous beds whatever, 'young' or 'old,' may be found occurring conformably on any other fossiliferous beds, 'older' or 'younger.'"[5] Whitcomb and Morris' *The Genesis Flood*, still in print, continues to foster Price's false perspective.[6]

---

4. Ritland, "Historical Development of the Current Understanding of the Geologic Column: Part I," 59–76; Ritland, "Historical Development of the Current Understanding of the Geologic Column: Part II," 28–50; Brand and Chadwick, *Faith, Reason, & Earth History*, 374–80. The references cited here are from creationist sources that accept the reality of the geologic column and its sequence of fossils.

5. Price. *The New Geology*, 296, 637–38.

6. Whitcomb and Morris, *The Genesis Flood: The Biblical Record and Its Scientific Implications*, 132–35, 169–211.

As historian Gary Wills put it, "Price deserves some kind of award for creative imagination, and for economy of argument: He countered all the Darwinian arguments with one simple chess move of the mind."[7] All geologists, and even better-informed young-age creationists, recognize that Price, for all his well-intentioned bluster, was simply wrong. Indeed, one of his most admiring former students, Harold W. Clark, became convinced of the order of fossils in the geologic column. He spent the summer of 1938 in the oil fields of Oklahoma and Texas where he learned that geologists use the orderly sequence of fossils to predict and locate deposits of oil. Petroleum geologists have no interest in competing philosophical or religious interpretations of earth history. Their only concern is what helps them find oil, and this is what the predictable order of fossils does well.[8]

In a 1938 letter to Price, Clark was quite direct regarding his discovery and change in perspective:

> The rocks do lie in a much more definite sequence than we have ever allowed. The statements in the *New Geology* do not harmonize with the conditions in the field... All over the middle West the rocks lie in great sheets extending over hundreds of miles, in regular order. Thousands of well cores prove this.[9]

Eight years later, Clark published *The New Diluvialism*, written from a flood geology perspective. But the book endorsed the view that fossils were found in a predictable order, and that the geologic column is real. In response, Price came unglued. All his anti-evolution arguments had been based in the assertion that the geologic column did not contain an orderly sequence of fossils. So when Clark—a disciple and former student, no less—contradicted the basic assumption of his life's work, Price was livid. He fought back by publishing a forty-seven-page diatribe entitled *Theories of Satanic Origin* aimed directly at Clark, and he filed heresy charges against him with the Seventh-day Adventist Church. In the end, however, Clark's view won the day among many young-age creationists, including most fellow Adventist science teachers.[10] Price, an "armchair geologist," had never spent much time in the field, whereas Clark enjoyed field work and recognized firsthand the orderly sequence of rocks and fossils. Where the order was disrupted, reasonable, data-based explanations were in place for the lack of order.

---

7. Wills, *Under God*, 121.
8. Numbers, *The Creationists*, 144.
9. Quoted by Numbers, *The Creationists*, 144.
10. Numbers, *The Creationists*, 144–48.

Clark had completed a master's degree in ecology at Berkeley and explained the occurrence of fossil order as the result of pre-flood ecological zones. The geologic column contains mostly marine fossils at the lowest levels, with terrestrial forms of life appearing gradually at higher levels along with more recognizable marine forms. Clark postulated a pre-flood earth with a large ocean at the lowest altitude, and smaller seas surrounded by land at higher altitudes. As the flood waters rose, these ecological zones were progressively buried yielding today's fossil record.[11]

Clark's "ecological zonation theory" was a clever, albeit not entirely original, explanation for the orderly nature of the geologic column. During the nineteenth century Reverend William Cockburn, a Cambridge-trained theologian and Dean of York, promoted a similar view, as did David and Eleazar Lord, American businessmen and writers.[12] As a naïve young creationist, I was impressed by the logic of ecological zonation, as were many other young-age creationists. But once I learned a little about geology and paleontology, numerous problems with the theory became glaringly apparent.

ONE SERIOUS PROBLEM WITH the theory of ecological zonation and flood geology relates to the sheer bulk of organic material represented in the geologic column. Massive limestone deposits, for example, are found in many places on earth—think, for example, of the White Cliffs of Dover, England, or the massive Thornton Quarry south of Chicago. Some limestone forms as a chemical precipitate from high concentrations of calcium carbonate in seawater, but most of this type of rock is formed from the accumulated remains of microscopic marine organisms that have drifted to the ocean floor following death. Many of these uplifted deposits are hundreds of feet thick and spread over large areas. Often the purity of such deposits is high, making them excellent building materials—indeed, the best place to show fossils to my Andrews University students was in the Paleozoic limestone blocks used to construct the campus church. The purity presents a problem for proponents of flood geology who envision violent water activity which would mix up organic remains. The thickness and vast areas covered by these deposits suggest deposition of tiny organisms under relatively calm conditions over very long periods of time.[13]

---

11. Numbers, *The Creationists*, 142–45; Clark, *The New Diluvialism*, 62–93, and graphically illustrated in Plate 7; Clark, *Skylines and Detours*, 198–203.

12. Ritland, "Ecological Zonation Theory," 145–50; Numbers, *The Creationists*, expanded edition, 30–32.

13. Plummer and Carlson, *Physical Geology*, 147–51.

Recently a group of friends and I hiked to a beautifully preserved stromatolite reef in Banff National Park. Stromatolites are formed by layers of cyanobacteria that sequester and cement sediment particles into characteristic mounds, columns, and sheets. Living stromatolites are uncommon today, although they still exist, most notably in Shark Bay, Australia. By contrast, fossil stromatolites are quite abundant. The Banff stromatolite bed, located in the Cambrian Pika Formation in Cambrian rocks, extends over 2,000 feet and exhibits a width of over thirty feet. The individual stromatolite structures are exquisitely preserved, each twelve to sixteen inches in diameter and height.[14] To raft such a reef, entirely intact, into place during a flood event would be physically impossible. The reef sits atop deep layers of rocks from earlier times, and thick layers once lay atop the reef before they eroded away and exposed it to view. This reef, along with numerous other fossil reefs at various levels within the geologic column, are clearly in their original positions of growth. To me, this type of evidence is impossible to account for as the result of a worldwide flood.

Vast deposits of coal and oil also belie the story presented by flood geologists. Coal is formed primarily from plant remains, fossils of which are commonly preserved in coal. As in the case of limestone, coal deposits often are quite pure, extensive in area, and very thick. The earth's coal reserves are enormous. Total recoverable coal deposits in the world were estimated in 2011 to equal 891,530,000,000 tons. (One ton equals 2,000 pounds)[15] That amount does not include all the coal *already* mined over the centuries, nor does it include non-recoverable coal deposits, which are abundant. Oil deposits, also derived from biomass, are equally impressive with an estimated 179,682,000,000 tons (1,339,617,000,000 barrels) of proven recoverable reserves in 2011, a figure that does not include the enormous volumes of oil already extracted and burned over the past century.[16] A 2012 estimate of the world's living plant and microorganism biomass is 785,948,605,796 tons.[17] On the basis of these admittedly rough estimates, it would take about 1.4 times the biomass of the *current* earth to form the *existing* amount of available coal and oil. Again, it is important to recognize this estimate is based on values determined *after* many years of fossil fuel extraction. Even

---

14. Dolph and Gibson, "Recent Discovery of an Extensive Stromatolite Outcrop in the Middle Cambrian Pika Formation, Lake Helen-Lake Katherine Area, Banff National Park."

15. World Energy Council, "Coal," 1.1–1.32 (Table 1).

16. World Energy Council, "Oil," 2.1–2.56 (Table 1).

17. Kallmeyer et al., "Global Distribution of Microbial Abundance and Biomass in Subseafloor Sediment," 6213–16.

more importantly, it does not include the biomass represented by the massive deposits of limestone in the earth, which are vast.

A second problem with ecological zonation theory and flood geology concerns vast areas covered by thick volcanic deposits, including the Deccan traps in India, the Siberian traps in Russia, and the Columbia River Basalts in Washington, Oregon, and Idaho. I once lived among the Columbia River Basalts, and I continue to spend lots of time visiting this intriguing region. Approximately 80,000 square miles are covered by thick beds of basalt which in places are over one mile deep. These beds were formed when molten lava flowed from great fissures and spread over the surrounding landscape. It is possible to determine whether these flows occurred over dry land or under water. Underwater lava flows produce pillow basalt, rounded mounds visible along vertical cliffs. By contrast, lava flowing over dry land produces columnar basalt, hexagonal columns which look very different from pillow basalt. Columbia Plateau basalt is primarily columnar. This means that the lava flowed mostly over land, except when it flowed through a body of water such as a lake. Furthermore, between some of the many flows are soil layers that built up between volcanic eruptions. The soil layers are associated with fossil trees, rhinoceroses, three-toed horses, and other organisms, some similar and some different than those we see today.[18]

Even before the great fissure eruptions that formed the Columbia Plateau occurred, volcanism played an important role in the development of the fossil record in the Pacific Northwest. The John Day fossil beds in northern Oregon provide impressive evidence of successive ecological communities, very different from those we see in the region today. The extensive deposits of sediment in this region are primarily terrestrial in nature, with volcanic ashfalls playing important roles. Just as Mount St. Helens' 1980 ashfall buried the nesting colony of gulls I was studying, much larger, repetitive eruptions buried a series of ecosystems in this region that contained all sorts of interesting plants and animals, many of which were beautifully preserved as fossils. Water-borne deposits, such as one would expect from a worldwide flood, are not a big part of this story.[19]

The problems described above are very serious from my perspective, but the most serious problem for ecological zonation and flood geology is the increase in percent of extinct types of organisms as we look deeper and deeper in the geologic column. In more superficial deposits of the column, fossil organisms are similar or identical to those living today. Go a little

18. Hooper, "The Columbia River Basalts," 1463–68; Alt and Hyndman, *Northwest Exposures*, 235–53.

19. Ritland, "Ecological Zonation Theory, 150–67"; Bishop, *In Search of Ancient Oregon*, 78–167.

deeper and the fossils look a bit strange. Go deeper yet and things look downright otherworldly.

Take plants, for instance. Many of the types of plants we see every day are called flowering plants, or angiosperms—grasses, petunias, tulips, blueberries, oaks, maples, and most of the other plants familiar to us. No flowering plants appear in the fossil record below the Mesozoic sediments. And even though pollen grains from flowering plants fossilize well and exhibit widespread distributions by riding the winds high in the atmosphere, no angiosperm pollen grains are found in rocks lower than those in middle Mesozoic. There are lots of plant and pollen fossils in the Paleozoic rocks, but they are of conifers, ferns, and other non-flowering species. Conditions were good for plants and their fossilization during these pre-Mesozoic times. If flowering plants had been around, they would have left some trace.[20]

Mammals provide another dramatic example. Mammal bones fossilize well. If mammals are around, they typically leave a fossil record. But no mammal fossils have been found in Paleozoic sediments, sediments that make up much of the geologic column. Close to the top of the Paleozoic strata, mammal-like reptiles appear. Not until the lower Mesozoic deposits do fossils with all the basic characteristics of modern mammals show up. Not until the Cenozoic rocks, very high in the column, do we find a great diversity of mammalian fossils. And not until almost the top of the Cenozoic sediments do we find fossils of mammals like those that are living today. It might be argued that most of the Paleozoic sediments are aquatic, so we would not expect to find the remains of mammals in those sediments; most mammals, after all, are terrestrial. Wouldn't we expect, however, to find an occasional whale, porpoise, or manatee bone in these marine sediments? Fossils of marine mammals are found in marine sediments at higher levels of the geologic column, the same levels at which we find fossils of land mammals, so it's hard to imagine they would not have been preserved in Paleozoic rocks had they been present.[21]

In short, there is a dramatic increase in the percent of extinct types of mammals—and in virtually all other types of organisms—as we look deeper and deeper in the geologic column. I have never seen a reasonable young-age creationist explanation for this most basic and obvious paleontological fact. This, I believe, is because a reasonable explanation from the perspective of young-age creationist is not possible. Ecological zonation theory and its derivatives were the best young-age creationists could come up with, but

---

20. Cutbill and Funnell, "Numerical Analysis of the Fossil Record," 801 (Figure 4).

21. Cutbill and Funnell, "Numerical Analysis of the Fossil Record," 813 (Figure 16a).

the shortcomings of these hypotheses are more sharply defined with each new fossil discovery.

IN ADDITION TO CHANGES in percentages of extinct types, other trends are apparent in the fossil record. Ammonites, mollusks related to octopuses, squid, and cuttlefish, are common as fossils in Mesozoic rocks, but they, along with dinosaurs and many other organisms, completely disappear as we move from Mesozoic up to Cenozoic deposits. Despite their abundance as fossils, no ammonites are known to be alive today. Ammonites function as important index fossils, fossils that serve as markers for specific levels of the geologic column.[22]

One of the features of ammonites that makes them ideal index fossils are the suture patterns in their shells. At lower levels of the column, many ammonites possessed relatively simple suture patterns. But at higher levels the suture lines often look more meandering and complicated. There seems to be no reason why this should be the case if successive ecological zones in the sea were wiped out by rising flood waters.[23]

We see some fascinating trends in the Cenozoic pattern of fossil mammals as well. Fossil horses, for example, first appear in lower levels of the Cenozoic rocks. These horses had four toes, were about the size of small dogs and possessed small teeth for browsing foliage and fruit. A bit higher in the Cenozoic rocks we find larger horses with three toes and with wider, grinding teeth, adaptations to the appearance of large, grassy regions. Finally, near to the top of the Cenozoic rocks, we see horses like those alive today, which possess only one well-developed toe, and have jaws fitted with tall, grinding teeth. Interestingly, modern horses still carry splint bones, vestiges of the two other toes carried by their three-toed predecessors. This is not to say there was a simple straight line of ascent from early four-toed to modern one-toed animals. No, horses represent a complex paleontological history. Despite the complexity, however, the general trends in size, foot structure, and tooth anatomy are obvious.[24]

PALEONTOLOGY, LIKE OTHER AREAS of modern science, is not only a *descriptive* endeavor, it is also a *predictive* enterprise. Prediction is a crucial aspect of science. If we make a prediction based on a pattern we observe in nature, and if the prediction is supported by data collected after the

---

22. Pojeta and Gordon, "Class Cephalopoda," 329, 353.
23. Pojeta and Gordon, "Class Cephalopoda," 336, 337, 345–53.
24. Colbert and Morales, *Evolution of the Vertebrates*, 352–64.

prediction is made, our confidence is strengthened that we understand the observed natural pattern. If, on the other hand, new information we collect does not support our prediction, we suspect we do not yet understand the observed pattern. Paleontologists have successfully made predictions from present life to past life, and also from past life to present life. Some examples have made this clear to me.

Back in the mid-1800s, paleontologists saw close similarities between modern birds and a group of dinosaurs called theropods, which included such animals as *Albertosaurus, Tyrannosaurus, Troodon,* and *Velociraptor*. Each of these animals had fused clavicles that formed a "wishbone," an s-shaped neck, semi-lunate carpel (wrist) bones, and an air sac system; moreover, they laid eggs in nests, brooded their young, used gizzard stones to grind their food, and slept with their heads under their forelimbs, all characteristics of modern birds. It was features like these that led nineteenth- and twentieth-century paleontologists to make the prediction that birds and theropod dinosaurs were closely related.[25]

Since about 1990, that prediction has been stunningly supported by a series of remarkable fossil finds. Most of these fossils have been found in the Liaoning Province in northeastern China, where animal remains have been beautifully preserved in layers of volcanic ash. The most spectacular finds have been of theropod dinosaurs with feathers, fossils that closed the link between dinosaurs and birds and provided strong support for the prediction that birds and dinosaurs are members of the same group.[26]

Another intriguing confirmation of a prediction from the present to the past has been the discovery of whales with legs. Modern whales and their relatives contain tiny hind leg and pelvic bones not connected to the main skeleton. These more or less useless bones were thought by early anatomists to indicate that early whales had hind legs. Since the 1970s paleontologists have found a series of fossil whales with functional hind legs.[27]

An interesting example of a prediction going the other direction, from characteristics of fossils to features of modern animals, involves teeth. One of the first things I learned in my undergraduate ornithology course was that today's birds have no teeth. Toothlessness has sometimes been thought to be a weight-reduction feature which enhances flight. But flying reptiles, the pterosaurs, had teeth, as do today's bats. And, birds preserved as fossils in Mesozoic rocks had teeth and could fly. So the weight-reduction hypothesis

25. Padian and Chiappe, "Bird Origins," 71–79.
26. Xu et al., "An Integrative Approach to Understanding Bird Origins," 1341; Chaippe and Qingjin, *Birds of Stone*.
27. Gingerich et al., "Origin of Whales from Early Artiodactyls," 2239–42; Thewissen, *The Walking Whales*.

HISTORY WRIT LARGE   157

does not really hold up. One thing is clear—birds once had teeth and now they do not. Consequently, the prediction was made that modern birds retain the genes to make teeth, although these genes have been silenced.[28]

The results of an intriguing experiment was reported in 1980 which demonstrated that avian oral epithelium can produce dental tissue if oral ectomesenchyme from a lizard or mouse is grafted underneath. A second experiment reported in 2006, however, was even more dramatic. It showed that a modern chicken mutant called *talpid* developed teeth similar to those of young alligators. In short, the prediction that modern birds retain the genes to make teeth has been confirmed.[29] This confirmation provides powerful evidence that modern birds are the descendants of toothed birds, which, in turn, closely resembled theropod dinosaurs. Indeed, most paleontologists today suggest that modern birds *are* theropod dinosaurs.[30]

AN ADDITIONAL ISSUE IMPRESSIVE to me concerns the geology and fossil record of the Holy Land. This region is of particular interest to Christians, given the biblical record. All the stories and events recorded in both the Old and New Testaments occurred in the Middle East and surrounding areas. All the writers of the biblical books lived there. Archaeologists and historians exhibit great interest in this region, for this is where all three monotheistic religions originated. The record of human history in the region is rich and varied.

Curiously, little attention has been paid by Christians to what lies *under* the land of the Bible, the rocks and the fossils on which Middle Eastern civilization was built. Geologists know a great deal about these rocks and fossils, but most young-age creationists seem to have ignored or are unaware of this information. Any understanding of the history of life from a biblical perspective must take this information into account. Every process that led to the deposition of these rocks and fossils occurred *before* the events depicted in scripture. These processes were complicated, highly varied, and left a detailed record.[31]

28. Meredith et al., "Evidence for a Single Loss of Mineralized Teeth in the Common Avian Ancester," 1254390-1-6.

29. Kollar and Fisher, "Tooth Induction in Chick Epithelium," 993-95; Harris et al., "The Development of Archosaurian First-Generation Teeth in a Chicken Mutant," 371-77.

30. Birkhead et al., *Ten Thousand Birds*, 12-17.

31. For a creationist perspective on the geology of Israel, however, see Snelling, "The Geology of Israel with the Biblical Creation-Flood Framework of History: 1. The Pre-Flood Rocks," 165-90; Snelling, "The Geology of Israel with the Biblical Creation-Flood Framework of History: 2. The Flood Rocks," 167-309. Snelling works for Answers in

In July 1996, a team of scientists was exploring the marsh region of Azraq Shishan, Jordan. For many years the water table in Jordan and surrounding countries had been dropping due to the increasing needs of a rising population. When the water table dropped in one of the area ponds, ʿAin Soda, hundreds of stone tools and fossil bones appeared in the exposed sediments. The tools included butchering implements and hand axes. Bones were those of camels, wild boars, and an extinct species of elephant, *Elephas hysudricus*. The nature of the stone tools, as well as the bones of the extinct elephant, suggest this site dates from the Lower Paleolithic period, a time interval that coincided with the Ice Age, when large portions of the northern hemisphere were glaciated and the first modern human fossils appear.[32]

Although the deposits of ʿAin Soda occur very near the surface, they were deposited long before the lives of Moses, Abraham, and Isaac. In fact, all the historic events recorded in the Bible occurred *after* these and similar fossils in the Middle East formed. Moreover, much deeper deposits in the region are rich with fossils, including of ammonites, mosasaurs, plesiosaurs, giant marine turtles, and other extinct animals. The marine fossils indicate this region was once covered by ancient seas. The Egyptian Sphinx and pyramids, located southwest of Israel, are in large part composed of marine limestone which contain numerous fossils. Dinosaur tracks are preserved in the town of Beit Zayit, just outside Jerusalem, and a dinosaur bone was discovered in Jordan during the 1990s.[33] In short, the pre-biblical geological

---

Genesis, a creationist think-tank. He earned a PhD in geology from the University of Sydney, Australia. His two very long articles contain professionally-rendered geologic maps of Israel and possess all the accouterments of a scholarly publication. However, statements like "It can easily be demonstrated that these granitic rock units in southern Israel were buried under thick sedimentary sequences during the Flood," (Part 1, page 184) and "The sedimentary strata that comprise and cover most of Israel provide and obvious record of the Genesis Flood" (Part 2, page 305) are not what one expects from a scientist working in the context of objectivity. Indeed, the geologic cross section and maps he presents underscore the geological complexity of the region and seriously undercut his interpretation. It should be noted that Snelling is the editor of the creationist journal within which his two papers appear.

32. Wright, "College Instructor Stumbles onto Important Archeological Site." See also Richter et al., "An Early Epipalaeolithic Sitting Burial from the Azraq Oasis, Jordan," 321–34; Nowell et al., "Middle Pleistocene Subsistence in the Azraq Oasis, Jordan: Protein Residue and Other Proxies," 36–44.

33. Gvirtzman et al., "Upper Cretaceous High-Resolution Multiple Stratigraphy, Northern Margin of the Arabian Platform, Central Israel," 107–35; Christiansen and Bonde, "A New Species of Gigantic Mosasaur from the Late Cretaceous of Israel," 629–44; Lewy and Gaffney, "First Record of a Possible Chelonioid Sea Turtle from the Upper Campanian of Southern Israel," 55–58; Emery, "Weathering of the Great Pyramid," 140–43; Avnimelech, "Dinosaur Tracks in the Lower Cenomanian of Jerusalem," 264; Martill et al., "The First Dinosaur from the Hashemite Kingdom of Jordan," 147–54.

record of the Holy Land represents an historical period far more extensive than the time covering biblical history. To suggest these very deep and complex deposits were formed during the Genesis flood, or during a few hundred years before the flood, is to ignore or misinterpret data indicating they were laid down over long periods of time.

ANOTHER FASCINATING PIECE OF evidence involving the Holy Land concerns the Mediterranean Sea, or "Great Sea," which borders this region. This body of water, mentioned multiple times in both the Old and New Testaments, is most famously associated with the missionary journeys of the Apostle Paul. As Paul plied the waters in sailing ships, he could not have imagined that nineteen centuries later another ship, the *Glomar Challenger*, would be probing the floor of that same sea. He would have been even less prepared to imagine what those probes discovered.

In 1970, scientists aboard the Glomar Challenger took numerous core samples from the floor of the Mediterranean Sea. The samples contained layers of gravel, silt, sand, gypsum, anhydrite, rock salt, and other materials which provided strong evidence for a period long before Paul's day—even long before the great Ice Age—when the Mediterranean Sea became an actual desert. The sea literally dried up. How could this have happened? It seems that during a very dry period, the Strait of Gibraltar closed up, isolating the Mediterranean. Conditions were so dry that nearly all the water evaporated from the sea, probably leaving only a few isolated and highly salty ponds in its place. At the same time rivers like the Nile eroded channels more 8,200 feet deep into the sides of the dry Mediterranean basin. Evaporation caused the salts to precipitate out of solution to form the layers of gypsum, anhydrite, and rock salt deposits beneath the drying sea. When the Strait of Gibraltar opened once again, water from the Atlantic refilled the basin. Evidence suggests this may have occurred more than once.[34]

There is still much to learn about this so-called Messinian Salinity Crisis of the Mediterranean and there is disagreement among scientists about the details. Most agree, however, that some type of drying event occurred. This event provides further evidence that the history of the Holy Land region has been far from simple. Our concepts of the past must be broad enough to account for these types of events.

---

34. Hsü et al., "Late Miocene Desiccation of the Mediterranean," 240–44; Hsü et al., "History of the Mediterranean Salinity Crisis," 399–403; Hsü, *The Mediterranean Was a Desert: A Voyage of the Glomar Challenger*.

THE SWEEP OF HISTORY depicted by geology and paleontology is breathtaking—truly, history writ large. Given the relatively small chance that an organism will be preserved as a fossil, paleontologists must contend with an incomplete history. Nonetheless, what we do see is impressive and informative, and it can teach us if we will look with an open mind.

The fossil record has led me to several important conclusions, conclusions that constrain my views on the history of life: 1) Fossils are arranged in a definite and predictable order in the geologic column, and this order can be seen throughout the world. 2) The biomass required to form the fossil record would require much more biological material than contained in the world today. 3) There is a pronounced increase in the percent of extinct types of organisms of all taxonomic groups as we look at progressively deeper rocks in the geologic column. 4) Within specific taxonomic groups, definite trends in size and structure occur in progressive layers of the column. 5) Most biblical stories took place on the presently recognizable landscape of the Holy Land, which sits atop a vast and complex set of rocks that involved many long-term processes. These conclusions, based upon multiple, converging lines of evidence, have led me away from the speculations posed by young-age creationists toward a perspective that is more in line with the history of life proposed by the majority of the scientific community.

12

What about Home?

"Nothing escapes the Creator's cycle... All living things emerge, gather, spark new life, fall apart, die, and emerge in new ways."
—Mark Nepo[1]

As I write, I'm perched in a screened-in porch overlooking our southwestern Michigan backyard. On this late September morning, a gentle breeze stirs the leaves of sweetgum, river birch, rhododendron, black walnut, and maple trees that form a canopy above the lawn and garden. Already some leaves are falling, a process hastened by rain pelting the lush greenery. Robins dart around the lawn seeking any breakfast item that wriggles in the moist topsoil or crawls along the blades of grass. A blue jay calls from somewhere up in the canopy. Chipmunks, red squirrels, and fox squirrels scurry through the yard, scoot along the top of the fence, and scamper up and down the trunks of trees as they search for food and chase one another out of claimed space. Presently the rain stops and shafts of sunlight break through the clouds, reminding me that the sun is the driving force behind all this vibrancy, both in our local ecosystem and in the entire biosphere.

I am a behavioral ecologist by training and by passion. The word "ecology," coined in 1869 by German biologist Ernst Haeckel, derives from the

---

1. Nepo, *The Book of Awakening*, 83.

Greek words *oikos*, which means "home," and *logos*, which means "study."[2] "Ecology," then, refers to "the study of home." Ecology is the most comprehensive of sciences—it involves mathematics, physics, chemistry, and biology at multiple levels of organization. Ecologists seek to understand how solar energy is shuttled from one organism to another before it radiates back into space as heat; how nutrients combine, recombine, cycle, and recycle within the earth; how water flows from one part of the system to another and serves as a universal matrix for the entire process; how a tangled web of interrelations operates among a myriad of species undergoing continual adaptations to their environments. Ecology, a beautiful science, nonetheless presents perplexing conundrums to me as a person of faith. These conundrums involve considerations regarding the long-range survivability of life, the distribution of organisms throughout the world, the universal processes of death and reproduction, the existence of a huge group of organisms that feed on dead organisms, the necessity of natural selection and adaptation which work only in conjunction with death, and the problem of pain and suffering.

I WILL START WITH the sun, the gravitational center of our solar system and the engine that drives the hydrologic cycle, powers weather systems, and energizes the photosynthetic process. Fusion of hydrogen molecules in the sun releases the energy to make things move, quickens the molecules of life, and generates the warmth that keeps us from freezing. Every second, over 660 million tons of hydrogen atoms in the sun are fused to form a similar quantity of helium, releasing massive amounts of electromagnetic radiation in the process.[3]

According to astrophysicists, the sun is a middle-aged star formed over four and a half billion years ago. It contains sufficient hydrogen to continue warming the earth for another five or six billion years. But as the sun ages, it eventually will turn into a "red giant," engulfing the earth with lethal quantities of heat.[4] This prospect raises important theological and ethical questions for me: Why would a good God create a system with intelligent beings capable of contemplating the future, a future that will eventually become unsustainable? What will happen to these beings when the sun turns into a red giant? Will life on earth simply burn out? Are we part of a divine experiment that will end in sizzling tragedy?

I could brush off these concerns as irrelevant—five billion years, after all, is a long time. But Christian theology teaches that God is eternal, with

---

2. Begon et al., *Ecology*, xi.
3. Hewitt et al., *Conceptual Physical Science*, 353.
4. Sagan, *Cosmos*, 231, 238.

no beginning and no end. So even though I don't need to worry about the prospect of a dying sun during my lifetime or during the lifetimes of my descendants far into the future, scientific facts about the sun raise disturbing questions about the nature of God. Where do I go with this? I grew up believing that God is a God of generosity and love. Is this notion simply wrong? Does God really care? Or are materialists right in contending there is no God and that I am here only as the result of chance? These are big questions that deserve satisfying answers.

A SECOND AREA OF concern involves biogeography, a subdivision of ecology and one that has received lots of attention over the past 150 years. Biogeographers ask questions such as, What ecological factors are involved in determining current distribution patterns of organisms? How have these patterns changed over time? What are the genetic consequences of these changing patterns? A topic so vast deserves much more attention than I can provide in this brief overview. So I will consider only one example, the mammals of Australia and New Zealand. These two islands, plus New Guinea, constitute what biogeographers call the Australian Region. When I studied biogeography in graduate school, it was this region that stood out as the most intriguing.

The most remarkable thing I learned about the Australian region is that most of its mammals are marsupials. Why should this be? Marsupials differ from other mammals in numerous anatomical and physiological characteristics—they're fascinatingly weird![5] The fossil record indicates that marsupials first diversified in South America, a continent that continues to exhibit significant marsupial variety. It appears that an ancestral group of marsupials migrated from South America to Australia via Antarctica when all three continents were connected in a supercontinent called Gondwanaland. From the initial set of migrants that moved into Australia, a mind-boggling level of diversification occurred, with marsupials filling nearly every ecological niche occupied by placental mammals[6] elsewhere in the world. Approximately 180 marsupial species are endemic to Australia and nearby islands today. These animals range in size from tiny marsupial mice to kangaroos standing well over six feet tall. Various marsupials look and

---

5. Stonehouse, "Introduction: The Marsupials," 1–5; Barbour, "Anatomy of Marsupials," 237–72

6. Placental mammals (eutherians) are born at a more advanced stage of development than in marsupials (metatherians), among other differences.

behave like shrews, flying squirrels, moles, badgers, and dogs. Others, such as koalas and kangaroos, exhibit no resemblance with any placental.[7]

A few non-marsupial land mammals are native to Australia, but these consist only of rodents and bats. Bats clearly flew to Australia, but how did rodents get there? Given their small size, they probably arrived by rafting on mats of vegetation that occasionally break away from continents or other islands during storms. Marine mammals—seals, manatees, whales, and porpoises—ply the waters around the island. Dogs (including dingos), cats, rabbits, squirrels, hares, goats, horses, and other familiar terrestrial mammals have been introduced by humans.[8]

Monotremes, bizarre mammals even more extraordinary than marsupials, are restricted to Australia and nearby New Zealand. This strange but tiny group consists only of one species of platypus and two species of echidnas. Monotremes lay eggs like birds and reptiles; have no teeth in their birdlike bills; possess jaws that are structured differently than those of other mammals; and use a common opening, the cloaca, for urination, defecation, and reproductive functions. Females have no nipples and male platypuses sport poisonous spurs on their ankles. Monotremes are the most un-mammal-like of all mammals. When the first platypus specimen was brought to England, naturalists thought it was a fake, assembled from parts of different animals.[9]

Both living and fossil distribution patterns for marsupials and monotremes match extremely well. How could this be if fossils were formed by the flood, as I once believed? If true, when released from the ark these animals would have needed to migrate huge distances back to the places where they lived before the flood. How would they have found appropriate food to eat along the way? How could they have traversed enormous water and mountain barriers? Flood enthusiasts resort to remarkable explanations for how, explanations that stretch one's credulity. George McCready Price, for example, posited that once off the ark, animals returned to their pre-flood distributions by "divinely-implanted instinct"; similarly, L. James Gibson opined that a miraculous post-flood redistribution process may have been responsible for the preponderance of marsupials in Australia; and John Woodmorappe suggested that "the postdiluvian peoples" were responsible for redistributing animals to where they lived before the flood.[10]

---

7. Brown and Gibson, *Biogeography*, 332; Darlington, Zoogeography, 335–39.

8. Brown and Gibson, *Biogeography*, 332; Darlington, Zoogeography, 335.

9. Brown and Gibson, *Biogeography*, 332; Colbert, *Evolution of the Vertebrates*, 236; Hall, "The Paradoxical Platypus," 211–18.

10. Price, *Outlines of Modern Science and Modern Christianity*, 188–91; Gibson, "Patterns of Mammals Distribution"; Woodmorappe, "Studies in Creationism and

An approach to truth in which one uses science when it agrees with one's presuppositions, but then resorts to miracles or ad hoc explanations when it does not, allows a person to defend any position, regardless of how outrageous or inconsistent with physical reality. There is no way to test postulates that involve this type of reasoning. While faith extends to things beyond our experience, it should not conflict with the reality we see around us. If it does, it's not faith.

A THIRD, ECOLOGY-BASED ISSUE involves reproduction and death. These two processes constitute fundamental properties of every ecosystem and of every living thing. They are two sides of the same coin. Every scrap of information from nature indicates that both death and reproduction have played important roles in the history of life all the way back to its beginning.[11]

Members of all species have the capacity to reproduce. Indeed, that capability is one of the fundamental properties of life. As a biologist I can't imagine organisms without the ability to reproduce.[12] What would such organisms look like? How would they function? How would they behave? So much of what organisms do is geared toward reproduction.

I have thought about this in relation to our human selves. What would we be like if we did not reproduce? Women would not have ovaries, Fallopian tubes, or wombs. They would have no need of hormonal cycles. They would not need breasts to feed babies. Their hips and pelvic bones would not be shaped for giving birth. Men would not have testes, seminal vesicles, or prostate glands. Their penises would not contain cavernous tissue for producing erections. Indeed, there would be no need for penises, vaginas, or sexual desire. Remove reproductive structures, physiologies, and behaviors from any type of organism, and it no longer would be that organism. It would not look the same, function the same, or behave the same.

Flood Geology."

11. Evidence of both reproduction and death occur early in the fossil record. Purported fossil embryos have been found in Precambrian rocks in China. See, for example, Li et al., "Precambrian Sponges with Cellular Structures," 879–82; and Chen et al., "Small Bilaterian Fossils from 40 to 55 Million Years Before the Cambrian," 218–22. Predators also plundered early forms of animal life. *Anomalocaris* was a large, arthropod predator found preserved in the Burgess Shale of Cambrian age. In 2018 another arthropod predator, *Cambroraster falcatus*, was discovered in the Cambrian rocks of British Columbia; similar animals also have been discovered in the Cambrian rocks of China. See Sokol, "Fossils Show Large Predator Prowled Cambrian Sediments," 417.

12. Some individuals within species are unable to reproduce due to sterility, developmental aberrations, or in the case of worker bees, members of special non-reproductive castes which foster reproduction by reproductive castes. But all species contain reproductive members.

The fact is, we humans and all other living things reproduce. Given that all living things do this, then all living things must die. If they kept on reproducing without dying, the world would fill up in a matter of days and resources would dwindle away quickly. Death is the fate of all things that reproduce.

We express joy at the birth of a baby, but we feel sadness at the death of a loved one. Ecological reality, however, tells us we cannot have one without the other. Perhaps it is good that we increasingly celebrate the lives of our dead in more upbeat "memorial services," rather than enduring the depressing old-fashioned "funerals" with which I grew up. It is normal to feel sad when loved ones pass away, but an understanding of ecology and the necessity of death may help us cope with these losses in a more positive manner. It is only through my death that space and resources become available for my children and grandchildren. Providing them with space and resources is a good—and necessary—thing to do.

Even religious writers have long recognized the necessity of both reproduction and death. The nineteenth-century Presbyterian minister, James Miller Killen, for example, noted that "Marriage in the world is the ordinance God hath appointed to repair the ravages of death: but in heaven there will be no death, so there is no such compensatory institution as marriage . . . to counterbalance the effects of dissolution." Another Presbyterian, John Kerr, was even more pointed: "As there shall be no more death [in heaven], neither will marriage, instituted to supply the waste of mortality, be any longer necessary, and of course have no place."[13]

THE FACT THAT ALL organisms die leads me to consider a fourth ecological reality: Dead organisms must be recycled. They can't just pile up. Thus ecosystems contain detritivores and decomposers, very large and diverse groups of organisms which do the recycling.[14]

Some organisms, like bald eagles, function as part-time detritivores. Where I work on Protection Island, harbor seal pups that are born dead or die usually are eaten by bald eagles. When eagles feed on dead seal pups, they function as detritivores, even though during much of their lives they function as predators.[15] The same is true for many other predatory animals. By contrast, almost all the food eaten by condors and vultures is already dead—they function as full-time detritivores. Other detritivores include

---

13. Cited by McDannell and Lang, *Heaven*, 260.

14. Smith and Smith, *Elements of Ecology*, 124–34, 648.

15. Hayward et al., "Foraging-Related Activity of Bald Eagles at a Washington Seabird Colony and Seal Rookery," 19–29.

sow bugs, earthworms, and many types of insects. Detritivores ingest dead plant or animal matter and digest this matter using internal processes.[16]

Decomposers, by contrast, break biological compounds down to simpler molecules which can be recycled within the ecosystem. The most important decomposers are fungi and some types of bacteria. Through decomposition, these organisms produce the nutrients that are taken up by plants and reconfigured into plant tissue. Plant tissue, in turn, becomes food for animals. Even small amounts of soil contains millions of bacteria and fungi ready to dissolve any dead plant or animal tissue that comes their way.[17] Detritivores and decomposers, then, are the undertakers of nature. Just like human undertakers, these organisms play crucial, but often uncelebrated, roles in our communities.

The existence and efficiency of hundreds of thousands of species of detritivores and decomposers provide an important indication that death is a fundamental natural process, an aspect of nature that from all indications has functioned since life's beginning.

A FIFTH ECOLOGICAL REALITY concerns the value and necessity of natural selection in a world of constant change. Without natural selection, all species would eventually go extinct because none of them could adapt to environmental change. Adaptation is a crucial genetic process. It lets members of populations exploit new food sources, live in new habitats, and survive under new climate conditions. The genetic restructuring of populations brought about by adaptation allows for the continuation of populations in face of environmental change, and under some circumstances it leads to the development of new species.[18]

Only populations can undergo adaptation, not individuals. Adaptation occurs when members of a population with favored genetic traits produce more offspring than members with less favorable traits. Offspring with the favored traits thrive and proportionately take over the population. In this way, populations track changes in the environment and thrive.[19] A crucial point here is that members of earlier generations must die in order for members of the new, better adapted, generations to thrive. Death, then, is an important and necessary component of the process of adaptation. Adaptation, in turn, is a crucial and necessary component of all populations

16. Terres, *The Audubon Society Encyclopedia of North American Birds* 956–58; Smith and Smith, *Elements of Ecology*, 124–25.

17. Smith and Smith, *Elements of Ecology*, 124–34.

18. Molles, *Ecology*, 77–96.

19. Molles, *Ecology: Concepts and Applications*, 79–87.

that endure over the long haul, because all populations face constant environmental change.

WITH AN UNDERSTANDING OF death as a creative ecological force in the world, I might be able to reassign death to the positive side of life's ledger. But death is often associated with pain and suffering. Also, much pain and suffering occurs without death. This fact confronts me with a sixth ecological reality, one that begs the most serious questions about the nature of God. Why is there pain and suffering—and so much of it—in ecological systems? If a good God is the creator of life on earth, why didn't he come up with a more benign plan? Death may be an ecological necessity, but why all the pain and suffering? This is the question of theodicy, an issue theologians have wrestled with for centuries, regardless of their views on the history of life.[20]

We have all watched, either in real life or on TV, violent scenes from nature in which predators like cheetahs, wolves, and snakes grab their prey and bite, strangle, or eviscerate their victims in what often is an agonizingly slow death. I have watched with horror many killings of prey by bald eagles. I will spare you details, only to say that these events can last for many long, bloody minutes during which time I wonder if I have chosen the right profession. What's particularly disturbing to me is the fact that predators often take their good old time with seeming indifference to the suffering of their victims—think of domestic cats and how they playfully bat around the mice they've injured before delivering the final killing bite.

Pain and suffering are not only physical. I have seen terror in the eyes of prey about to meet their end, observed the dread of female gulls who react to attempts by male gulls to rape them, watched seal mothers who have just given birth to stillborn pups behave with distress. Many animals, including killer whales, chimpanzees, monkeys, cats, and crows, grieve the deaths of their companions.[21] We humans are no different. Think of the terror expressed by a passenger on a sinking ship, the grief a parent suffers after the loss of a child, and the depression that drives a person with bipolar disorder to suicide. Fear, distress, depression, terror, remorse, guilt, grief—physical pain often is easier to endure than emotional suffering. Why do we live in a world where, as many scientists believe, mammals, birds, fish, and even crabs experience pain and suffering?[22]

20. Osborn, *Death before the Fall*, 11–21.
21. Coghlan, "Monkey seen caring for dying mate then grieving after she dies"; Simon, "Tour of Grief Is Over."
22. Low, "The Cambridge Declaration on Consciousness"; Sneddon, "Evolution

In one of the most philosophically profound books of the Bible, Job explores the question of theodicy. The book opens with God asking Satan[23] if he has considered Job, a resident in the land of Uz, whom God says is blameless and upright. Satan, however, is unimpressed with God's depiction of Job as righteous:

> Does Job fear God for nothing? Have you not put a fence around him and his house and all that he has, on every side? You have blessed the work of his hands, and his possessions have increased in the land. But stretch out your hand now, and touch all that he has, and he will curse you to your face. (Job 1:9–11, NRSV)

So God decides to back up his claims to Satan with a demonstration. He tells Satan to do with Job as he likes, except Satan is not to harm Job himself. Satan gets to work.

First, Sabeans sweep down and carry off Job's children's oxen and asses, killing the herdsmen in the process; second, fire from heaven kills their sheep and shepherds; third, Chaldaeans steal their camels and put the camel drivers to the sword; and fourth, a whirlwind destroys the house in which the children are partying, killing them all. Job, hearing all this bad news, shaves his head, falls prostrate to the ground, and says: "Naked I came from my mother's womb, and naked shall return there; the Lord gave, and the Lord has taken away; blessed be the name of the Lord. (Job 1:21, NRSV) "In all this," notes the text, "Job did not sin or charge God with wrongdoing." (Job 1:22, NRSV)

Satan and God again meet, and God asks Satan if he has considered his blameless servant Job. Satan, still unimpressed, responds that if Job were physically afflicted, he will curse God. So God said, go ahead and make him miserable, but spare his life.

Once again, Satan gets to work. He afflicts Job with loathsome sores head to toe. The pain is now physical *and* emotional. Job's wife implores her anguished husband, "Curse God, and die" (Job 2:9, NRSV). Job retorts that he did not expect God to always make life easy, a response by which Job demonstrates his loyalty to God. "In all this," the text reports, "Job did not sin with his lips" (Job 2:10, NRSV).

---

of Nociception and Pain: Evidence from Fish Models," 2019029; Elwood and Adams, "Electric shock causes physiological stress responses in shore crabs, consistent with prediction of pain," 20150800;

23. The name "Satan" in Job does not refer to the supernatural character known as the "devil" in later Jewish and Christian literature. Rather it refers to "any one of the angels sent by God for the specific purpose of blocking or obstructing human activity" (Pagels, *The Origin of Satan*, 39). The Hebrew expression might best be translated as "the satan."

Three friends of Job hear about his plight and come to comfort him. But there is little comfort in their words. They are certain Job is simply getting his just dues. He has been sinful and this is his reward. Job protests that he has done nothing to deserve this suffering, but to no avail. His friends continue to pile on abuse and guilt.

Meanwhile a tempest arises, and out of the tempest God responds to everyone's accusations, assertions, questions, and justifications. Ironically, God's response is not in the form of justifications or answers, but in the form of questions, questions that highlight Job's—and all humankind's—lack of understanding concerning the universe and its inhabitants.

> Where were you when I laid the foundation of the earth? Tell me, if you have understanding. Who determined its measurements—surely you know? Or who stretched the line upon it? On what were its bases sunk, or who laid its cornerstone when the morning stars sang together and the heavenly beings shouted for joy? (Job 38:4-7, NRSV).

And God's questions continue—on and on.

In face of a finite sun, reproduction, death, pain, and suffering, we are left only with questions. That is our humble lot. Our attempt to decipher the meaning of these things is futile—like trying to measure the extent of eternity. It is beyond our ken.

THE SCIENCE OF ECOLOGY presents multiple challenges to young-age creationism, challenges often ignored by well-meaning fundamentalists. Yet these challenges highlight processes so basic to life and its existence that it is impossible to conceive of a reasonable model of life and its history without addressing them. As an ecologist who has spent many years studying ecological systems firsthand, I am troubled by how these challenges have been glossed over by fundamentalists. Facile claims are no substitute for serious grappling with, or at least acknowledgment of, these challenges. It is one thing to admit we don't understand why certain aspects of reality occur, it's quite another to act as though they don't exist.

13

Life Changes

"The truth is incontrovertible. Panic may resent it; ignorance may deride it; malice may distort it; but there it is."

—Winston Churchill[1]

"Daddy, check this out!" An email from my daughter, Shanna, nearly leapt off the screen. The attachment was a black-and-white photo of two indistinct blobs encircled within a larger structure. It was a few seconds before I realized what I was seeing—an ultrasound image of forthcoming twins—my first grandkids!

At this stage there wasn't much to look at, for there wasn't much detail. But as days and weeks sped by, heads formed from large swellings, fingers emerged from paddle-like hands, eyes appeared where earlier there had been only depressions, hair grew atop now well-formed heads—the two blobs began to look like tiny human beings.

At nine months, Shanna, otherwise slim and trim, sported an enormous, protruding abdomen. Contractions began none too soon, leading to the appearance of Dominique and Etienne, squirming, bloody, beautiful masses of flesh and bone—all this from a single fertilized egg, smaller than a pinhead, which early on split into two identical cells.

---

1. Churchill, "Speech in the House of Commons."

Now, thirteen years later, Dominique and Etienne are teenagers, and thirteen years hence, they will be grown men—intelligent, productive, talented adults.

All multicellular organisms, just like my grandsons, go through a process of development. In Dominique and Etienne's case, what started out as a single cell ended up as two complicated kids, rapidly growing human beings who build Lego castles, play classical piano, do flips off the high dive, read voraciously, ride bikes, learn math, and act out the stories they invent. Change is part and parcel of life, a truly miraculous process in which one type of thing morphs into another.

As the fossil record clearly indicates, change also occurs over generations, one generation at a time. And just as the change in Dominique and Etienne is imperceptible from one day to the next, so are the changes that occur in all species from generation to generation. But looked at over the course of many days or many generations, change becomes apparent.

YEARS AGO WHILE VISITING Chicago's Field Museum of Natural History, I was admiring the mounted mammal specimens on the main level. Presently, I came across a display of mustelids, the family of carnivores that includes weasels, wolverines, badgers, martins, otters, minks, and polecats. As I studied the display, I was struck by the physical resemblances of various members of this group to one another. Each possessed short legs, stubby round ears, thick brown fur, and similar faces. Not that these animals were nearly identical—some were large, some small; some were skinny, and some rotund. Instead, it was like seeing a human family reunion, with aunts, uncles, cousins, and grandparents displaying similar and distinctive noses, skin color, and body shapes, yet dissimilar in other ways. For the first time in my life the sight of a group of diverse, but "related," species seemed to shout out with utmost clarity, "We all descended from a common ancestor!"

Years later, I arrived in Frankfurt, Germany, to make a presentation at an avian paleontology conference. It was my first visit to Germany. Upon arriving at my hotel, I was anxious to shake off jet lag and get a sense of the local vegetation and wildlife. So I took a walk in a nearby park. Oddly, it seemed as if I were walking through a park in Michigan—the feel was much the same. In particular, birds hopping about the lawns captured my attention. They exhibited the same body shape as American robins yet they were black. Even more striking was their behavior—they moved like robins. After a few hops across the grass, they stopped, cocked their heads, yanked up a worm, or pounced on some other prey item—the same behavior as the robins in my Michigan backyard. These were common blackbirds, classified with American robins in the same genus. Two species of birds, occupying different continents, exhibiting almost the same body form and behaviors—visual confirmation for me that these birds descended from a common ancestor sometime in the past.

I should not have been surprised. Even young-age creationists whom I had read believed that entire groups of animals evolved from single "created kinds."[2] The process of speciation is not a problem for many young-age creationists. But never had I been struck so forcefully by physical evidence that underscored this type of diversification.

"[F]OR THERE IS IN this Universe a Stair, or manifest Scale of creatures, rising not disorderly, or in confusion, but with a comely method and proportion." So proclaimed Sir Thomas Browne, the seventeenth-century English polymath and physician. He, along with many of his contemporaries, believed that God had created a highly organized universe, the "Great Chain of Being," in which every rock, plant, animal, human, and angel had its divinely-ordained place. Every link in the Chain had been created by God and fit perfectly in its appointed place.[3]

A scheme such as this had no place for ancestral mustelids diversifying into weasels, badgers, and wolverines, or ancestral birds giving rise to robins and blackbirds. Aside from undeniable changes like the development of individuals from conception to death and the decay of dead bodies, natural process was not a dominant theme of the medieval mindset. Some fundamentalists today hold much the same perspective.

As a high school freshman studying biology, I learned about Carolus Linnaeus, the eighteenth-century classifier of living things. Naturalists before Linnaeus used long strings of Latin words to designate particular plants and animals. Linnaeus came up with a much more efficient *binomial* expression for species names, in which each species name consisted of a *genus* name, a noun, and a specific epithet, an adjective. A particular genus could contain one or many species, but the binomial species name was unique for a given species.[4] Thus, the genus *Quercus* contains contains all oak trees, and the species *Quercus alba* refers specifically to the white oak. "*Quercus*" means "oak" and "*alba*" means "white."

---

2. Price, *Genesis Vindicated*, 173; Marsh, *Variation and Fixity in Nature*, 34–35; Coffen, *Creation—Accident or Design?*, 336–37; Brand, *Faith, Reason, and Earth History*, 179.

3. Eiseley, *Darwin's Century*, 7; Prest, *The Garden of Eden*, 51–52.

4. Koerner, *Linnaeus*, 43–55.

But Linnaeus did more than tack names onto species. He was a keen observer who recognized that groups of living things appeared to be related to one another. He grouped genera into *orders*, and orders into *kingdoms*, higher taxonomic categories still in use today. Linnaeus believed that, in the beginning, God had created individual species, forms of life that remained fixed through time. Linnaeus himself immodestly claimed to be the organizer of God's creation.[5] Later in life he did acknowledge the possibility that different species within the same genus may have split away from the original created kind, but for the most part he was confident that living things had remained pretty much the same since the beginning.[6]

Despite his belief in "special creation,"[7] Linnaeus' recognition of hierarchical categories of organisms was an important break from Great-Chain-of-Being thinking. Instead of a linear scale of organisms, he saw organisms as members of nested groups. This conceptual advance made a great deal of sense, one which later biologists would use as a basis for their notion of evolution which involves ancestral groups radiating out into descendent species.[8] Linnaeus, however, would not have liked the idea that modern-day whales descended from land animals with hind legs, or that fish evolved into four-legged beasts—so-called "macroevolutionary" changes. To the day he died he remained what we would today call a "conservative creationist," someone who rejects the concept of large-scale change through time.

As a kid, I was happy to remain in Linnaeus' camp. I would have rejected the idea that modern whales evolved from land animals with hind legs, or that descendants of fish sprouted legs. But the more I learned about life, the fossil record, and the amazing things that happen at the level of genes and chromosomes, the more I began to see convincing evidence for large-scale change.

MY OBSERVATIONS RECOUNTED AT the beginning of this chapter provided visual evidence of biological change, but they did not document the appearance of new features. What I had observed were relatively simple modifications of pre-existing features. If large-scale change really happens, I would

---

5. Linneaus was not modest. Referring to himself in the third person, he wrote *Deus creavit Linnaeus disposuit*—"God creates, Linnaeus ordered" (Charwat, "'God Created, Linnaeus Ordered'" *CILIP Update* (August 2013, 34).

6. Koerner, *Linnaeus*, 44.

7. "Special creation" refers to the belief that, except for inconsequential within-species variation, species have remained unchanged and separate since creation. See Herron and Freeman, *Evolutionary Analysis*, 38–39.

8. Eiseley, *Darwin's Century*, 6–10; Moore, *Science as a Way of Knowing*, 127; Futuyma, *Evolutionary Biology*, 9, 107–108, 288; Koerner, *Linnaeus*, 44.

expect to find examples of new structures and functions making their appearance in fossil lineages.

It is important to note that no modern evolutionary biologist expects a new feature to suddenly appear, *de novo*, or "out of nowhere." Instead, new structures and behaviors are modified from previously existing features. With the exception of DNA mutations, so-called "macroevolutionary"[9] changes are not about the "sudden appearance" of brand new characteristics.

One example of a purported macroevolutionary change was the appearance of feathers. Feathers are unique structures today that are found only on birds. All birds have feathers, and feathers are important to birds in several ways: 1) they keep birds warm; 2) they act as airfoils during flight; 3) they make birds lightweight; and 4) they are used by birds in communication, especially during courtship and aggressive encounters.[10]

Archaeopteryx, the famous reptile-like bird from late Jurassic rocks in Germany, had feathers. The reptilian features of *Archaeopteryx* led paleontologists to think that *Archaeopteryx* and other birds evolved from a group of dinosaurs called theropods. Paleontologists also predicted that fossil animals intermediate between dinosaurs and modern birds would be discovered. That is precisely what happened. More than a dozen species of theropods, discovered since the 1990s, had feathers, probably for warmth and communication. Moreover, the feathers found on earlier examples of these reptiles looked like they had been derived from simpler structures.[11]

Huge numbers of fossil organisms have been found in rocks older than Jurassic rocks, but none have contained feathers. Through the years of thinking about the nature of the fossil record, starting in graduate school, I asked myself, if the origin of new features by evolution is impossible, why wouldn't we find at least the occasional feather on animals preserved in older rocks? Why did feathers first appear in rocks where evolutionists expected them to appear? And why would the more recent fossil feathers show more complexity than the earliest fossil feathers?

A second example involves the origin of tetrapody, the possession of four limbs. Long ago evolutionary biologists believed that amphibians evolved from fish. This would have required that fish-like intermediates develop legs where none existed before. Paleontologists predicted that fossils exhibiting features intermediate between fish and tetrapods eventually

---

9. "Macroevolution" is a loosely defined term that often refers to large changes in organisms above the genus level. See Herron and Freeman, *Evolutionary Analysis*, 818.

10. Terres, *The Audubon Society Encyclopedia of North American Birds*, 110, 279.

11. Huxley, "On the Animals which Are Most Nearly Intermediate between Birds and Reptiles," *Annals and Magazine of Natural History*, 66–75; Herron and Freeman, *Evolutionary Analysis*, 52–53; Chiappe and Qingjin, *Birds of Stone*.

would be discovered in Paleozoic rocks. Once again, that's what happened. Not only were the fossils with intermediate leg-like structures found, but they were found in rocks dating to the "right" time period, in Upper Devonian rocks of the Paleozoic Era, above where bony fish first appear and below where full-blown tetrapods first appear.[12]

Although there is some debate over exactly when the first tetrapods appeared, there is little question that a group of animals known as lobe-finned fish exhibit intermediate characteristics. One of the important fossils in this group, *Tiktaalik roseae*, was discovered in 2004 on Ellesmere Island, Canada by Neil Shubin, a biologist from the University of Chicago. *Tiktaalik* possessed features that strongly suggested it was structurally and behaviorally intermediate between fish and amphibians—it possessed scales like a fish; a head hinged by the neck to the rest of the body so that, unlike most fish, it could peer around to its surroundings; a horizontally flattened head; spiracles (holes) atop its snout, implying it had lungs for breathing; and front limb bones consisting of a scapula, coracoid, humerus, ulna, radius, and wrist bones—the same bones found in tetrapod limbs. But *Tiktaalik*, along with a constellation of ancient fossil fish with similar characteristics, was a scaly fish with gills. These animals apparently lived in the shallow bodies of freshwater where they hunted along the edge for prey. Today, mudskippers, fish unrelated to lobe-finned fish and without limb bones, engage in amphibious behavior similar to what was probably exhibited by *Tiktaalik*.[13]

In short, not only do organisms make small, structural adjustments over time through shifts in structure and loss of function, but they also develop new structures and behaviors modified from earlier characteristics. These new structures and behaviors confer distinct advantages. No one would argue against the fact that feathers provide advantages to birds, or that limbs provide advantages to terrestrial animals. Evidence for the appearance of new features at the "right" times in the fossil record is for me supportive of the theory of macroevolutionary change.

A POPULAR CREATIONIST RESPONSE to the origin of new features in organisms involves "intelligent design," or "ID." The notion of intelligent design suggests that features with multiple working parts show evidence of a designer. In order for something to function properly, all its parts must be present for it to work. What advantage would accrue to an organism if it possessed only a half-formed eye, feather, or limb? How would natural

---

12. Zimmer, *At the Water's Edge*, 35–85;

13. Daeschler et al., "A Devonian tetrapod-like fish and the evolution of the tetrapod body plan," 757–63.

selection favor a partially-formed modality?[14] Usually behind this question is the belief that God is the designer, an attractive concept to Christians.

The "argument from design" has enjoyed a long and venerable history, extending back at least to the teachings of Socrates. One of the best known examples of this type of argument was by the Reverend William Paley in his book *Natural Theology*. Paley began his book with an analogy. If someone finds a watch lying on the ground, the finder will assume the watch had a maker. A watch is a highly organized object, one that suggests purpose, and purpose can only be generated by a mind with intent. Thus, when one observes an organism which is highly organized and seems to exhibit purpose, one should assume the organism had a designer. Paley argued that the designer is God.[15]

Intelligent design advocates argue that "incompletely" formed structures could not possibly function correctly in ancestral forms of life. In other words, functional structures are "irreducibly complex." In his book, *Darwin's Black Box*, Michael J. Behe used the example of a mousetrap to explain the principle of irreducible complexity. Behe noted that a common mousetrap contains five parts, each of which is necessary if the trap is to do its job. Remove even one of these parts from the trap and the trap will not work—in other words, it is irreducibly complex.[16]

Behe then proceeded to apply the concept of irreducible complexity to several examples including cilia, which provide the *Paramecium* and other single-celled organisms with the ability to move; flagella, which move bacteria through fluid by propeller-like spinning motions; the complex cascade of proteins which coordinate the blood-clotting process; and the formation of antibodies which combat disease-forming proteins.[17] There is no question that these molecular machines are impressive in terms of formation, complexity, and function. According to Behe, each of these systems is irreducibly complex because, just like the mousetrap, if any component of the system were to be removed, the system could not work. So his question was, how could such a system evolve unless it initially appeared completely intact with all its components in place—unless, that is, it was created?

Behe's book provided a fun-to-read challenge to macroevolution that was impressive to many people. I wondered how evolutionary biologists would respond to his arguments. But as I read and listened to their

---

14. A recent, popular example of this argument is Michael Behe's *Darwin's Black Box*, 39–73.
15. Paley, *Natural Theology*, 1–3.
16. Behe, *Darwin's Black Box*, 42–45.
17. Behe, *Darwin's Black Box*, 51–139.

responses, I became convinced that Behe's clever premise of irreducible complexity provided only cardboard caricatures of the systems he addressed, caricatures that greatly oversimplified reality.

Behe claimed that because "the complexity of the cilium is irreducible, then it can not have functional precursors," and therefore had to have been designed.[18] But as cell biologists know, there are many different types of cilia, some with considerably fewer parts and different arrangements than the common, more complicated, type described by Behe. What's more, all these forms, whether simple or complex, work just fine. Consequently, Behe's claim that the complex cilium he described is irreversibly complex is false—there are much simpler ways to make a functional cilium, ways that abound in nature.[19]

Claims by Behe that various proteins, like certain enzymes, and biochemical pathways like Kreb's cycle which produces ATP,[20] are irreducibly complex also have been shown to be overblown or false. Biochemists have experimentally demonstrated that if genes for particular proteins are mutated so they no longer work, instead of destroying the entire system as the concept of irreducible complexity might predict, other genes step in and manufacture different proteins that do the same job as the original proteins—and sometimes even do a better job. Moreover, biochemists also have shown how intermediate stages within the Krebs cycle and the blood-clotting mechanism could have been cobbled together from existing, component parts.[21]

All this is not to deny the possibility of divine design. But to make a "faith claim" that *any particular* structure or function exists only because it has been specially designed is a setup for disappointment, or even disillusionment. Natural process is surprisingly "adept" at accomplishing amazing feats of organization. Using science to "prove" the direct intervention of God because of the occurrence of some structure or process is risky business. Just because a gap occurs in our understanding of a particular structure or process, does not mean a rational explanation based on physical principles is unavailable.

---

18. Behe, "Molecular Machines."

19. Miller, *Finding Darwin's God*, 140–43.

20. ATP stands for adenosine triphosphate, a molecule that captures energy during Krebs cycle, and stores that energy temporarily before it is used to carry out some type of activity.

21. Miller, *Finding Darwin's God*, 143–58.

A MORE PERPLEXING PROBLEM for the argument from design is that it cuts two ways. If fairly applied to the natural world, it must be applied to both "good" and "obnoxious" features of organisms. As a biologist I am keenly aware of the existence of literally millions of obnoxious types of organisms that cause pain and death to other organisms. If God is responsible for intelligently designed organisms, he is responsible for both those that are "good" and those that are "obnoxious." I have had to ask myself, do I want to blame God for all the obnoxious organisms I know about, organisms that feature complicated and exquisitely-designed structures and behaviors that make them obnoxious? What kind of God would make such things?

Before pursuing this issue further, however, I have had to think about what makes something obnoxious. Is something obnoxious simply because I don't like it? Is mold, for example, obnoxious? I don't like mold on my bread, but in nature mold helps to break down dead materials. Some people hate blue jays because they seem so haughty and noisy, but I know someone who thinks they are among the most delightful of birds. Are yellow jackets obnoxious? Recently I thought so when I got stung by one while mowing my lawn. But these feisty, predatory wasps keep insect pests in check; we might regret their loss should they suddenly disappear. Are humans obnoxious? They are overpopulating the earth, spewing toxic chemicals, and changing the physical nature of the planet in very harmful ways. Yet humans also make love, art, music, and civilization. So deciding which organisms are obnoxious and which are beneficial is not really possible. All living things occupy niches within complex ecosystems where each organism plays a role. For purposes of this chapter, however, I will consider an organism to be obnoxious if it causes pain, disease, or death to another organism. Predators and parasites clearly fit within this category.

The other day I watched my neighbor's cat, Rosy, proudly carrying the limp body of a little gray rodent. I thought to myself, "How obnoxious!" I doubt Rosy even ate the rodent which she took back to my neighbor's back door—Rosy's owner provides her with plenty of nutritious food. No, Rosy killed the rodent simply because that's what cats do. Rosy is an amazingly well-adapted predator. Her eyes are set in front of her skull for 3D-vision; her saberlike, carnivorous teeth line powerful jaws perfectly designed for killing bites; her digestive tract, typical of meat-eating animals, is relatively short and made for processing meat; and her razor sharp retractable claws allow her to climb to arboreal ambush sites from which she springs and firmly grasps her prey.[22] Rosy, along with all other cats, is an exquisitely designed killing machine. Remove the killer attributes from a cat and you no longer

---

22. Macdonald, *Carnivores*, 18–19, 42

have a cat. Anti-evolutionists like to assert that all cats today are variations of the originally created "cat kind." If that is true, then God created exquisitely-designed killers. What does this say about the goodness of God?

The same thing could be said about eagles. I have studied bald eagles for many years—Protection Island typically supports at least one nesting pair, and many transient eagles hang around the island during the spring and summer when the seabirds and seals are breeding. When they are not soaring majestically against blue skies, eagles do not appear particularly bright. Nonetheless, eagles are very big, very strong, and very effective predators. I have watched eagles capture and kill hundreds of adult gulls and chicks, and even watched an eagle kill and begin to eat a dying harbor seal pup.[23] These are highly unpleasant, bloody events; the act of killing is often slow and drawn out.

Eagles, like cats, are amazingly well adapted killing machines. Their size alone is enough to strike terror into the hearts of potential prey. Eagle eyes are set in front of their heads giving them excellent depth perception, and their visual acuity is remarkable—at least twice that of humans.[24] They are agile fliers. I have watched eagles chase gulls, agile fliers in their own right, for several minutes; sometimes they capture gulls midair. Their great, curved, pointed beaks serve as efficient meat hooks which they use to tear open the flesh of even tough-skinned prey. Recently I examined the fresh carcass of an adult eagle which had died on Smith Island National Wildlife Refuge north of Protection Island. What impressed me most were the feet. Not only were they huge, with a spread nearly the size of my open hand, but they contained rough scales which allowed them to grip slippery salmon and other prey.

Then consider spiders. "For a display of nature's diabolical inventiveness, it's hard to beat spiders," opened a 2017 cover story in the journal *Science*. All of the estimated 90,000 species of spiders are predatory, and all spiders produce deadly venom which they deliver to their victims via an effective pair of fangs. Also, all spiders produce the amazingly strong, elastic, and versatile material we call silk, which can be made of many different chemical formulations for different purposes, even by the same animal.[25]

Spiders are found on every continent except Antarctica. They are abundant residents of most ecosystems. Given their ability to balloon for long distances, suspended beneath gossamer threads of silk, spiders are

---

23. Hayward et al., "Foraging-Related Activity of Bald Eagles at a Washington Seabird Colony and Seal Rookery," 19–29; Hayward, "Eagle Predation on Harbor Seal Pups," 51–53.

24. Shlaer, "An Eagle's Eye," 922.

25. Pennisi, "Untangling Spider Biology," 288–91.

among the first animal colonizers of islands.[26] One morning on Protection Island, I awoke to a dense fog, a common occurrence in the Strait of Juan de Fuca. I looked out the window to see hundreds of spider webs in the tall prairie grass, each highlighted by shimmering beads of condensed fog. I was curious as to the density of the webs, so I laid out a long line and randomly picked ten points along the line. At each of the ten points I laid square frame, which encompassed a ten-foot-square area, over the grass. Within each framed area I counted all the spider webs. I then determined the average number of webs per framed area—over thirty-three, more than three webs per square foot. This value, multiplied by the multiple millions of square feet making up the island, suggested the existence of an enormous number of webs. Each web was tended by a voracious, eight-legged predator ready to paralyze and suck the life out of anything unlucky enough to fly or hop into the sticky, silky, deadly network.

Spiders, cats, weasels, toads, dragon flies, grizzly bears, cormorants, sturgeon, boa constrictors, brook trout, timber wolves, sand wasps, tyrannosaurs, anteaters, harbor seals, sharks, bald eagles, pterodactyls—the world is crawling and swimming with predators, and it has been this way as far back as we have fossil evidence. Does the existence and abundance of predators such as these serve as evidence for design by God?

As a graduate student, I enrolled in a parasitology course, one of the most eye-opening classes I ever took. The massive impact of parasites on virtually all free-living organisms, including humans, is mind-boggling. A parasite is any organism that lives on or in the body of another "host" organism, and taps into the host's hard-earned resources to the detriment of the host. As I noted in a previous chapter, virtually all animals harbor parasites, and usually multiple species of them. Humans over the world, for example, collectively carry over a thousand different types. Moreover, some parasites harbor their own parasites, and some parasites of parasites harbor parasites! Thus, there are more types of parasites in the world than there are free-living species. What's more, parasites have "devised" amazingly bold, intricate, and insidious strategies for the successful infection of their hosts. I've been stunned by some of the examples that I've come across.[27]

In 2017, malaria infected an estimated 219 million people, of whom more than 4 million died from the disease.[28] The malarial parasite, *Plasmodium*, is a protozoan that uses another parasite, the *Anopheles* mosquito,

26. Pennisi, "Untangling Spider Biology," 289; Foelix, *Biology of Spiders*, 287.
27. Noble and Noble, *Parasitology*, 3, 5–6.
28. *World Malaria Report 2018*, iv.

as an intermediate host. Four species of *Plasmodium* infect humans, and more than 100 others infect non-humans, including other mammals, reptiles, and birds.[29] When a female *Anopheles* mosquito draws blood from an infected human, she takes in *Plasmodium* sex cells called gametocytes. Male gametocytes produce sperm-like structures which fertilize female gametocytes; the resultant zygotes move through the mosquito's gut wall and form oocysts. The oocysts, in turn, churn out large numbers of sporozoites which enter the mosquito's tissues. When an infected mosquito takes another blood meal from a human, it first injects sporozoite-infused saliva. The sporozoites invade the human blood stream and travel to the liver, where they penetrate red blood cells. In the blood cells they go through a series of transformations, and divide into myriads of merozoites. The merozoites, in turn, infect other red blood cells in repeating cycles, a process only too familiar to anyone suffering from malaria. Some of the merozoites develop into gametocytes and complete the cycle.[30]

The *Plasmodium* life cycle is one of the most complicated among parasites. From the point of view of the parasite, its byzantine way of life is hugely successful. Each zygote has the potential of spreading its genes into enormous numbers of mosquito and human hosts. As with all parasite-host interactions, each stage must be chemically and physiologically compatible with the cell or organ within which it finds itself, or it would quickly die. The genetic interactions and cell-to-cell signaling involved are truly mind-bending. As Columbia University parasitologist O. Roger Anderson wrote, the *Plasmodium* life cycle "is indeed a remarkable sequence of ordered transformations, producing cells uniquely adapted to each of the specialized sites where they must survive or grow—design on steroids."[31]

Then, of course, there are the *Anopheles* mosquitoes that shuttle *Plasmodium* and other parasites from human to human. These remarkable ectoparasites exhibit incredibly complex design in their own right. They start out as floating eggs laid on the water. The eggs hatch into legless, aquatic larvae that swim around and feed on algae and bacteria. The larvae do not have gills but must come to the surface frequently to obtain oxygen through their specialized breathing siphons. Once large enough, they transform into active pupae called tumblers. Tumblers mature into adults with legs, wings, and the all-important blood-sucking proboscis. The transformation—all within a few days, from aquatic egg, larva, and pupa—into an aerodynamically-sophisticated, sexually-motivated, human-bound, blood-sucking

---

29. Wernsdorfer, "The Importance of Malaria in the World," 13.
30. Anderson, *Comparative Protozoology*, 169–72.
31. Anderson, *Comparative Protozoology*, 172.

adult appears nothing short of miraculous.[32] Sometimes when I slap one of these annoying pests, I think about the astonishing level of complexity and design I've just destroyed.

The obnoxiousness of parasites knows no bounds. Consider *Cymothoa exigua*, or the tongue-mimicking crustacean. This little aquatic animal enters snapper fish through the fish's gills. It then moves from the gills to the fish's mouth where it cuts through the blood vessels that supply nutrients to the tongue. The dead tongue soon falls off, and the crustacean now attaches itself to the stump of the tongue. There, firmly attached, it functions as the fish's new tongue, now in a most convenient location to steal food taken in by the fish.[33]

Ichneumons make up an enormous family of wasps, with more species than all fish, amphibians, reptiles, birds, and mammals combined. All ichneumons are *parasitoids*. Parasitoids function as parasites only during the larval stage—adult parasitoids are free-living animals. Most ichneumons have not been classified, but the more than 24,000 species that have been classified make taxonomists think it is the largest family of hymenopterans—the group that contains ants, bees, and wasps. Ichneumons occur on every continent except Antarctica. Female ichneumons lay their eggs on or in other insects, most commonly larval insects. Some female ichneumons first paralyze their "host" with a sting while depositing their eggs. The egg-laying organ, the ovipositor, doubles as a stinger. Once the eggs hatch, the larval ichneumons begin to feed on the flesh that is closest to them—the living, quivering flesh of their host.[34]

Planiceps hirsutus is an ichneumon that lays her eggs on California trapdoor spiders. When she finds a trapdoor, she makes a commotion outside the spider's home which causes the spider to emerge from its burrow. When it does so, the female ichneumon stings the spider and lays a single egg on its abdomen. Then she stuffs the paralyzed host back into its own burrow—being careful to shut the trapdoor behind her. The tiny larval wasp soon hatches and devours the body of the spider—immobile but still alive at the beginning of the meal. In an act of macabre efficiency, some relatives of *Planiceps* first amputate the legs of their spider victims before tucking them back in their burrows.[35] Designed by God? Really?

---

32. Noble and Noble, *Parasitology*, 407–08.

33. Brusca, "Tongue Replacement in a Marine Fish (*Lutjanus guttatus*) by a Parasitic Isopod (Crustacea: Isopoda)," 813–16.

34. Wahl and Gauld, "Genera Ichneumonorum Nearcticae," http://www.amentinst.org/GIN/, lines 7–15; Gould, *Hen's Teeth and Horse's Toes*, 32–44.

35. Gould, *Hen's Teeth and Horse's Toes*, 37.

"What a book a devil's chaplain might write on the clumsy, wasteful, blundering, low, and horribly cruel work of nature!" wrote Charles Darwin, a kind-hearted gentleman who looked closely at nature and recoiled at the sight of brutality.[36] And despicable members of the natural world are hardly the exceptions. Instead, they are the most common of all creatures. And each one engages in intricacies made possible by remarkably well-designed lances, prongs, fangs, darts, stings, lassos, bolas, bludgeons, poisons, claws, traps, and other instruments of torture and doom.

Should I blame God for making such a rogues' gallery of creatures? Actually, some Christians *have* attributed the design of such creatures to God. Reverend William Kirby, a nineteenth-century entomologist and rector of Barham, England, saw ichneumon parasitoids as exemplars of motherly love. "When you witness the solicitude with which they [adult female ichneumons] provide for the security and sustenance of their future young, you can scarcely deny to them love for a progeny they are never destined to behold." Kirby praised these wasps for controlling the populations of "those . . . that would destroy us," such as a wheat-eating fly that "is rendered harmless, by the goodness of Providence, by not less than three [species] of these little benefactors of our race."[37] Kirby was one of the leading Christian apologists of his day.

Perhaps Mark Twain had been reading Kirby when he wrote the satirical short story titled "Little Bessie Would Assist Providence." Precocious Bessie has heard some well-meaning religious explanations about pain, suffering, and death, and she is pummeling her pious mother with questions:

> "Mamma, Mr. Burgess said in his sermon that billions of little creatures are sent into us to give us cholera, and typhoid, and lockjaw, and more than a thousand other sicknesses and—mamma, does He send them?"
>
> "Oh, certainly, child, certainly. Of course."
>
> "What for?"
>
> "Oh, to *dis*cipline us! haven't I told you so, over and over again?"
>
> "It's awful cruel, mamma! And silly! and if I—"
>
> "Hush, oh *hush!* do you want to bring the lightning?"
>
> "You know the lightning *did* come last week, mamma, and struck the new church, and burnt it down. Was it to discipline the church?"
>
> (Wearily). "Oh, I suppose so."

---

36. Charles Darwin to J. D. Hooker.

37. Kirby, *The Bridgewater Treatises on the Power, Wisdom, and Goodness of God as Manifested in the Creation*, 62, 63, 333.

"But it killed a hog that wasn't doing anything. Was it to discipline the hog, mamma?"

"Dear child, don't you want to run out and play a while? If you would like to—"

"Mama, only think! Mr. Hollister says there isn't a bird or fish or reptile or any other animal that hasn't got an enemy that Providence has sent to bite it and chase it and pester it, and kill it, and suck its blood and discipline it and make it good and religious. Is that true, mother—because if it is true, why did Mr. Hollister laugh at it?"

"That Hollister is a scandalous person, and I don't want you to listen to anything he says."

"Why, mamma, he is very interesting, and I think he tries to be good. He says the wasps catch spiders and cram them down into their nests in the ground—*alive*, mamma!—and there they live and suffer days and days and days, and the hungry little wasps chewing their legs and gnawing into their bellies all the time, to make them good and religious and praise God for His infinite mercies. I think Mr. Hollister is just lovely, and ever so kind; for when I asked him if he would treat a spider like that, he said he hoped to be damned if he would; and then he—"

"My child! oh, do for goodness' sake—"[38]

I suggest the answers to little Bessie's questions are best found in evolutionary biology, not in theology or demonology. I prefer to think that lethal microbes, predators, parasites, and parasitoids are the result of natural processes, processes that result in features that are highly beneficial to the success of the organisms involved, even though these features are not something I like. Although this explanation is not completely satisfying, it seems to be the most straightforward, honest, and parsimonious explanation of any we could come up with. Moreover, this explanation lets God off the hook for creating such things, and allows for the acceptance of reasonable interpretations of scientific data.

Although a scientific explanation does not provide a satisfying theological explanation for obnoxiousness in nature, the existence of bad things is a fact of life—regardless of what approach I take to the history of life. The "problem of evil" is a long-standing problem irrespective of how anyone looks at it. There is no good theological explanation for the origin of pain, suffering, and evil.[39] Every time someone attempts such an explanation,

---

38. Twain, "Little Bessie Would Assist Providence."
39. Polkinghorne, *Exploring Reality*, 140; Osborn, *Death before the Fall*, 150.

fatal flaws appear in the logic. This, indeed, is one of the messages of the book of Job.

EVOLUTIONARY BIOLOGY OFFERS POWERFUL explanations for the processes by which new features—obnoxious or not—arise. Unfortunately, the concept of evolution is widely misunderstood. Evolution means simply "change," something anyone who knows anything about life accepts. Even Harold W. Clark, a prominent young-age creationist, admitted back in 1940 that "The theory of 'divergent evolution' . . . is apparently a valid one within actually observable limits."[40] And more recently Leonard Brand wrote that "even an interventionist [a creationist who believes that God intervenes in the history life] recognizes that microevolution and a certain amount of macroevolution does occur."[41] Thus, it is puzzling that the term "evolution" gets such a bad rap among conservative Christians. Most likely this is because evolution is often associated with "materialism," the philosophical notion that there is no reality beyond what we can sense in the material universe. While it is true that materialists believe in evolution, so do many non-materialists.

No one denies that humans develop from a fertilized egg—a mere single cell—into walking, thinking, talking beings capable of remarkable feats. We become adults through a long and complicated process of development. In fact, we never stop changing from conception to death—we look completely different at the beginning of life than at the end. And we develop new features and behaviors all along the way. The process of evolution should be no more difficult to accept than the process of development, except that evolution occurs over multiple generations and, consequently, is more difficult for us to visualize directly.

The physical world is constantly undergoing change—including the appearance of new habitats, alterations of climate, shifting of populations, increasing or decreasing food supplies—even new islands and continents. Without the ability to adapt to these changes, all species would go extinct. The capacity of species to adapt in response to changes in their surroundings is one of the most amazing characteristics of living things. We should not look at evolution with suspicion or negativity, even though at times we may not like what it has produced. We should celebrate the occurrence and capacity of biological change as a remarkable process, certainly one of the most remarkable capacities of living things.

---

40. Clark, *Genes and Genesis*, 56.
41. Brand, *Faith, Reason, and Earth History*, 161.

A variety of interacting processes promote evolutionary change in species, just as a variety of interacting processes promote developmental change in an individual. Two of the most basic of these processes are mutation and natural selection. Mutations are *random* changes in the DNA which makes up the genes. Mutations sometimes create disease, but often they result in the production of alternate, functional proteins, the building blocks and control molecules in organisms. Natural selection, by contrast, is a *nonrandom* process whereby organisms with particular variant proteins survive and reproduce more effectively than those with other variant proteins in a given environment. Processes such as gene duplication, genetic drift, horizontal gene transfer, hybridization, gene regulation, and heterochrony interact with mutation and natural selection and lead to adaptation.[42] Adaptation allows organisms to thrive as environments change. We still have a lot to learn about how these processes work and interact, but biologists have unequivocally demonstrated their existence and impact on species. And each of these processes is measurable, just like growth, respiration, reproduction, homeostasis, and the other characteristics common to living things.

The weight of biological evidence, looked at objectively and considered in conjunction with an interconnected web of evidence from plate tectonics, the geologic column, the fossil record, radiometric dating, and other important sources of data, strongly suggests that evolution happens and happens with truly remarkable, often largescale, results.

---

42. Any contemporary introductory evolutionary biology text will explain some of the mechanisms behind these processes. One of the best such texts, one that provides evidence-based explanations, is Herron and Freeman's *Evolutionary Analysis*.

PART FOUR

Conclusion

190 PART FOUR: CONCLUSION

The first line of a popular movie theme song by Burt Bacharach and Hal David during the mid-1960s was "What's It All about Alfie?" Against the backdrop of the Vietnam War, racial unrest, assassinations, drugs, sexual promiscuity, and moon-walking humans, it was a question on the minds of many people, What is it all about? There is no deeper philosophical question. Each of us has grown up within a belief system, whether religious or secular, that attempts to address this question. Regardless, the uncertainties and contingencies of life continue to raise conundrums about love, life, suffering, death, and existence. How do we answer these questions? In a final chapter, I explore what I think it's all about from my admittedly limited, biased, and personal perspective.

14

Voyage of Discovery

"There is a source of wonderment greater than stellar magnitudes, the tricks of time, or the miracle of growth. It is that we are here and have within us the ability to know beauty, to be kind, to experience patience, peace, and deep piety."

—Sam Campbell[1]

"In awe, mystery and humility, I stand solidly with you before an amazing miraculous universe, and I believe most other atheists stand before nature with the same posture."

So wrote my friend, now retired, who taught biology for many years in Christian colleges. He is a master teacher and an articulate interpreter of nature who has thought deeply about life. And he no longer believes in God.

"If you are to help me to 'find God' again," he continued, "you must offer me other reasons [than awe, mystery, and humility], and Jim . . . there are times I really do wish I could find 'Him' again."

I have received many such communications, both in writing and in person. Each one is from someone with integrity who, like me, appreciates the beauty, intricacy, and remarkable diversity of the natural world, but

---

1. Campbell, *Nature's Messages*, 95.

understands the evidence for deep time and extensive change while recognizing the specter of pain and death integral to life.

The solution offered by fundamentalists is to simply accept the authority of a "plain reading" of selected scriptures, and assent to the half-truths and hollow assertions of "creation science." If evidence from the natural world seems to contradict that "plain reading," simply discount the evidence.[2]

Some of us are unable to take that approach. Evidence from the physical universe remains important to us. We cannot close our eyes to the reality of shifting tectonic plates, radiometric dates, fossil sequences, ecological systems, and evolutionary processes, and simply "believe." We can't allow ourselves to sort, twist, and constrain evidence so it fits some form of wishful thinking or superficial "plain reading" of scripture. We value intellectual integrity more than group conformity, although we continue to revere the deep resonances of scripture.

Within a three-year period, 2011 to 2014, I lost my mother, my father, and one of my best friends. I watched helplessly as they drew their last, labored breaths. The finality was palpable. With each heaving breath I felt a sharp sense of loss. And with each loss I was confronted directly with questions of meaning and purpose.

I have just turned seventy-one. Not a day passes when I fail to anticipate my own demise. The anticipation comes with more puzzlement than dread. Why was I born those many years ago? Why have I spent so much time living, learning, and growing in wisdom when it will all end? Have I made a difference? Is this all there is? How do I traverse the remaining days, months, years, or decades of my life? Can I do so with both integrity *and* hope? Is there meaning in the past? How do I live as both a scientist and as a believer? Is there promise for the future?

When I learn about a tsunami that snuffs out hundreds of thousands of lives, when I hear that a mass shooting destroys dozens of innocent victims, or when I discover that a colleague tragically loses a young child, I ask myself, does anyone or anything care? Is the universe "benignly indifferent" to

---

2. See, for example, Whitcomb and Morris, *The Genesis Flood*, xxv–xxix. The authors state that "We believe that the Bible, as the verbally inspired and completely inerrant Word of God, gives us the true framework of historical and scientific interpretation, as well as of so-called religious truth. . . We take this revealed framework of history as our basic datum, and then try to see how all the pertinent data can be understood in this context." See also Hasel, "The Meaning of the Chronogenealogies of Genesis 5 and 11," 68. Hasel, a conservative Old Testament scholar, opined that "whenever biblical information impinges on matters of history, age of the earth, origins, etc., the data observed must be interpreted and reconstructed in view of this superior divine revelation which is supremely embodied in the Bible."

pain and suffering?[3] Does anything like a God really exist? Life presents conundrums from which doubts arise in every honest and thoughtful person.

My friend and other atheists may be right—the universe and everything in it is the result of chance; there is no meaning, no reason for hope, no higher power; we have evolved as a result of chance collisions of stardust; and if we don't destroy ourselves first, the sun will burn out and humans, with their consciousness and creativity, will puff out of existence with the rest of life. Sociobiologist David Barash expressed this perspective well:

> We are all sitting at a cosmic poker game in which the house has an infinite supply of chips. Neither we nor our genes can ever really win, since we can never cash in our chips and go home. As for the compulsive gambler, there is nothing but the game, and since it has been going on for a long time, only the best players are left. It is an existential game, the only one in town, and all we can do is stay in as long as possible.[4]

I easily comprehend why knowledgeable nonbelievers like David Barash and my atheist friend have arrived at this conclusion. Yet I choose not to join them. The reasons for my choice—and for their choice—are not based on objective, airtight logic, nor can they be. But the reasons for my choice are subjectively compelling for me, and through them I derive a sense of purpose, meaning, and hope.

When doubts play on my mind, which they often do, I ask, Wait a minute, how does "such-and-such" fit into this picture? Is it reasonable to assume this part of reality exists because of pure chance? Is the assumption that there is someone or something beyond chance any *less* reasonable than the alternative? Below I briefly explore several reasons I believe in a larger reality.

THE LARGEST, OVER-ARCHING, MIND-BENDING reason is simply that we are here, that we are aware, and that we communicate with one another about why we are here. Why should this be? Why is there something instead of nothing? This is the ultimate question.

If I assume the existence of "something," I then wonder how a lump of "something" could achieve self-consciousness. Assuming it gains self-consciousness, I then wonder how the lump could achieve the ability to exchange thoughts on ultimate questions with other lumps? Why wouldn't a lump be perfectly content, pardon the anthropomorphism, to remain

---

3. Camus, *The Stranger*, 154. In this most famous of Camus' novels, the soulless Monsieur Meursault awaits the guillotine without remorse for his crime and opens his heart to the "benign indifference of the universe."

4. Barash, *The Whisperings Within*, 26–27.

unconscious, like a lump of wet mud? What would drive or pull it to become anything other than inanimate? What would stimulate it to communicate?

Everything we do, think, feel, or believe is predicated on the assumption that there is something instead of nothing. Why this should be? Why are we here to even ask the question? The biggest reason for why I believe in a larger reality, then, is simply that we exist.

But there are other reasons as well.

As I descended the steps of the university library, I encountered my friend and colleague, Abraham Terian. We were busy academics working in different corners of campus, and we hadn't seen one another for many weeks. We both expressed our regrets and Abraham, always wise, added with his delightful Armenian accent, "I have come to believe that friends are *thē* most important things in life!" I'll never forget his words.

Friends, broadly speaking, include spouses, members of our family, and other people whose company we enjoy. Friends stick together because of a mysterious affinity for one another, an affinity that for want of a better term we call *love*. Whether we actually use the word to refer to our various relationships, love forms the basis of these strong attachments.

I am part of an informal group of four couples that meets for a simple meal of soup, salad, and bread every other Monday evening. We call ourselves the "soup group." We have met like this for the past twelve years. We are comprised of an attorney, psychologist, musician, anthropologist, physical therapist, physician, mathematician, and biologist. No topic is off the table for discussion: family, spirituality, food, meaning, history, culture, globalization, marriage, art, science, doubt, politics, struggles, faith, death—you name it, we've talked about it. Except for the simple but delicious soup-centered meal, our two- to three-hour, biweekly get-togethers are completely spontaneous. Yet conversation flows effortlessly. Once or twice a year, we rent a large house at a beautiful location away from home, and for several days we live communally. We are bound together by friendship. Research on the importance of friends suggests that our chances of living longer and healthier lives are improved as a result of that friendship.

Scientists try to explain friendship and love as a consequence of things like neurochemical transmitters, kin selection, and reciprocal altruism. No doubt all of these play a role. And there's little doubt that natural selection shapes the outcome of these influences in various populations of animals and humans. Still, I wonder if this is the total story, for the power of love extends even toward individuals we don't know—we donate billions of dollars each year to feed the hungry, clothe the naked, house the homeless, dispense health to the underprivileged, and aid victims of disasters in faraway places.

The selflessness of truly loving persons appears limitless. Think of Francis of Assisi, Florence Nightingale, Clara Barton, Mahatma Gandhi, Martin Luther King, Mother Teresa—individuals motivated by a desire to help others, regardless of the cost to themselves. All the world's great religions honor their selfless saints. Can this outpouring of love and care be explained simply in terms of neurochemistry and a deep level of masked selfishness masquerading as altruism? I doubt it.

When I say, "I love you!" I extend myself into one of the richest, most meaningful relationships possible in life, but it also makes me vulnerable to hurt, deception, and loss. Liabilities such as these make it even more remarkable that we form tight friendships bound by love. Science has yet to plumb the depths of friendship and love. There are undefined elements here that transcend neurotransmitters and self-interest.

I AM STANDING AT the ship's bow as we make our way slowly through a corridor of rocks and ice. I am overwhelmed by the beauty, and I wish that everyone could experience what I'm experiencing. The stark, pristine beauty of Paradise Bay in the Antarctic Peninsula is stunning, riveting, without peer. Clouds of white and gray shroud parts of the mountains, while here and there splashes of blue sky poke through. Rounded, jagged, bold, subdued, towering,—you name it—every possible shape is represented. Icebergs punctuate the channel between us and the mountains and provide platforms for groups of chinstrap and Gentoo penguins. Sea lions lounge on floating bergs and great whales surface and dive, surface and dive, exhaling giant plumes of mist. Shearwaters and petrels race about, gliding just above the water's surface, searching for nutritious morsels. I have visited hundreds of beautiful places during my life, but nothing—simply nothing—compares with the scene opening before me.

Now I am sitting with friends in the balcony of Hill Auditorium at the University of Michigan. It's December, and we've come to engage in a great Christmas tradition—participation in George Frideric Handel's "Messiah." I say *participation* because one can't listen to this music without emotional involvement. I am untrained musically, but training is unnecessary to respond to the grandeur of this work. The full-voiced oratorio, with words from the King James Version of the Bible and the Book of Common Prayer, begins with words in Isaiah about the coming Messiah and in Luke describing an angelic appearance to shepherds at Jesus' birth. It continues with texts concerning the Passion of Christ and the "Hallelujah" chorus, and concludes with the resurrection of the dead and Christ's heavenly reinstatement. The stirring melodies, swelling crescendos, and emphatic repetitions infuse my being. The oratorio, created more than 250 years ago, remains unspeakably powerful. I wonder what it must be like to be part of the choir or orchestra. At the conclusion, I exit the concert hall elevated, confident that I have partaken of another reality.

And now, at the National Gallery of Art in Washington, DC, I stand transfixed before one of my favorite paintings, Claude Monet's *La Femme à l'ombrelle—Madame Monet et son fils* ("Woman with a Parasol—Madame Monet and Her Son"). The oil-on-canvas work, painted in 1875 by the celebrated impressionist, uses light, color, shade, and illusion to capture the essence of femininity. From behind wisps of light, the hauntingly large eyes of the lady's indistinct but hypnotizing face peer directly into my own eyes. It is a look that kindles romance. I sense the warm breeze of the summer day as it tugs at her full skirt. Her shadow, along with her glance, reaches toward me across the uncut grass and wildflowers. She stands elevated, raised above the commonplace in life. I am not only the recipient of her gaze, I am also the small boy pictured behind her, overpowered by her mysterious presence.

Nature, music, and painting, along with literature, poetry, theater, dance, sculpture, opera, architecture, taste, touch—all the remarkable modalities of beauty that inspire my life—could I live without them? Yes, I could live as a purely mechanical entity—a fleshy machine of pumps, bellows, pipes, levers, tanks, and chemical reactions—but mine would be an impoverished life, one barren of loveliness, empty of meaning, devoid of purpose. Where did esthetic sensibility, the drive to create, the urge to look, hear, taste, and feel that which is pleasing—where did it come from? Why is it part of my life?

Among biologists, there is growing interest in the notion of beauty and its appreciation. Charles Darwin himself was interested and believed that non-human animals were capable of appreciating beauty. This belief formed the basis of his theory of sexual selection, which contrasted with his better known theory of natural selection. According to Darwin, sexual selection is primarily a two-pronged process that includes both competition among males for females, and pickiness on the part of females for attractive males. "A great number of male animals," opined Darwin, "have been rendered beautiful for beauty's sake."[5] While his notion of male-male competition found ready support in male-dominated Victorian society, many readers

---

5. Quoted by Jabr, "How Beauty Is Making Scientists Rethink Evolution."

panned Darwin's belief that female animals choose males simply on the basis of beauty—there must be a more utilitarian reason, critics argued.[6]

Richard Prum, a prominent ornithologist at Yale University, has revitalized Darwin's belief in beauty for beauty's sake. According to Prum, animals are drawn to beauty, not because beauty communicates information about other attributes like health or reproductive vigor, but because animals simply like what is beautiful. Prum considers the subjective experience of desire in response to beauty to be an important component of the sexual lives of both humans and nonhumans. Decisions are made on the basis of this desire, decisions that impact mate choice and thus the genetic makeup of the next generation. This focus on subjective experience, however, has earned Plum the ire of other biologists who believe it is impossible to use science to explore the subjective appreciation of beauty in the minds of animals. But Prum cheerfully presses on with what many consider an outdated Darwinian view.[7]

I don't know if Prum is correct, but I do know that beauty and its appreciation serve as essential, subjective ingredients for joy in my life, and in the lives of most humans. Along with all other life forms, I could live at some level without the existence of beauty, but life without it would be an impoverished one. Despite the fact that esthetics is an unnecessary component of biological existence, it contributes in a large way to my satisfaction and possibly to the satisfaction of nonhuman animals. But why does it exist if it is unnecessary?

"WE HOLD THESE TRUTHS to be self-evident, that all Men are created equal, that they are endowed by their Creator with certain unalienable Rights, that among these are Life, Liberty and the pursuit of Happiness."[8]

The second sentence of the United States Declaration of Independence is one of the most familiar in the English language. The fact that this "self-evident" truth does not translate into equal rights and opportunities for all people—men, women, whites, and nonwhites—is a sad reminder that our loftiest aspirations often fail to be realized in practical life. Indeed, Thomas Jefferson, who crafted the first draft of this famous document, was himself a slave owner.[9] Nonetheless, I find it intriguing that the United States of America was founded on the principle of human equality, and that other nations have adopted similar statements of egalitarian idealism.

6. Prum, *The Evolution of Beauty*, 17–53.
7. Prum, *The Evolution of Beauty*, 54–88.
8. *The Formation of the Union*, 26.
9. Bailey, *The American Pageant*, 115.

There is hardly anything more obvious, however, than the fact that we humans are decidedly *not* equal. We exhibit nearly limitless diversity in terms of personal characteristics, strengths, weaknesses, talents, abilities, and potential. Our inequalities become obvious when teaching a class, during a summer visit to the beach, or while strolling down a city sidewalk. People are quick, slow, tall, short, wide, narrow, dark, light, young, and old. Some folks seem preternaturally happy, while others remain in a constant state of gloom or anxiety. People are either easy to get along with or cantankerous. Colleagues may be highly organized or seemingly random. Mozart, the musician, was composing at age five, and Ted Kaczynski, the "Unabomber," was accepted at Harvard at age sixteen. Some children are born developmentally disabled, whereas others are born savants or picture perfect. "One size" does not "fit all." Human diversity is one of the facts of life that makes life colorful, pathetic, intriguing, and scary.

It is not "self-evident" that "all men are created equal"—*unless*, that is, we're thinking about human value. Indeed, the concept that all human life is equally valuable constitutes a basic assumption on the part of most ethicists. Although practical life and death decisions are made difficult by variables such as age, health, personal responsibility, etc., the theoretical principle that all human life is of equal, intrinsic worth is behind all medical practice, search-and-rescue operations, ambulance services, and other aspects of human society. Where does this sentiment come from? Could natural selection have created it? For what reason? For what advantage? It's not clear to me that natural selection, or any other evolutionary process, could have generated such an unselfish concept as egalitarianism.

FOR TWENTY YEARS I taught an undergraduate course in general genetics, and for two of those years a course in molecular genetics. Genetics is a foundational topic in life science, one that explains a great deal about living things, especially the process of information transfer and the alteration of that information over time. The concepts of genetics excite me.

Unlike some beginning biology courses, which feature boring lists of terms to memorize, genetics is rooted in principles of mathematics, statistics, and biochemistry. The logical progression of ideas involved in genetics makes it a joy to teach. Fascinating storylines in the science capture one's imagination.

The central player in these stories is deoxyribonucleic acid—DNA. Most people are at least superficially acquainted with DNA, the molecule with the beautiful double helical structure discovered by Rosalind Franklin, James Watson, and Francis Crick in the early 1950s. If you took a long, weakly constructed ladder and twisted the vertical rails around one another, you would form a rough model of the double helix.

The two rails of the DNA molecular ladder are comprised of a string of organic molecules called nucleotides, and each rung consists of two "nitrogen bases," molecules extending toward and loosely tied to one other by a weak chemical bond. These chemical bonds keep the two rails, with their nitrogen bases, zipped together. The sequence of nitrogen bases, of which there are four (A, T, C, and G), create the "genetic code." Remarkably, this same code, variously arranged, makes a bacterium a bacterium, an oak tree an oak tree, and a human being a human being.

In order for the genetic code to shape and continue life, it needs to replicate itself and provide instructions for the manufacture of the myriad of biochemicals that quicken life. Accomplishment of all this involves a maze of processes still being worked out. The basics, however, are well understood.

DNA "replication" is the process by which DNA makes copies of itself for new generations of cells. Manufacturing DNA for regular cells versus reproductive cells requires somewhat different processes ("mitosis" versus "meiosis"), but this detail need not concern us here.

DNA serves as a template for the "transcription" of another, quite similar molecule, ribonucleic acid—RNA. RNA, in turn, serves as a template for the "translation" of proteins from the RNA code. Proteins exhibit virtually limitless variety and form body frameworks, act as hormones, function as antibodies, and serve as enzymes. DNA replication, RNA transcription, and protein translation are intricate, precise, and mindboggling. A vast toolbox of enzymes and other molecules is involved in these processes.

All these processes depend on enzymes to work—enzymes that are the end products of the very manufacturing processes they control. This is a chicken-and-egg puzzle for molecular evolutionists who rightly wonder which came first, DNA, RNA, or enzymes. Some tentative answers have been proposed, but huge leaps of "faith" are necessary to envision them— leaps no less significant than those made by members of the "intelligent design" community. From whatever perspective, it is very difficult for me imagine how all this intricate molecular machinery—which is essentially the same in bacteria, oak trees, and humans—could have come about by pure chance.[10]

---

10. Basic principles concerning DNA, RNA, proteins, and their functions can be found in any general biology text. For an excellent review of theories and speculations regarding an evolutionary origin of life, see Herron and Freeman, *Evolutionary Analysis*, 645–90.

IF THERE IS MEANING and purpose to life, if there is someone or something behind existence, if there is reason for optimism and hope, how much can I understand about who or what might be behind all this? Given the tremendous variety of conflicting religious beliefs and the limitation of human understanding, I think there is very little we can know and understand objectively. Holy books like the Bible are profound attempts to reach out to an essence beyond. But none of these works provides an objective treatise on the nature of that ineffable essence.

I am not convinced, however, that objective knowledge would provide an adequate basis for religious experience and faith. As Karen Armstrong has noted, "it was a modern Western fallacy, dating only from the eighteenth century, to equate faith with accepting certain intellectual propositions about God." Instead, she says, faith is "the cultivation of a conviction that life had some ultimate meaning and value."[11] Martin Luther would have agreed. "Faith does not require information, knowledge and certainty," he preached, "but a free surrender and a joyful bet on [God's] unfelt, untried and unknown goodness."[12] This view contrasts starkly with the stance of today's young-age creationists who believe that faith requires belief in a short-term chronology, a worldwide flood, and limited evolutionary change, claims concerning physical reality which have been roundly rejected on the basis of vast accumulations of scientific evidence.

While I think there is room for doctrine as a way of summarizing what groups of people perceive about transcendent reality, when doctrine is defined as "Truth," we run into trouble. Doctrine too often promotes arrogance instead of humility, divides rather than unites, makes enemies instead of friends. It is a sad fact of history that many of the world's armed conflicts have been rooted in doctrinal differences. I once heard Hans Küng, the renowned Swiss Catholic theologian, give a talk entitled "No World Peace without Religious Peace." Doctrine can be, and often is, toxic.

WE LIVE IN A wide, wide world with an amazing variety of cultures, histories, and ethical commitments. I grew up in a Christian culture with Christian parents and Christian education. It is no surprise, then, that I am a follower of the teachings of Jesus. In a classical sense this makes me a Christian. Unfortunately, in recent years the term "Christian" has been co-opted by people who oppose the very essence of Jesus' challenging teachings to love one's enemies, to minister to the poor, and to make peace. They are bedazzled by fast-talking salesmen who plunder the poor, preach

---

11. Armstrong, *The Spiral Staircase*, 292.
12. Quoted in Armstrong, *A History of God*, 278.

a "Prosperity Gospel," and lead dissolute lives. They refuse to acknowledge the findings of science—that climate change is real, vaccinations prevent disease, and dinosaurs and people never walked the earth together. In view of these distortions, I prefer to simply call myself a follower of Jesus.

I am on a voyage of discovery.[13] I believe in beauty, curiosity, generosity, kindness, hope, and love. I possess deep commitments to my family, my friends, my science, and my faith in a transcendent, undefinable reality I call God. I believe in living a quality life, in assuming responsibility, and in communicating and behaving with integrity. I believe in trying to make the world a better place, ecologically, socially, and spiritually. I refuse to categorize myself. As I've indicated, I'm not a young-age creationist, flood geologist, or biblical literalist, but neither am I an atheist, deist, materialist, theistic evolutionist, or many of the other philosophical "-ists." Self-categorization limits one's ability to explore life with integrity, and to adjust one's outlook responsibly when faced with new information, novel ideas, and fresh experiences.

When a person takes a lifelong voyage of discovery, conflicts can arise with people who want you to agree with their views. This is a natural human response—good people want the people they love and respect to be part of their belief system, their clan. While we cannot live a fulfilled life if we constantly strive to fulfill the wishes of others, we can relate to others with kindness, understanding, and acceptance.

I have a young-age creationist friend who is deeply committed to flood geology and a recent six-day creation. In terms of earth history perspectives we could not be more dissimilar. Yet we treat each other with courtesy, kindness, and respect. I want him to thrive, and I'm sure he feels the same way about me. He has stood up for me when it would have been politically advantageous to go along with the crowd and be critical. I have done the same for him. This, I believe, is how peace is achieved in a world of bitter division. I don't need to give up my principles in order to be kind and accepting of people who think and believe differently than I. Each of us experiences a limited understanding of reality.

---

13. Dunne, *Time and Myth*, 37. Dunne writes, "The question for me is not 'Is there a God?' so much as 'What is God?' The question 'Is there a God?' supposes that one already understands what God would be if there were a God. It supposes that no voyage of discovery is necessary. The question 'What is God?' on the contrary, calls for a voyage of discovery, for a whole lifetime of discovery. As I explore the height and the depth and the breadth of life, each discovery I make about life is a discovery about God, each is a step with God, a step toward God."

IN VIEW OF WHAT I have shared in this book, I ask myself, do I have faith? Hebrews 11:1 declares faith to be "the substance of things *hoped for*, the evidence of things *not seen*." Faith, then, has nothing to do with things I can measure, count, compare, and evaluate—dinosaurs, plate tectonics, radiometric dates, volcanoes, fossil sequences, ecological relationships, biogeographic distribution patterns, evolution, and the like. No, faith reaches out in hope toward what I cannot see, to an undefinable, ineffable, transcendent reality, yet a reality that also exists deep within me and in all of life. It involves a hope that things can and will be better, even though at this moment they may not be trending in that direction. Faith does not ask me to believe things which evidence suggests are unlikely or untrue—"idols of fundamentalism," Karen Armstrong calls them.[14] Instead, faith bids me to receive grace and to humbly open my life to goodness, beauty, love, and behave responsibly toward the rest of creation. I still have a long way to travel, but my journey so far, as well as what remains, has been and will be made with faith.

The University of Notre Dame is located just a few minutes south of where I live. When I'm on campus, I enjoy visiting the Jordan Hall of Science, Notre Dame's largest building devoted to undergraduate education. Upon entering the building, I'm enveloped by what appears to be the nave of an enormous Gothic cathedral, except there are no pews and there is no chancel. Along the walls are displays depicting the history of the universe and life as understood by the best of contemporary science. As I raise my eyes above the displays, however, I am moved by the sight of a simple crucifix which hangs on the wall above. The message to me is profound: Life and its history are complex, even problematic, but above all that we know and understand about the past and present, there exists a reality that transcends the rational, yet one with which we can participate in faith.

It is in this context that I wish to conclude with a favorite text, one that makes clear to me how I should think and act in a world of unanswered questions, conflicting views, and divided allegiances. It is a familiar passage, one that encourages me to recall what is most important in this life-long voyage of discovery:

> "He has told you, O mortal, what is good; and what does the LORD require of you but to do justice, and to love kindness, and to walk humbly with your God?" (Mic 6:8, NRSV).

If there is a solution to the puzzles that complicate my quest for meaning, purpose, and understanding, it is to cultivate a resilient life, a life

---

14. Armstrong, *A History of God*, 399.

committed to integrity, open to evidence, and guided by the principles of justice, mercy, humility, and faith. This is how I find personal peace and joy within a miraculous, but often bewildering, universe.

Acknowledgments

I am indebted to the host of people who have stimulated my thought, corrected my mistakes, and supported my maturation as a scholar and human being. I am particularly grateful to my late parents, James L Hayward, Sr. and Jane B. Hayward, who fostered my educational pursuits from first grade through graduate school. They, like others who survived the Great Depression, were pragmatic folk. Yet they nurtured values in me that extended far beyond the pragmatic—values of integrity, industry, and faith. If they were alive today they would take exception with some of my assumptions and conclusions, but without their love and provision this book would not have been written.

Unnumbered teachers, students, writers, friends, and family members have influenced my thinking. I particularly wish to acknowledge the influence of John Baldwin, Deborah Berecz, John Berecz, Gerald Bryant, Brian Bull, Donald Casebolt, Dale Clayton, Richard Coffen, Joseph Galusha, Glen Greenwalt, Carrie Grellmann, David Grellmann, Jerry Gladson, Cheryl Hayward, Shandelle Henson, the late Karl Hirsch, Billy Hughes, Harold James, Warren Johns, Gene Johnson, Asta LaBianca, Øystein LaBianca, the late Gary Land, John McLarty, Larry McCloskey, Ronald Numbers, Juanita Ritland, the late Richard Ritland, Art Robertson, Clark Rowland, John Stout, Abraham Terian, Richard Tkachuck, the late Joe Willey, Tom Wehtje, and Dennis Woodland. Some of these individuals hold or held views very different from my own, but each of them has taught me valuable perspectives and lessons.

John Berecz, Donald Casebolt, Beverly Cobb, Cheryl Hayward, John Hayward, Calvin Hill, Gene Johnson, Øystein LaBianca, Ronald Numbers, Ken Tkachuck, Richard Tkachuck, Tom Wehtje, and the late Joe Willey read all or parts of the manuscript and offered feedback which encouraged me to continue the project. Penny Tkachuck and Richard Coffen, both perceptive readers and gifted writers, provided numerous and helpful comments and suggestions on early drafts of the manuscript.

I owe a large debt of gratitude to Shandelle Henson, my wife, research colleague, and editor-in-chief of *Natural Resource Modeling*, who read through the manuscript several times and provided insightful criticism, advice, and support every step of the way. Her red-inked comments like "weak sentence," "awkward progression," "doesn't make sense," "redundant," and "find a different word" made the text flow more logically and smoothly than otherwise would have been the case.

It has been a pleasure to work with the fine professionals at Wipf & Stock. I am especially grateful to Matthew Wimer, Editorial Production Manager, and Daniel Lanning, Editorial Administrator, who expertly guided this project through to publication. I have appreciated their proficiency, timely feedback, and advice.

Finally, over the decades, members of my family have provided generous support through the joys and perils of life. They are a most loving, forgiving, and encouraging bunch, despite the fact that too often I have been physically present but emotionally distant, immersed in yet another of my projects. In ways too many to enumerate, they have shaped my thoughts, commitments, and perspectives. Shandelle, Cheryl, and Shanna—thank you. I am truly grateful to you.

Bibliography

Aamodt, Terrie Dopp. *Bold Venture: A History of Walla Walla College*. College Place, WA: The College, 1992.
Abelson, Philip H. "Creationism and the Age of the Earth." *Science* 215 (January 8, 1982) 119.
———. "Paleobiochemistry." *Scientific American* 195 (July 1956) 83–92.
"About Us." Hewitt Homeschooling. https://hewittlearning.org/about-us/.
Allee, W. C., and Karl P. Schmidt. *Ecological Animal Geography*. New York: Wiley, 1951.
Allégre, Claude. *The Behavior of the Earth: Continental and Seafloor Mobility*. Translated by Deborah Kurmes Van Dam. Cambridge, MA: Harvard University Press, 1988.
Allen, Sarah Addison. *The Girl Who Chased the Moon: A Novel*. New York: Bantam, 2010.
Alley, Richard B. *The Two-Mile Time Machine: Ice Cores, Abrupt Climate Change, and Our Future*. Princeton, NJ: Princeton University Press, 2000.
Alt, David, and Donald W. Hyndman. *Northwest Exposures: A Geologic Story of the Northwest*. Missoula, MT: Mountain, 1995.
Amlaner, Charles J., Jr., and John F. Stout. "Aggressive Communication by *Larus glaucescens*. Part VI: Interactions of Territory Residents with a Remotely Controled, Locomotory Model." *Behaviour* 66 (1978) 223–51.
Anderson, Bernhard W. "From Analysis to Synthesis: The Interpretation of Genesis 1–11." *Journal of Biblical Literature* 97 (1978) 23–39.
Anderson, Godfrey T. "Sectarianism and Organization 1846–1864." In *Adventism in America*, edited by Gary Land, 36–65. Grand Rapids, MI: Eerdmans, 1986.
Anderson, O. Roger. *Comparative Protozoology: Ecology, Physiology, Life History*. New York: Springer-Verlag, 1988.
Andrews, J. N. *History of the Sabbath and First Day of the Week*. 3rd ed. Battle Creek, MI: Review & Herald, 1887.
Anonymous. "Karl Hirsch: Anything but Ordinary." *Rockwell News* 11 (February 1, 1985) 2–3.
———. "Patient Donates to Hospital Building Program." *Atlantic Union Gleaner* 67 (March 19, 1968) 16.
———. "Prophet or Plagiarist?" *Time* 108 (August 2, 1976), 43.
———. *Seventh-day Adventists Believe . . .: A Biblical Exposition of 27 Fundamental Doctrines*. Washington, DC: Ministerial Association, General Conference of Seventh-day Adventists, 1988.
Armstrong, Karen. *A History of God: The 4,000-Year Quest of Judaism, Christianity and Islam*. New York: Ballantine, 1993.

———. *The Spiral Staircase: My Climb out of Darkness*. New York: Knopf, 2004.

———. *Through the Narrow Gate: A Memoir of Spiritual Discovery*. New York: Book-of-the-Month Club, 1994.

Atkins, Gordon J., et al. "Copulation Song Coordinates Timing of Head-Tossing and Mounting Behaviors in Neighboring Glaucous-winged Gulls." *Wilson Journal of Ornithology* 129 (2017) 560–67.

———. "How Do Gulls Synchronize Their Ovipositions?" Manuscript in preparation.

Avnimelech, M. "Dinosaur Tracks in the Lower Cenomanian of Jerusalem." *Nature* 196 (1962) 264.

Bailey, Thomas A. *The American Pageant: A History of the Republic*. 4th ed. Lexington, MA: Heath, 1971.

Barash, David. *The Whisperings Within: Evolution and the Origin of Human Nature*. New York: Harper & Row, 1979.

Barbour, R. A. "Anatomy of Marsupials." In *The Biology of Marsupials*, edited by Barnard Stonehouse and Desmond Gilmore, 237–72. Baltimore, MD: University Park, 1977.

Barnes, Ross O. "Thermal Consequences of a Short Time Scale for Sea-Floor Spreading." *Perspectives on Science and the Christian Faith* 32 (June, 1980) 123–25.

Bauer, David "Assistant Seminary Dean Approved." *Lake Union Herald* 65 (June 19, 1973) 16.

———. "Horn Appointed Dean of Seminary." *Lake Union Herald* 65 (March 6, 1973) 16.

———. "Three New Scholarships Endowed at Andrews." *Lake Union Herald* 65 (February 27, 1973) 8.

Begon, Michael, et al. *Ecology: From Individuals to Ecosystems*. 4th ed. Malden, MA: Blackwell, 2006) xi.

Behe, Michael J. *Darwin's Black Box: The Biochemical Challenge to Evolution*. New York: The Free Press, 1996.

———. "Molecular Machines—Experimental Support for the Design Inference." Talk for the C. S. Lewis Society, summer 1994 (cited by Miller. *Finding Darwin's God*. 140).

Benedict, Warren V. *History of White Pine Blister Rust Control—A Personal Account*. Washington, DC: U.S. Department of Agriculture, Forest Service, 1981.

Benn, Douglas I., and David J. A. Evans. *Glaciers & Glaciation*. London, UK: Hodder Education, 2007.

Benton, Roy. "Odyssey of an Adventist Creationist." *Spectrum* 15 (August, 1984) 46–53.

Bird, Roland T. "Thunder in His Footsteps." *Natural History* 43 (May, 1939) 254–61.

Birkhead, Tim, et al. *Ten Thousand Birds: Ornithology since Darwin*. Princeton, NJ: Princeton University Press, 2014.

Bishop, Ellen Morris. *In Search of Ancient Oregon: A Geological and Natural History*. Portland, OR: Timber, 2003, 78–167.

Bond, Gerard, et al. "Correlations between Climate Records from North Atlantic Sediments and Greenland Ice." *Nature* 365 (1993) 143–47.

Booth, Ernest S. *Biology, the Story of Life*. Mountain View, CA: Pacific, 1950.

———. *How to Know the Mammals*. Dubuque, IA: W. C. Brown, 1961.

Bottomley, Richard J. "Age Dating of Rocks." *Spectrum* 27 (Autumn, 1999) 44–47.

Bradley, Sculley, et al. *The American Tradition in Literature*. Vol. 1 and 2. 3rd ed. New York: Norton, 1967.

Brand, Leonard. *Faith, Reason, and Earth History: A Paradigm of Earth and Biological Origins by Intelligent Design.* Berrien Springs, MI: Andrews University Press, 1997.

———. "Field and Laboratory Studies on the Coconino Sandstone (Permian) Vertebrate Footprints and Their Paleoecological Implications." *Palaeogeography Palaeoclimatology Palaeoecology* 28 (December, 1979) 25–38.

———. "Fossil Vertebrate Footprints in the Coconino Sandstone (Permian) of Northern Arizona: Evidence of Underwater Origin." *Geology* 20 (December, 1991) 668–70.

———. "The Vocal Repertoire of Chipmunks (Genus *Eutamias*) in California." *Animal Behaviour* 24 (May, 1976) 319–35.

———. "Vocalizations and Behavior of the Chipmunks (Genus *Eutamias*) in California." PhD diss., Cornell University, 1970.

Brand, Leonard, and Arthur Chadwick. *Faith, Reason, & Earth History: A Paradigm of Earth and Biological Origins by Intelligent Design.* 3rd ed. Berrien Springs, MI: Andrews University Press, 2016.

Brand, Leonard R., et al. "Fossil Whale Preservation Implies High Diatom Accumulation Rate in the Miocene-Pliocene Pisco Formation of Peru." *Geology* 32:165–68.

Briggs, J. C. *Biogeography and Plate Tectonics.* Amsterdam, Netherlands: Elsevier, 1987.

Brown, James H., and Arthur C. Gibson. *Biogeography.* St. Louis, MO: Mosby, 1983.

Brown, R. H. "Can Tree Rings Be Used to Calibrate Radiocarbon Dates?" *Origins* 22 (1999) 47–52.

———. "Correlation of C-14 Age with the Biblical Time Scale." *Origins* 17 (1990) 56–65.

———. "Ion Formation and Decay in a Mercury Resonance Cell as Evidenced by Electrical Image Forces." PhD diss., University of Washington, 1950.

———. "R. H. Brown Comments on Radioactive Age Panel." *Report of the Fifth Quadennial* [sic] *Session of the Applied Arts and Sciences.* Lincoln, NE, August 22–28, 1956, 22–24.

———. "Radiocarbon Dating." In *Creation—Accident or Design?* by Harold G. Coffin, 299–316. Washington, DC: Review and Herald, 1969.

———. "Radioactive Time Clocks." In *Creation—Accident or Design?* by Harold G. Coffin, 273–96. Washington, DC: Review and Herald, 1969.

———. "Scientific Creationism?" *Origins* (1981) 57–58.

Brusca, Richard C. "Tongue Replacement in a Marine Fish (*Lutjanus guttatus*) by a Parasitic Isopod (Crustacea: Isopoda)." *Copeia* 1983 (1983) 813–16.

Bull, Brian, and Fritz Guy. *God, Land, and the Great Flood: Hearing the Story with 21st-Century Christian Ears.* Roseville, CA: Adventist Forum, 2017.

———. *God, Sky & Land: Genesis 1 as the Hebrews Heard It.* Roseville, CA: Adventist Forum, 2011.

———. *God, the Misreading of Genesis, and the Surprisingly Good News.* Roseville, CA: Adventist Forum, 2019.

Bull, Malcolm, and Keith Lockhart. *Seeking a Sanctuary: Seventh-day Adventism and the American Dream.* 2nd ed. Bloomington, IN: Indiana University Press, 2007.

Bullard, Fred M. *Volcanoes of the Earth.* Revised ed. Austin, TX: University of Texas Press, 1976.

Burdick, Clifford L. "Ararat—The Mother of Mountains." *Creation Research Society 1967 Annual* 4 (1967) 5–12.

———. "Were the First Americans Giants? More Huge Footprints Discovered." *Signs of the Times* (February, 1958) 23–24
Butler, Jonathan. "The Historian as Heretic." In *Prophetess of Health*, by Ronald L. Numbers, 3rd ed. Grand Rapids, MI: Eerdmans, 2008.
———. "The Making of a New Order: Millerism and the Origins of Seventh-day Adventism." In *The Disappointed: Millerism and Millenarianism in the Nineteenth Century*, edited by Ronald L. Numbers and Jonathan M. Butler, 189–208. Bloomington, IN: Indiana University Press, 1987.
———. "Seventh-day Adventist Historiography: A Work in Progress." *Church History* 87 (March, 2018) 149–66.
Cahalane, Victor H. *Mammals of North America*. New York: Macmillan, 1947.
Cain, Susan. *Quiet: The Power of Introverts in a World that Can't Stop Talking*. New York: Crown, 2012.
Campbell, Sam. *How's Inky? A Porcupine and His Pals Offer Some Highlights on Happiness*. Indianapolis, IN: Bobbs-Merrill, 1943.
———. *Natures Messages: A Book of Wilderness Wisdom*. New York: Rand McNally, 1952.
"Campus Ethnic Diversity." *U.S. News & World Report*. https://www.usnews.com/best-colleges/rankings/national-universities/campus-ethnic-diversity.
Camus, Albert. *The Stranger*. Translated from the French by Stuart Gilbert. New York: Vintage, 1946.
Canadian Centre for Home Education. "Raymond & Dorothy Moore: Homeschool Pioneers." https://cche.ca/raymond-dorothy-moore-homeschool-pioneers/
Carpenter, Kenneth. *Eggs, Nests, and Baby Dinosaurs: A Look at Dinosaur Reproduction*. Bloomington, IN: Indiana University Press, 1999.
Carpenter, Kenneth, et al. "Introduction." In *Dinosaur Eggs and Babies*, edited by Kenneth Carpenter et al., 1–11. Cambridge, UK: Cambridge University Press, 1994.
"Certificate of Baptism," Takoma Park, MD: General Conference of Seventh-day Adventists n.d.
Chadwick, Arthur V. "Precambrian Pollen in the Grand Canyon—A Reexamination." *Origins* 8 (1981) 7–12.
Charles Darwin to J. D. Hooker, July 13, 1856. Darwin Correspondence Project. https://www.darwinproject.ac.uk/letter/?docId=letters/DCP-LETT-1924.xml;query=what%20a%20book%20a%20devil%27s%20chaplain%20might%20write;brand=default;hit.rank=1#hit.rank1.
Charwat, Elaine, "'God Created, Linnaeus Ordered' . . . and Linnaeus Link Delivers." *CILIP Update* (August, 2013) 34–36.
Chen, Jun-Yuan, et al. "Small Bilaterian Fossils from 40 to 55 Million Years before the Cambrian." *Science* 305 (July 9, 2004) 218–22.
Chiappe, Luis, and Meng Qingjin. *Birds of Stone: Chinese Avian Fossils from the Age of Dinosaurs*. Baltimore, MD: Johns Hopkins University Press, 2016.
Chiappe, Luis, et al. "Sauropod Eggs and Embryos from the Late Cretaceous of Patagonia." In *First International Symposium on Dinosaur Eggs and Babies*, edited by A. M. Bravo and T. Reyes, 23–29. Isona, Spain, 2000.
Christiansen, Per, and Niels Bonde. "A New Species of Gigantic Mosasaur from the Late Cretaceous of Israel." *Journal of Vertebrate Paleontology* 22 (2002) 629–44.

Church of the Ascension in the City of New York. "Parish History." https://ascensionnyc.org/history/.
Churchill, Winston. "Speech in the House of Commons, May 17, 1916." https://api.parliament.uk/historic-hansard/commons/1916/may/17/royal-assent#column_1578.
Clague, David A., and G. Brent Dalrymple. "The Hawaiian-Emperor Volcanic Chain: Part I: Geologic Evolution." In *Volcanism in Hawaii*, edited by Robert W. Decker, US Geological Survey Paper 1350 (1987) 5–54.
Clark, Harold W. *Genes and Genesis*. Mountain View, CA: Pacific Press, 1940.
———. *The New Diluvialism*. Angwin, CA: Science Publications, 1946.
———. *Skylines and Detours*. Washington, DC: Review and Herald, 1959.
Colbert, Edwin H. *Evolution of the Vertebrates: A History of the Backboned Animals through Time*. New York: Wiley, 1964.
Coffin, Harold. *Creation—Accident or Design?* Washington, DC: Review and Herald Publishing Association, 1969.
———. "A Preliminary Report on the Carboniferous of Nova Scotia." Unpublished manuscript, Geoscience Research Institute, Berrien Springs, Michigan, 1967.
———. "Research on the Classic Joggins Petrified Trees." *Creation Research Society Annual* 6 (June, 1969) 35–44, 70.
Coghlan, Andy. "Monkey Seen Caring for Dying Mate then Grieving after She Dies." *NewScientist*, May 23, 2016. https://www.newscientist.com/article/2089522-monkey-seen-caring-for-dying-mate-then-grieving-after-she-dies/.
Colbert, Edwin H., and Michael Morales. *Evolution of the Vertebrates: A History of the Backboned Animals through Time*. 4th ed. New York: Wiley, 1991.
Cole, Bruce. "The Danger of Historical Amnesia: A Conversation with David McCullough." *Humanities* 23 (July/August, 2002) 4.
"College Clinic." *Southwestern Union Recorder* 62 (September 11, 1963) 10.
Colson, F. H., and G. H. Whitaker, translators. *Philo, Volume I*. Cambridge, MA: Harvard University Press, 1929.
Connolly, John. *The Book of Lost Things*. New York: Simon & Schuster, 2006.
Conover, M. R., et al. "Female-Female Pairs and Other Unusual Reproductive Associations in Ring-billed and California Gulls." *The Auk* 96 (1979) 6–9.
Cook, Melvin A. "William J. Meister Discovery of Human Footprint with Trilobites in a Cambrian Formation of Western Utah." *Creation Research Society Quarterly* 5 (December, 1968) 97.
Coulson, Ken P., and Leonard R. Brand. "Lithistid Sponge-Microbial Reef-Building Communities Construct Laminated, Upper Cambrian (Furongian) 'Stromatolites.'" *Palaios* 31 (June, 2016) 358–70.
Cushing, J. M., et al. *Chaos in Ecology: Experimental Nonlinear Dynamics*. San Diego, CA: Academic Press, 2003.
Cutbill, John Louis, and Brian Michael Funnell. "Numerical Analysis of the Fossil Record." In *The Fossil Record: A Symposium with Documentation*, edited by W. B. Harland, et al., 791–820. London, UK: Geological Society of London, 1967.
Daeschler, Edward B., et al. "A Devonian Tetrapod-Like Fish and the Evolution of the Tetrapod Body Plan." *Nature* 440 (April 6, 2006) 757–63.
Dalrymple, G. Brent. *The Age of the Earth*. Stanford, CA: Stanford University Press, 1991.
Damsteegt, P. Gerard. *Foundations of the Seventh-day Adventist Message and Mission*. Grand Rapids, MI: William B. Eerdmans, 1977.

Darlington, Philip J. *Zoogeography: The Geographical Distribution of Animals.* New York: Wiley, 1965.
Dart, John. "Seventh-day Adventist Prophet White Is Called Plagiarist." *Los Angeles Times,* November 7, 1980.
Darwin, Charles. *On the Origin of Species.* Edited with an introduction and notes by Gillian Beer. Oxford, UK: Oxford University Press, 2008.
Darwin, Charles, to J. D. Hooker, July 13, 1856, Darwin Correspondence Project. https://www.darwinproject.ac.uk/letter/DCP-LETT-1924.xml.
Davis, William B. *The Mammals of Texas.* Austin, TX: Texas Game and Fish Commission, 1960.
DeMets, Charles, et al. "Geologically Current Plate Motions." *Geophysical Journal International* 181 (2010) 1–80.
Dethier, D. P., et al. "Late Wisconsinan Glaciomarine Deposition and Isostatic Rebound, Northern Puget Lowland, Washington." *GSA Bulletin* 105 (1995) 1288–1303.
Dillard, Annie. *An American Childhood.* New York: Harper & Row, 1987.
Dolph, James Allan, and David Gibson. "Recent Discovery of an Extensive Stromatolite Outcrop in the Middle Cambrian Pika Formation, Lake Helen-Lake Katherine Area, Banff National Park." Abstract, Back to Exploration, 2008 CSPG CSEG CWLS Convention. http://www.searchanddiscovery.com/pdfz/abstracts/pdf/2013/90170cspg/abstracts/ndx_dolph.pdf.html.
Downing, Lawrence. "The Art and Practice of Biblical Proof-Texting." *Adventist Today,* January 22, 2017. https://atoday.org/the-art-and-practice-of-biblical-proof-texting/.
Dunbar, Carl O., and Karl M. Waagé, *Historical Geology.* 3rd ed. New York: Wiley, 1969.
Dunne, John S. *Time and Myth: A Meditation on Storytelling as an Exploration of Life and Death.* Notre Dame, IN: University of Notre Dame Press, 1973.
Easterbrook, Don J. "Stratigraphy and Chronology of Quaternary Deposits of the Puget Lowland and Olympic Mountains of Washington and the Cascade Mountains of Washington and Oregon." *Quaternary Science Reviews* 5 (1986) 145–59.
EGW Writings. "Some Hermeneutical Principles Bearing on the Ellen G. White Writings." https://m.egwwritings.org/en/book/699.190#192.
Eiseley, Loren. *Darwin's Century: Evolution and the Men Who Discovered It.* New York: Doubleday, 1958.
———. *The Night Country.* New York: Charles Scribner's Sons, 1971.
Einstein, Albert. *The Essential Einstein: His Greatest Works.* New York: Penguin, 2008.
Einstein, Albert, and Alice Calaprice. *The Ultimate Quotable Einstein.* Princeton, NJ: Princeton University Press, 2011.
Ellen G. White Estate. *Comprehensive Index to the Writings of Ellen G. White.* Three volumes. Mountain View, CA: Pacific Press, 1962.
———. "Ellen G. White Statements Relating to Geology and Earth Sciences." Unpublished manuscript, Washington, DC, March, 1982
———. *The Spirit of Prophecy Treasure Chest: An Advent Source Collection of Materials Relating to the Gift of Prophecy in the Remnant Church and the Life and Ministry of Ellen G. White.* Glendale, CA: Prophetic Guidance School of the Voice of Prophecy, 1960.
Elwood, Robert W., and Laura Adams. "Electric Shock Causes Physiological Stress Responses in Shore Crabs, Consistent with Prediction of Pain." *Biology Letters* (November 1, 2015). 11:20150800. http://dx.doi.org/10.1098/rsbl.2015.0800.

Emerson, Ralph Waldo. "Nature." In *The American Tradition in Literature*, Vol. 1, 3rd ed., edited by Sculley Bradley et al., 1064-98. New York: Norton, 1967.
In *Galileo Goes to Jail and Other Myths about Science and Religion*, edited by Ronald L. Numbers, 68–78. Boston, MA: Harvard University Press, 2009.
Emery, Kenneth O. "Weathering of the Great Pyramid." *Journal of Sedimentary Research* 30 (1960) 140–43.
Erickson, Gregory M., et al. "Giantism and Comparative Life-History Parameters of Tyrannosaurid Dinosaurs." *Nature* 430 (August 12, 2004) 772–75.
Evans, Rachel Held. *Evolving in Monkey Town: How a Girl Who Knew All the Answers Learned to Ask the Questions.* Grand Rapids, MI: Zondervan Education, 2010.
Farlow, J. O., et al. "Dinosaur Tracksites of the Paluxy River Valley (Glen Rose Formation, Lower Cretaceous), Dinosaur Valley State Park, Somervell County, Texas." *Jornadas Internacionales sobre Paleontología de Dinosaurios y su Entorno*, 2012, Salas de los Infantes, Burgos, Spain. https://www.researchgate.net/publication/230897131_Dinosaur_Tracksites_of_the_Paluxy_River_Valley_Glen_Rose_Formation_Lower_Cretaceous_Dinosaur_Valley_State_Park_Somervell_County_Texas.
Finley, Bruce. "'Addition' Hatched from Dinosaur Egg." *The Denver Post* (May 15, 1989) 1B–2B.
Finocchiaro, Maurice A. "That Galileo Was Imprisoned and Tortured for Advocating Copernicanism." In *Galileo Goes to Jail and Other Myths about Science and Religion*, edited by Ronald L. Numbers, 68–78. Boston, MA: Harvard University Press, 2009.
Foelix, Rainer F. *Biology of Spiders*. 3rd ed. Oxford, UK: Oxford University Press, 2011.
"Footprints in Stone: A Comprehensive Review of Human Footprints in Stone." Restoring Genesis Ministries. https://www.footprintsinstone.com.
"Footprints in Stone: Forbidden History II." Restoring Genesis Ministries. https://www.footprintsinstone.com/the-movie/.
"Footprints in Stone: The Controversy." Restoring Genesis Ministries. https://www.footprintsinstone.com/the-controversy/.
Formation of the Union (The), National Archives Publication No. 70–13. Washington, DC: National Archives Trust Fund Board, National Archives and Records Service, General Services Administration, 1970.
Forsyth, D. W., and S. Uyeda. "On the Relative Importance of the Driving Forces of Plate Motion." *Geophysical Journal of the Royal Astronomical Society* 43 (1975) 163–200.
Fortin, Denis. "'I Have Had to Adjust My View of Things.'" *Spectrum* 48 (No. 1, 2020) 16–27.
Fritz, William J. "Comment and Reply on 'Yellowstone Fossil Forests: New Evidence for Burial in Place.'" *Geology* 12 (1984) 638–39.
———. "Reinterpretation of the Depositional Environment of the Yellowstone 'Fossil Forests.'" *Geology* 8 (1980) 309–13.
Fritz, William J., and Robert C. Thomas. *Roadside Geology of Yellowstone Country*. 2nd ed. Missoula, MT: Mountain Press, 2011.
Futuyma, Douglas J. *Evolutionary Biology*. 2nd ed. Sunderland, MA: Sinauer, 1986.
Gardner, Martin. *The Flight of Peter Fromm*. Los Altos, CA: William Kaufmann, 1973.
Gavin, William Morris Bauer. "A Paleoenvironmental Reconstruction of the Cretaceous Willow Creek Anticline Dinosaur Nesting Locality: North Central Montana." MS thesis, Montana State University, Bozeman, 1986.

Geisler, Norman L., ed. *Inerrancy*. Grand Rapids, MI: Zondervan, 1979.
General Conference of Seventh-day Adventists. *2018 Seventh-day Adventist Yearbook*. Silver Spring, MD. http://documents.adventistarchives.org/Yearbooks/Forms/AllItems.aspx.
Geraty, Lawrence T. "How the Adventist Church Changed Its Fundamental Beliefs in San Antonio," *Spectrum* 43 (Summer, 2015) 69–72.
———. "The Genesis Genealogies as an Index of Time." *Spectrum* 6 (Nos. 1–2, 1974) 5–18.
Gibson, L. J. "Patterns of Mammals Distribution." Unpublished manuscript. Loma Linda CA: Geoscience Research Institute, n.d.
Gingerich, Philip D., et al. "Origin of Whales from Early Artiodactyls: Hands and Feet of Eocene Protocetidae from Pakistan." *Science* 293 (September 21, 2001) 2239–42.
Gladson, Jerry. "Taming Historical Criticism: Adventist Biblical Scholarship in the Land of the Giants." *Spectrum* 18 (April, 1988) 19–34.
Gosse, Edmund. *Father and Son: A Study of Two Temperaments*. New York: Norton, 1963. First published 1907.
Gould, Stephen J. *Hen's Teeth and Horse's Toes: Further Reflections on Natural History*. New York: Norton, 1983.
———. *Time's Arrow, Time's Cycle*. Boston, MA: Harvard University Press, 1987.
———. *Wonderful Life: The Burgess Shale and the Nature of History*. New York: Norton, 1989.
Greene, Mott T. *Alfred Wegener: Science, Exploration, and the Theory of Continental Drift*. Baltimore, MD: Johns Hopkins University Press, 2015.
Greenleaf, Floyd, and Jerry Moon. "Builder." In *Ellen Harmon White: American Prophet*, edited by Terrie Dopp Aamodt et al., 126–43. Oxford, UK: Oxford University Press, 2014.
Gross, M. Grant, and Elizabeth Gross. *DataStreme Ocean*. Beta edition. Boston, MA: American Meteorological Society, 2004.
"Guy Herbert Winslow." At Rest. *Accent on AUC* 24 (1974).
Gvirtzman, Gdaliahu, et al. "Upper Cretaceous High-Resolution Multiple Stratigraphy, Northern Margin of the Arabian Platform, Central Israel." *Cretaceous Research* 10 (June, 1989) 107–35.
Hall, Brian K. "The Paradoxical Platypus." *BioScience* 49 (March, 1999) 211–18.
Hall, E. Raymond, and Keith R. Kelson. *The Mammals of North America*, Vols. 1 and 2. New York: Ronald, 1959.
Hallam, A. *A Revolution in the Earth Sciences: From Continental Drift to Plate Tectonics*. Oxford, UK: Clarendon, 1973.
Hamilton, W. J., Jr., *American Mammals: Their Lives, Habits, and Economic Relations*. New York: McGraw-Hill, 1939.
Hammill, Richard J. "Fifty Years of Adventist Creationism: The Story of an Insider." *Spectrum* 15 (August, 1984) 32–45.
Hare, P. E. "Amino Acid Dating of Fossils." In *Creation Reconsidered: Scientific, Biblical, and Theological Perspectives*, edited by James L. Hayward, 104–9. Roseville, CA: Association of Adventist Forums, 2000.
Hare, P. E., et al. "Analyses for Amino Acids in Lunar Fines." *Proceedings of the Apollo 11 Lunar Science Conference* 2 (1970) 1799–1803.
Harris, Judith A. "Presentation of the Harrell L. Strimple Award of the Paleontological Society to Karl F. Hirsch." *Journal of Paleontology* 65 (1991) 527–28.

Harris, Matthew P., et al. "The Development of Archosaurian First-Generation Teeth in a Chicken Mutant." *Current Biology* 16 (February 21, 2006) 371–77.

Hasel, Gerhard F. "The Meaning of the Chronogenealogies of Genesis 5 and 11." *Origins* 7 (1980) 68.

Hawking, Stephen, ed. *A Stubbornly Persistent Illusion: The Essential Scientific Works of Albert Einstein.* Philadelphia, PA: Running, 2007.

Hayward, James L. "The Biologist—His History and Future." Unpublished manuscript, April 17, 1967.

———. "Breath of Vulcan." *The Living Bird Quarterly* 4 (Winter, 1985) 4–8.

———. "A Closer Look at Dinosaurs." *Journal of Adventist Education* 67 (February/March, 2005) 29–36.

———. "Dinosaurs." *Adventist Review* 170 (August 12, 1993) 12–14.

———. "Eagle Predation on Harbor Seal Pups." *Northwestern Naturalist* 90 (2009) 51–53.

———. "Effects of Nest Habitat, Behavior, and Volcanic Ash on Reproductive Success in Ring-billed and California Gulls," PhD diss., Washington State University, 1982.

———. "Genes and Genesis, by Harold W. Clark." Unpublished manuscript, January 17, 1968.

———. "Man's Quest for Truth." Unpublished manuscript, October 15, 1970.

———. "The Many Faces of Adventist Creationism: '80–'95." *Spectrum* 25 (March, 1996) 16–34.

———. "Nest-site Selection and Reproductive Success of Ring-billed Gulls at Sprague Lake, Washington." *Northwestern Naturalist* 74 (Winter, 1993) 67–76.

———. "Noah's Ark or 'Jurassic Park'?" *Spectrum* 23 (August, 1993) 6–14.

———. "A Philosophy on God and Nature." Unpublished manuscript, June 1, 1971.

———. "Trends in Adventist Creationism." *Adventist Today* 7 (September–October, 1999) 15.

———. "Vertical Position of Certain Fossil Trees in Light of Flotation Principles." Unpublished manuscript, Spring 1969.

———. "Volcanic Ash Fallout: Its Impact on Breeding Ring-billed and California Gulls." *The Auk* 99 (1982) 623–31.

Hayward, James L., and Donald E. Casebolt. "The Genealogies of Genesis 5 & 11: A Statistical Study." *Origins* 9 (1982) 75–81.

Hayward, James L., et al. "Aggressive Communication by *Larus glaucescens*. Part V. Orientation and Sequences of Behavior." *Behaviour* 62 (1977) 236–76.

———. "Egg Cannibalism in a Gull Colony Increases with Sea Surface Temperature." *Condor: Ornithological Applications* 116 (2014) 62–73.

———. "Eggshell Taphonomy at Modern Gull Colonies and a Dinosaur Clutch Site." *Palaios* 15 (2000) 343–55.

———. "Eggshell Taphonomy: Environmental Effects on Fragment Orientation." *Historical Biology* 23 (2011) 5–13.

———. "Foraging-Related Activity of Bald Eagles at a Washington Seabird Colony and Seal Rookery." *Journal of Raptor Research* 44 (2010) 19–29.

———. "Mount St. Helens Ash: Its Impact on Breeding Ring-billed and California Gulls." *The Auk* 99 (1982) 623–31.

———. "Rapid Dissolution of Avian Eggshells Buried by Mount St. Helens Ash." *Palaios* 6 (1991) 174–78.

———. "Turning Eggs to Fossils: A Natural Experiment in Taphonomy." *Journal of Vertebrate Paleontology* 9 (1989) 196–200.

———. "Volcanic Ash Fallout: Its Impact on Breeding Gulls." In *Mount St. Helens: One Year Later*, edited by S. A. C. Keller, 141. Cheney, WA: Eastern Washington University Press, 1982.

Hayward, James Lloyd, Sr., *Memoirs*. Unpublished manuscript, 2014.

———. *The Time of the End: A Study for the Last Days from the Word of God and the Spirit of Prophecy*. Revised edition. Harrisburg, PA: American Christian Ministries, 2013.

Henson, Shandelle M. *Sam Campbell: Philosopher of the Forest*. Brushton, NY: Teach Services, 2002.

Henson, Shandelle M., and James L. Hayward. "The Mathematics of Animal Behavior: An Interdisciplinary Dialogue." *Notices of the American Mathematical Society* 57 (November, 2010) 1249–58.

Henson, Shandelle M., et al. "Modeling Animal Behavior in a Changing Environment." *Resource Modeling Association Newsletter*, Spring, 2016, 3–12. http://resourcemodeling.org/spring-2016-2http://resourcemodeling.org/spring-2016-2/.

———. "Predicting Dynamics of Aggregate Loafing Behavior in Glaucous-winged Gulls (*Larus glaucescens*) at a Washington Colony." *The Auk* 121 (2004) 380–90.

———. "Socially Induced Ovulation Synchrony and Its Effect on Seabird Population Dynamics." *Journal of Biological Dynamics* 5 (September, 2011) 495–516.

———. "Socially-Induced Synchronization of Every-Other-Day Egg-Laying in a Seabird Colony." *The Auk* 127 (2010) 571–80.

Herron, Jon C., and Scott Freeman, *Evolutionary Analysis*. 5th ed. Boston, MA: Pearson, 2014.

Hewitt, Paul G., et al. *Conceptual Physical Science*. 2nd ed. Menlo Park, CA: Addison Wesley Longman, 1999.

Hirsch, Karl F. "Response by Karl F. Hirsch," *Journal of Paleontology* 65 (1991) 528.

Hoenes, Gregory. "Letters: Dino and Other Saurs (cont.)." *Adventist Review* 170 (October 14, 1993) 2.

Holden, Constance. "Vindication for Galileo." *Science* 258 (November 20, 1992) 1303.

Hooper, Peter R. "The Columbia River Basalts." *Science* 215 (March 19, 1982) 1463–68.

Horner, John R. "Ecologic and Behavioral Implications Derived from a Dinosaur Nesting Site." In *Dinosaurs Past and Present II*, edited by Sylvia J. Czerkas and Everett C. Olson, 51–63. Seattle, WA: Natural History Museum of Los Angeles County in Association with University of Washington Press, 1987.

Horner, John R., and James Gorman. *Digging Dinosaurs: The Search that Unraveled the Mystery of Baby Dinosaurs*. New York: Workman, 1988.

Horner, John R., and Robert Makela. "Nest of Juveniles Provides Evidence of Family Structure among Dinosaurs." *Nature* 282 (November 15, 1979) 296–98.

Horowitz, Wayne. *Mesopotamian Cosmic Geography*. Winona Lake, IN: Eisenbrauns, 1998.

Hsü, Kenneth J. *The Mediterranean Was a Desert: A Voyage of the Glomar Challenger*. Princeton, NJ: Princeton University Press, 1983.

Hsü, K. J., et al. "History of the Mediterranean Salinity Crisis." *Nature*, 267 (1977) 399–403.

———. "Late Miocene Desiccation of the Mediterranean." *Nature* 242 (1973) 240–44.

Hughes, Bill. "Darwin: 100 Years On." *Student Movement* 68 (No. 7, 1982) 8–9.

Hutchinson, John R., and Kevin Padian. "Carnosauria." In *Encyclopedia of Dinosaurs*, edited by Philip J. Currie and Kevin Padian, 94–97. San Diego, CA: Academic Press, 1997.

Huxley, T. H. "On the Animals which Are Most Nearly Intermediate between Birds and Reptiles," *Annals and Magazine of Natural History*, 4th, 2 (1868) 66–75.

———. "On the Reception of the 'Origin of Species.'" In *The Life and Letters of Charles Darwin, Including an Autobiographical Chapter*, Vol. 1, edited by Francis Darwin, 535–58. New York: Appleton, 1911.

Hyer, Marjorie. "Adventists Facing Financial Crisis." *Washington Post*, August 24, 1981.

Hyers, Conrad. "Biblical Literalism: Constricting the Cosmic Dance." *Christian Century* 99 (August 4–11, 1982) 823–27.

Jabr, Ferris. "How Beauty Is Making Scientists Rethink Evolution." *The New York Times Magazine* (January 9, 2019). https://www.nytimes.com/2019/01/09/magazine/beauty-evolution-animal.html.

James, Harold E. "Should We Drift with the Drifting Continents?" Unpublished manuscript.

Jung, Carl. *Letters [of] C. G. Jung*, Vol. 2, 1951–1961. London, UK: Routledge & Kegan Paul, 1976.

Kallmeyer, Jens, et al. "Global Distribution of Microbial Abundance and Biomass in Subseafloor Sediment." *Proceedings of the National Academy of Sciences* 109 (October 2, 2012) 6213–16.

"Karl Hirsch and the Hirsch Eggshell Collection." UC Museum of Paleontology. https://ucmp.berkeley.edu/science/eggshell/eggshell_hirsch.php.

Kirby, William. *The Bridgewater Treatises on the Power, Wisdom, and Goodness of God as Manifested in the Creation. Treatise VII: On the History, Habits and Instincts of Animals*. Vol. 2. London: Pickering, 1835.

KJV Old Testament Hebrew Lexicon. "*erets*." https://www.biblestudytools.com/lexicons/hebrew/kjv/erets.html.

Kollar, E. J., and C. Fisher. "Tooth Induction in Chick Epithelium: Expression of Quiescent Genes for Enamel Synthesis." *Science* 207 (February 29, 1980) 993–95.

Koerner, Lisbet. *Linnaeus: Nature and Nation*. Cambridge, MA: Harvard University Press, 1999.

Kuban, Glen J. "A Summary of the Taylor Site Evidence." *Creation/Evolution* 6 (1986) 10–18.

Leopold, Aldo. *A Sand County Almanac and Sketches Here and There*. Oxford, UK: Oxford University Press, 1949.

Lewis, C. S. *Voyage of the Dawn Treader*. New York, NY: Macmillan, 1952.

Lewy, Ze'ev, and Eugene S. Gaffney. "First Record of a Possible Chelonioid Sea Turtle from the Upper Campanian of Southern Israel." *Israel Journal of Earth Sciences* 54 (January, 2005) 55–58.

Li, Chia-Wei, et al. "Precambrian Sponges with Cellular Structures." *Science* 279 (February 6, 1998) 879–82.

Liu, Xin, and Dapeng Zhao. "P and S Wave Tomography of Japan Subduction Zone from Joint Inversions of Local and Teleseismic Travel Times and Surface-Wave Data." *Physics of the Earth and Planetary Interiors* 252 (March, 2016) 1–22.

Low, Philip. "The Cambridge Declaration on Consciousness." http://fcmconference.org/img/CambridgeDeclarationOnConsciousness.pdf.

Ludman, Allan, and Nicholas K. Coch. *Physical Geology*. New York: McGraw-Hill, 1982.

Lugenbeal, Edward. "The Conservative Restoration at Geoscience." *Spectrum* 15 (No. 2, 1984) 23–31.

Luther, Martin. *Luther's Works. Vol 54. Table Talk.* Edited by Helmut T. Lehmann. Philadelphia: Fortress Press, 1967.

Malahoff, Alexander. "Geology of the Summit of the Loihi Submarine Volcano." In *Volcanism in Hawaii*, edited by Robert W. Decker et al., 133–44. U.S. Geological Survey Paper 1350, 1987.

Markell, Howard. *The Kelloggs: The Battling Brothers of Battle Creek.* New York: Pantheon, 2017.

Marks, Peter S. "Letters: Dinos and Other Saurs." *Adventist Review* 170 (October 7, 1993) 2.

Marsden, George. *Fundamentalism and American Culture.* Oxford, UK: Oxford University Press, 1980.

Marsh, Frank Lewis. *Evolution, Creation, and Science.* 2nd ed. Washington, DC: Review and Herald, 1947.

———. *Life, Man, and Time.* Escondido, CA: Outdoor Pictures, 1967.

———. *Variation and Fixity in Nature.* Mountain View, CA: Pacific Press, 1976.

Martill, D. M., et al. "The First Dinosaur from the Hashemite Kingdom of Jordan." *Neues Jahrbuch für Geologie und Paläontologie Monatshefte* 199 (1996) 147–54.

Maxwell, Arthur S. *The Bible Story: More than Four Hundred Stories in Ten Volumes Covering the Entire Bible from Genesis to Revelation.* Vol. 1. Mountain View, CA: Pacific Press, 1953.

Mayr, Ernst. *Systematics and the Origin of Species from the Viewpoint of a Zoologist.* Cambridge, MA: Harvard University Press, 1999.

McAdams, Donald R. "Ellen G. White and the Protestant Historians: A Study of the Treatment of John Huss in *Great Controversy*, Chapter Six 'Huss and Jerome.'" Unpublished manuscript, October, 1977.

———. "Shifting Views of Inspiration: Ellen G. White Studies in the 1970s." *Spectrum* 10 (No. 4, 1980) 27–41.

McDannell, Colleen, and Bernhard Lang, *Heaven: A History.* New Haven, CT: Yale University Press, 1988.

Macdonald, David, editor. *Carnivores.* New York: Torstar, 1984.

Megna, Libby C., et al. "Equal Reproductive Success of Phenotypes in the *Larus glaucescens-occidentalis* complex." *Journal of Avian Biology* 45 (2014) 410–16.

Meister, William J., Sr. "Discovery of Trilobite Fossils in Shod Footprint of Human in 'Trilobite Beds'—A Cambrian Formation, Antelope Springs, Utah." *Creation Research Society Quarterly* 5 (December, 1968) 97–102.

Meredith, Robert W., et al. "Evidence for a Single Loss of Mineralized Teeth in the Common Avian Ancestor." *Science* 346 (December 12, 2014) 336.

Miller, Gifford H. "Obituary. Peter Edgar Hare (1933–2006)." *Quaternary Geochronology* 1 (2006) 87–88.

Miller, Kenneth R. *Finding Darwin's God: A Scientist's Search for Common Ground between God and Evolution.* New York: Harper Perennial, 2007.

Minkin, Jacob S. *The Teachings of Maimonides.* Northvale, NJ: Aronson, 1987.

Molles, Manuel C. *Ecology: Concepts and Applications.* 7th ed. New York: McGraw-Hill, 2016.

Moncrieff, Andre E., et al. "Mating Patterns and Breeding Success in Gulls of the *Larus-glaucescens-occidentalis* Complex, Protection Island, Washington, USA." *Northwestern Naturalist* 94 (2013) 67–75.

———. "A New Species of Antbird (Passeriformes: Thamnophilidae) from the Cordillera Azul, San Martín, Peru." *The Auk: Ornithological Advances* 135 (2017) 114–26.

Montgomery, David R. *The Rocks Don't Lie: A Geologist Investigates Noah's Flood.* New York: Norton, 2012.

"Moore Home Schooling." https://www.moorehomeschooling.com/about/moore-foundation/history/raymond.

Moore, John A. *Science as a Way of Knowing: The Foundations of Modern Biology.* Cambridge, MA: Harvard University Press, 1993.

Moore, Raymond S., and Dennis R. Moore. "The Dangers of Early Schooling." *Harper's Magazine* 245 (July, 1972) 58–62.

Moore, Raymond S., and Dorothy N. Moore. *Better Late than Early: A New Approach to Your Child's Education.* Chappaqua, NY: Reader's Digest, 1989.

Myrow, Paul M., et al. "Stratigraphic Correlation of Cambrian–Ordovician Deposits along the Himalaya: Implications for the Age and Nature of Rocks in the Mount Everest Region." *Geological Society of America Bulletin* 120 (2009) 323–32.

Nagata, Judith. "Beyond Theology: Toward an Anthropology of 'Fundamentalism.'" *American Anthropologist* 103 (June, 2001) 481–98.

Nearing, Helen, and Scott Nearing. *Living the Good Life: How to Live Sanely and Simply in a Troubled World.* New York: Schocken, 1954.

Nedelman, J. et al. "The Statistical Demography of Whooping Cranes." *Ecology* 68 (1987) 1401–11.

Nepo, Mark. *The Book of Awakening: Having the Life You Want by Being Present to the Life You Have.* San Francisco, CA: Conari, 2011.

Neufeld, B. "Dinosaur Tracks and Giant Men." *Origins* 2 (1975) 64–76.

Noble, Elmer R., and Glenn A. Noble. *Parasitology: The Biology of Animal Parasites.* Philadelphia, PA: Lea & Febiger, 1973.

Nowell, A., et al. "Middle Pleistocene Subsistence in the Azraq Oasis, Jordan: Protein Residue and Other Proxies." *Journal of Archaeological Science* 73 (2016) 36–44.

Numbers, Ronald L. "Creationism in 20th-Century America." *Science* 218 (November 5, 1982) 538–44.

———. *The Creationists: From Scientific Creationism to Intelligent Design.* Expanded ed. Cambridge, MA: Harvard University Press, 2006.

———. *Prophetess of Health: A Study of Ellen G. White.* New York: Harper & Row, 1976.

———. *Science and Christianity in Pulpit and Pew.* Oxford, UK: Oxford University Press, 2007.

———. "'Sciences of Satanic Origin': A History of Adventist Attitudes toward Evolutionary Biology and Geology." *Spectrum* 9 (January, 1979) 17–30.

Odell, N. E. "The Highest Fossils in the World." *Geological Magazine* 104 (February, 1967) 73–74.

Odum, Eugene P. *Fundamentals of Ecology.* Philadelphia, PA: Saunders, 1971.

Olson, Steve. *Eruption: The Untold Story of Mount St. Helens.* New York: Norton, 2016.

Osborn, Ronald E. *Death before the Fall: Biblical Literalism and the Problem of Animal Suffering* Downers Grove, IL: InterVarsity, 2014.

Padian, Kevin, and Luis M. Chiappe. "Bird Origins." In *Encyclopedia of Dinosaurs*, edited by Philip J. Currie and Kevin Padian, 71–79. San Diego, CA: Academic Press, 1997.

Pagels, Elaine. *The Origin of Satan*. New York: Random House, 1995.

Parchman, Frank. *Echoes of Fury: The 1980 Eruption of Mount St. Helens and the Lives It Changed Forever*. Kenmore, WA: Epicenter, 2005.

Paley, William. *Natural Theology; or Evidences of the Existence and Attributes of the Deity Collected from the Appearances of Nature*, 12th ed. Charlottesville, VA: Ibis, 1986. First published 1809.

Patrick, Arthur. "Author." In *Ellen Harmon White: American Prophet*, edited by Terrie Dopp Aamodt et al., 91–109. Oxford, UK: Oxford University Press, 2014.

Pennisi, Elizabeth. "Untangling Spider Biology." *Science* 358 (October 20, 2017) 288–91.

Phelps, Libby, with Sara Stewart. *Girl on a Wire: Walking the Line between Faith and Freedom in the Westboro Baptist Church*. New York: Skyhorse, 2017.

Pierce, Kenneth L., and Lisa A. Morgan. "The Track of the Yellowstone Hot Spot: Volcanism, Faulting, and Uplift." In *Regional Geology of Eastern Idaho and Western Wyoming*, edited by P. K. Link et al., 1–52. Geological Survey of America Memoir 179, 1992.

Plummer, Charles C., and Diane H. Carlson, *Physical Geology*. 12th ed. New York: McGraw-Hill, 2008.

Pojeta, John, Jr., and Mackenzie Gordon, Jr. "Class Cephalopoda," In *Fossil Invertebrates*, edited by Richard S. Boardman et al., 329–58. Cambridge, MA: Blackwell Science, 1987.

Polkinghorne, John. *Exploring Reality: The Intertwining of Science and Religion*. New Haven, CT: Yale University Press, 2005.

Powell, Horace B. *The Original Has This Signature—W. K. Kellogg*. Englewood Cliffs, NJ: Prentice-Hall, 1956.

Press, Frank, and Raymond Siever *Earth*. 4th ed. New York, NY: Freeman, 1986.

Prest, John. *The Garden of Eden: The Botanic Garden and the Re-Creation of Paradise*. New Haven, CT: Yale University Press, 1981.

Preus, Robert. "The Inerrancy of Scripture." In *The Proceedings of the Conference on Biblical Inerrancy* 1987. 47–60. Nashville, TN: Broadman, 1987.

Price, George McCready. *Genesis Vindicated*. Takoma Park, MD: Review and Herald, 1941.

———. *The New Geology*. Mountain View, CA: Pacific, 1923.

———. *Outlines of Modern Science and Modern Christianity*. Oakland, CA: Pacific, 1902.

———. *Theories of Satanic Origin*. Loma Linda, CA: Self-published, n.d.

Price, Ira M., et al. *The Ancestry of Our English Bible: An Account of Manuscripts, Texts, and Versions of the Bible*. New York: Harper & Row, 1956.

Prum, Richard O. *The Evolution of Beauty: How Darwin's Forgotten Theory of Mate Choice Shapes the Animal World—and Us*. New York: Doubleday, 2017.

Ramm, Bernard. *The Christian View of Science and Scripture*. Grand Rapids, MI: Eerdmans, 1954.

"Raymond S. Moore." https://www.goodreads.com/author/show/581991.Raymond_S_Moore.

Reimer et al. "Intcal13 and Marine13 Radiocarbon Age Calibration Curves 0–50,000 Years Cal BP." *Radiocarbon* 55 (2013) 1869–87.

Richter, T., et al. "An Early Epipalaeolithic Sitting Burial from the Azraq Oasis, Jordan." *Antiquity* 84 (2010) 321–34.

Ritland, Richard M. "Ecological Zonation Theory." In *Creation Reconsidered: Scientific, Biblical, and Theological Perspectives*, edited by James L. Hayward, 145–50. Roseville, CA: Association of Adventist Forums, 2000.

———. "Historical Development of the Current Understanding of the Geologic Column: Part I." *Origins* 8 (1981) 59–76.

———. "Historical Development of the Current Understanding of the Geologic Column: Part II." *Origins* 9 (1982) 28–50.

———. *Meaning in Nature*. Tacoma Park, MD: The Department of Education, General Conference of Seventh-day Adventists, 1966.

———. *A Search for Meaning in Nature: A New Look at Creation and Evolution*. Mountain View, CA: Pacific Press, 1970.

Ritland, Richard M., and Stanley L. Ritland, "The Fossil Forests of the Yellowstone Region." *Spectrum* 6 (Nos. 1–2, 1974) 19–66.

Ryder, J. P., and P. L. Somppi. "Female-Female Pairing in Ring-billed Gulls." *The Auk* 96 (1979) 1–5.

Sagan, Carl. *Cosmos*. New York: Random House, 1980.

Sakai, Harutaka, et al. "Geology of the Summit Limestone of Mount Qomolangma (Everest) and Cooling History of the Yellow Band under the Qomolangma Detachment." *The Island Arc* 14 (December, 2005) 297–310.

Schwarz, Richard W. *John Harvey Kellogg: Pioneering Health Reformer*. Hagerstown, MD: Review and Herald, 2006.

Schwarz, Richard W., and Floyd Greenleaf. *Light Bearers: A History of the Seventh-day Adventist Church*. Revised and updated edition. Nampa, ID: Pacific Press, 2000.

Segell, Michael. *The Devil's Horn: The Story of the Saxophone, from Noisy Novelty to King of Cool*. New York: Picador, 2006.

Shlaer, Robert. "An Eagle's Eye: Quality of the Retinal Image." *Science* 176 (May 26, 1972) 920–22.

Simon, Darran. "'Tour of Grief Is Over' for Killer Whale no longer Carrying Dead Calf." CNN, August 13, 2018. https://www.cnn.com/2018/08/12/us/orca-whale-not-carrying-dead-baby-trnd/index.html

Smith, Robert Leo, and Thomas M. Smith. *Elements of Ecology*. 5th ed. San Francisco, CA: Benjamin Cummings, 2003.

Smithsonian. "Smithsonian Exhibition 'Life in One Cubic Foot' Dives into Mosaic of Life from Around the Globe Starting March 4." https://www.si.edu/newsdesk/releases/smithsonian-exhibition-life-one-cubic-foot-dives-mosaic-life-around-globe-starting-march-4.

Sneddon, Lynne U. "Evolution of Nociception and Pain: Evidence from Fish Models." Philosophical Transactions of the Royal Society B 374:20190290. http://dx.doi.org/10.1098/rstb.2019.0290.

Snelling, Andrew A. "The Geology of Israel with the Biblical Creation-Flood Framework of History: 1. The Pre-Flood Rocks." *Answers Research Journal* 3 (2010) 165–90. https://assets.answersingenesis.org/doc/articles/pdf-versions/arj/v3/geology-israel-pre-flood.pdf.

———. "The Geology of Israel with the Biblical Creation-Flood Framework of History: 2. The Flood Rocks." *Answers Research Journal* 3 (2010) 267–309. https://assets.answersingenesis.org/doc/articles/pdf-versions/arj/v3/geology-israel-flood.pdf.

Sobel, Dava. *Galileo's Daughter: A Historical Memoir of Science, Faith, and Love.* New York: Penguin, 2000.

Sokol, Joshua. "Fossils Show Large Predator Prowled Cambrian Sediments." *Science* 365 (August 2, 2019) 417.

Spencer, Irene. *Shattered Dreams: My Life as a Polygamist's Wife.* New York: Center Street, 2007.

Stein, Kent. "Harry Anderson (1906–1996): The Art of Loose Realism." American Art Archives. http://www.americanartarchives.com/anderson,harry.htm.

Stonehouse, B. "Introduction: The Marsupials." In *The Biology of Marsupials*, edited by Barnard Stonehouse and Desmond Gilmore, 1–5. Baltimore, MD: University Park, 1977.

Stott, Rebecca. *In the Days of Rain: A Daughter, a Father, a Cult.* New York: Spiegel & Grau, 2017.

Stout, John F., et al. "Aggregations of gulls (Laridae) on aerodromes and behavioral techniques for dispersal." In *Proceedings of the Conference Biological Aspects of the Bird/Aircraft Collision Problem*, edited by S. A. Gauthreaux, Jr. Clemson, SC: Clemson University, 1974) 125–48.

Tate, W. Randolph. *Handbook for Biblical Interpretation: An Essential Guide to Methods, Terms, and Concepts.* 2nd ed. Grand Rapids, MI: Baker Academic, 2012.

Taylor, Ervin. "Peter Edgar Hare (1933–2006): American Scientist and Committed Adventist Layman." *Adventist Today* 14 (July–August, 2006) 16.

Taylor, Kendrick. "Rapid Climate Change." *American Scientist* 87 (July-August, 1999) 320–27.

Terian, Abraham. *The Armenian Gospel of the Infancy, with Three Early Versions of the Protevangelium of James.* Oxford, UK: Oxford University Press, 2008.

———. *The Festal Works of St. Gregory of Narek: Annotated Translation of Odes, Litanies, and Encomia.* Crestwood, NY: St Vladimir's Seminary Press, 2016.

———. *Macarius of Jerusalem: Letter to the Armenians, AD 335.* Avant Series, Book 4. Crestwood, NY: St Vladimir's Seminary Press, 2008.

Terres, John K. *The Audubon Society Encyclopedia of North American Birds.* New York: Wings, 1991.

Thewissen, J. G. M. Hans. *The Walking Whales: From Land to Water in Eight Million Years.* Oakland, CA: University of California Press, 2014.

Thompson, D'Arcy. *On Growth and Form.* Cambridge, UK: At the University Press, 1942.

Tigay, Jeffrey H. "Genesis, Science, and 'Scientific Creationism.'" *Conservative Judaism Journal* 40 (Winter, 1987–1988) 20–27.

Twain, Mark. "Little Bessie Would Assist Providence." Little Bessie, 1908. https://en.wikisource.org/wiki/Little_Bessie.

Twersky, Isadore, ed. *A Maimonides Reader.* Springfield, NJ: Behrman, 1972.

Uyeda, Seiya. *The New View of the Earth: Moving Continents and Moving Oceans.* San Francisco, CA: Freeman, 1978.

"Vacation Plans Announced by Administration." *Southwestern Union Recorder* 62 (October 9, 1963) 7.

Vanderwalker, John G. "Tektite II: Part One: Science's Window on the Sea." *National Geographic* 140 (August, 1971): 256–96.

Vande Vere, Emmett K. *The Wisdom Seekers.* Nashville, TN: Southern Publishing Association, 1972.

Vardiman, Larry. "Ice Cores and the Age of the Earth." *Acts & Facts*, (April 1, 1992). Institute for Creation Research. https://www.icr.org/article/ice-cores-age-earth/.
Volpe, E. Peter. *Understanding Evolution*. 2nd ed. Dubuque, IA: Wm. C. Brown, 1970.
Wahl, D. B., and I. D. Gauld, "Genera Ichneumonorum Nearcticae." http://www.amentinst.org/GIN/.
Waitt, Richard B. *In the Path of Destruction: Eyewitness Chronicles of Mount St. Helens*. Pullman, WA: Washington State University Press, 2014.
Walters, Jim. "Richard Hammill: The Interview." *Adventist Today* 5 (March-April, 1997) 17–19.
Walton, John H. *Ancient Near Eastern Thought and the Old Testament: Introducing the Conceptual World of the Hebrew Bible*. Grand Rapids, MI: Baker, 2006.
———. *The Lost World of Genesis One: Ancient Cosmology and the Origins Debate*. Downers Grove, IL: InterVarsity, 2009.
Wells, Donald A. *God, Man, and the Thinker: Philosophies of Religion*. New York: Dell, 1962.
Wegner, Paul D. *A Student's Guide to Textual Criticism of the Bible: Its History, Methods & Results*. Downers Grove, IL: InterVarsity, 2006.
Wegener, A. "Die Entstehung der Kontinente." *Geologische Rundshau* 3 (1912) 276–92.
———. "Die Entstehung der Kontinente." *Dr. A. Petermanns Mitteilungen aus Justus Perthes' Geographischer Anstalt* 63 (1912) 185–195, 253–256, 305–309.
———. *Die Entstehung der Kontinente und Ozeane*. Braunschweig, Germany: Sammlung Vieweg, 1915.
———. "Die Herausbildung der Grossformen der Erdrinde (Kontinente und Ozeane) auf geophysikalische Grundlage." Address to the German Geological Association, Frankfurt am Main, January 6, 1912.
———. *The Origin of Continents and Oceans*. Translated from the Fourth Revised German Edition by John Biram. New York: Dover, 1966.
Wehtje, Tom. "Too Adventist to be Adventist? Catch-44: The Paradox of Adventist Atheism." *Spectrum* 43 (Fall, 2015) 16–25.
Wenham, Gordon J. "The coherence of the Flood narrative." *Vetus Testamentum* 28 (July, 1978) 336–48.
Wernsdorfer, Walther H. "The Importance of Malaria in the World." In *Malaria: Volume 1: Epidemology, Chemotherapy, Morphology, and Metabolism*, edited by Julius P. Kreier, 1–93. New York: Academic Press, 1980.
Westover, Tara. *Educated: A Memoir*. New York: Random House, 2018.
Whitcomb, John C., Jr. "The Creation of the Heavens and the Earth." *Creation Research Society Quarterly* 4 (September, 1967) 69–74.
Whitcomb, John C., Jr., and Henry M. Morris. *The Genesis Flood: The Biblical Record and its Scientific Implications*. Philadelphia, PA: Presbyterian and Reformed, 1961.
White, Ellen G. *Colporteur Ministry*. Mountain View, CA: Pacific, 1953.
———. *Counsels on Diet and Foods*. Takoma Park, MD: Review and Herald, 1946.
———. *Messages to Young People*. Nashville. Nashville, TN: Southern, 1930.
———. *Real Happiness Is: A Guide to Discovery for the Young Who Love Life*. Washington, DC: Missionary Volunteers International, n.d.
———. *Selected Messages*. Book 1. Washington, DC: Review and Herald, 1980.
———. *Selected Messages*. Book 3. Washington, DC: Review and Herald, 1980.
———. *Spiritual Gifts*. Volume III. Battle Creek, MI: Steam Press of the Seventh-day Adventist Publishing Association, 1945. First published 1864.

———. *The Story of Patriarchs and Prophets.* Mountain View, CA: Pacific, 1958. First published 1890.

———. *Testimonies for the Church*, Vol. 1. Mountain View, CA: Pacific, 1948.

———. *Testimonies for the Church*, Vol. 2. Mountain View, CA: Pacific, 1948.

———. "To Those Who Are Receiving the Seal of the Living God." Broadside dated January 31, 1849, Topsham, Maine. Cited by Ronald L. Numbers, *Prophetess of Health: A Study of Ellen G. White.* New York: Harper & Row, 1976 (page 219, note 1).

Widmer, O. Kris. "Letters: Dino and Other Saurs (cont.)." *Adventist Review* 170 (October 14, 1993) 2.

Williams, Emmett L., Jr., "A Simplified Explanation of the First and Second Laws of Thermodynamics: Their Relationship to Scripture and the Theory of Evolution." *Creation Research Society Quarterly* 5 (March, 1969) 138–47.

Wills, Garry. *Under God: Religion and American Politics.* New York: Simon and Schuster, 1990.

Wilson, Edward O. *Naturalist.* Washington, DC: Island, 1994.

———. *The Creation: An Appeal to Save Life on Earth.* New York: Norton, 2006.

Winslow, Guy Herbert. "Ellen Gould White and Seventh-day Adventism." PhD diss., Clark University, 1933.

Woodmorappe, John. "Studies in Creationism and Flood Geology." *Acts & Facts* (April 1, 1993). www.icr.org/article/studies-creationism-flood-geology/.

World Energy Council. "Coal." *World Energy Resources: 2013 Survey.* London, UK: World Energy Council. 2013. https://www.worldenergy.org/assets/images/imported/2013/10/WER_2013_1_Coal.pdf.

———. "Oil." *World Energy Resources: 2013 Survey.* London, UK: World Energy Council. 2013. https://www.worldenergy.org/assets/images/imported/2013/10/WER_2013_2_Oil.pdf.

World Malaria Report 2018. Geneva, Switzerland: World Health Organization, 2018.

Wright, Scott W. "College Instructor Stumbles onto Important Archeological Site." *Community College Week* (December 16, 1996).

Xu, Xing, et al. "An Integrative Approach to Understanding Bird Origins." *Science* 346 (December 12, 2014) 1341.

Young, Davis A., and Ralph F. Stearley. *The Bible, Rocks and Time: Geological Evidence for the Age of the Earth.* Downers Grove, IL: InterVarsity, 2008.

Young, Opal. "Andrews Dedicates Science Complex." *Lake Union Herald* 66 (November 26, 1974) 4–5.

Yuretich, R. F. "Comment and Reply on 'Yellowstone Fossil Forests: New Evidence for Burial in Place'." *Geology* 12 (1984) 639.

———. "Yellowstone Fossil Forests: New Evidence for Burial in Place." *Geology* 12 (1984) 159–62.

Zimmer, Carl. *At the Water's Edge: Macroevolution and the Transformation of Life.* New York: Free Press, 1998.

Zinke, E. Edward. "Theistic Evolution: Implications for the Role of Creation in Seventh-day Adventist Theology." In *Creation, Catastrophe, & Calvary: Why a Global Flood Is Vital to the Doctrine of Atonement,* edited by John Templeton Baldwin, 159–71. Hagerstown, MD: Review and Herald, 2000.

Index

Abelson, Philip H., 138-39
acelerator mass spectrometry (AMS) carbon-14 dating, 136
Acrocanthosaurus theropod tracks, 28
Adam, pictured with newly created animals, 7
Adam and Eve, xii, xiv, 14
adaptation, 167, 187
adaptive radiation, 45, 78
Adventism. *See* Seventh-day Adventist Church
age of the earth, xii, 28, 45, 73
'Ain Soda, Jordan, Lower Paleolithic site, 158
Albertosaurus, 147
Alley, Richard, 143
"all Men are created equal" ideal, 196
American homeschool movement, 56, 58
American Mammals (Hamilton, Jr.), 6
American Museum of Natural History, New York, 28
American robins and common blackbirds, 172-73
American Tradition in Literature, The (Bradley et al., eds.), 115
amino acid racemization dating, 139, 142
amino acids in fossils, 138-39
Amlaner, Charles, 84-85, 88
ammonites, 155
Ancestry of Our English Bible (Price), 107
Anderson, Bernhard W., 116

Anderson, Harry, 7
Anderson, O. Roger, 182
Andrews University, Michigan, 49, 53-66, 68-75, 77-83, 93, 95, 122, 151
Andrews, J. N., 54
angiosperm pollen grains, 154
animal phyla, 10
Anopheles mosquito, 181-82
antibody formation, 177
anti-intellectual cultural forces, xvi, 201
Antiochus Epiphanes, 107
apocalypticism, xv, 3, 11
Apocrypha, 108
appreciation of beauty, 11, 195-97
Aquinas, Thomas, 45
Archaeopteryx, reptilian and avian features of, 175
Armstrong, Karen, 200, 202
asthenosphere, 130
atheism, 191-93
Atkins, Gordon, 100-101
Atlanta, Georgia, 11
Atlantic Union College, Massachusetts, 5-10, 34, 55
Australia, 63, 125, 152, 163-64
Australian biogeographic region, 63, 163-64
Azraq Shishan, Jordan, 158

Baker, Gil, 120-21
Banff National Park, Alberta, fossil stromatolite reef, 152

Barash, David, 193
Barron, Dick, 21
Barton, Clara, 195
bats, 164
Battle Creek College, Michigan, 54
Battle Creek Sanitarium, Michigan, 53
Battle Creek, Michigan, 53-54
Battle of the Bulge, World War II, 5
Beary, Dexter, 29, 37-39
beauty and the arts, 196
behavioral ecology, 36
Behe, Michael, 177-78
benign indifference of the universe, 192-93
Beta Analytic, Inc., 136-37
Better Late than Early (Moore and Moore), 56-57
Beverly Road Seventh-day Adventist Church, Atlanta, Georgia, 11
Bible, xii, 7, 10, 31-32, 44, 55, 72-73, 75, 105-19, 140-41, 146, 157-58, 169-70, 195, 200
Bible and other holy books, 200
Bible proof-texting, 107
Bible Story, The (Maxwell), 7
biblical inerrancy, 109
biblical interpretation, xiii-xv, 81, 109, 115, 141, 146
biblical literalism, xii, 12, 32, 75, 82, 105, 108, 110, 113-15
Big Island of Hawaii, 129
biogeographic regions, 63
biogeography, 63, 122, 163-64
biological diversity, 6, 10, 18, 45-46, 63-64, 77, 95, 149, 154, 191, 198
Biology, the Story of Life (Booth), 14-15, 28
biomass of living organisms, 152-53, 160
Bird, Roland T, 28
birds
    ancestry and relationships of, 28, 85, 156-57, 172-73, 175-76
    author's interest in, xii, 9-10, 12-13, 15, 30, 48
    biology and characteristics of, 30, 64, 85, 91, 156-57, 164, 168, 179, 182-83, 185
    distribution of, 63
    fossil, 89, 149, 156-57
    research on, 18, 58, 64-66, 69, 84, 91-101, 136, 180
Blister Rust Control program, 34-35
blood-clotting mechanism, 177
Blue Mountains, Oregon, 41
"Book of Life," xiii
Booth, Ernest S., 14-19, 23, 28, 38-39, 42-43, 49
Booth, Lowell, 17-18, 43
Boston, Massachusetts, 11
Brand, Leonard, 35, 113-14, 133, 141, 186
Bray, Emily, 147
Brown, Milford O., 15
Brown, Robert H., 75, 140-41
Browne, Thomas, 173
Bull, Brian, 111-14
Burdick, Clifford, 29, 31, 39
Burke Museum, University of Washington, 43

Calvin, John, 45
Camp Winnekeag, Massachusetts, 48
Campbell, Sam, 10-13, 16, 94, 191
canonization of scripture, 108
carbon-14 dating, 136-39, 141-42
Casebolt, Donald, 74
cataclysmic evolution, 45
Catholic Church. *See* Roman Catholic Church
cats, 179-80
Cenozoic Period, 122, 144
Cenozoic rocks, 59, 122, 144, 149, 154-55
centrifugal force on tectonic plates, 131
ceratopsians, 148
Chadwick, Arthur, 141
change, 33-34, 44-45, 62, 64, 78, 109, 146, 149, 155, 163, 167-68, 171-87, 192, 200
chiastic structure in the Bible, 116-17
Chobotar, Bill, 64
Christian Scientists, 10

"Christian" label coopted by those who oppose Jesus' principles, 200–201
Christian View of Science and Scripture, The (Ramm), 31
Christians, oppose geocentric universe today, 146
cilium, 177
Cincinnati Dome, 59
civil rights movement, 11
Civil War centenary, 11
Clark University, Massachusetts, 8–9
Clark, Harold W., 33–34, 150–51, 186
Clayton, Dale, 45
climate history using ice core data, 143–45
coal, vast deposits of, 152
Cockburn, William, 151
Coffen, Richard, 8–9, 48
Coffin, Harold G., 36, 60–61, 75
Colahan Seamount, 129
collaboration in scientific research, 87
College Place, Washington, 41
Columbia Plateau, 153
Columbia River Basalts, 153
columnar basalt, 153
common blackbird and American robins, 172–73
communication, 64, 93
compassion for the needy, xv
continental drift, 122–26, 130, 133. *See also* plate tectonics,
convection currents, 130–31
Coon, Glenn, 72
Copernican revolution, 132
Copernicus, Nicholaus, 145
"created kinds," 31, 173
Creation Research Society Quarterly, 32
Creation Research Society, 32, 55
"creation science," hollow assertions of, 192
creation
   author and, 7, 12, 44–46, 71, 146, 202
   belief in literal, xv, 12, 32, 75, 82, 110, 140, 201
   days of, 31, 115–19
   Genesis account of, 44, 73, 111, 115–19
   Sabbath and, xiv, 12, 33, 116
   science and, 45, 63, 113, 174
   Seventh-day Adventists and, xiv, 12, 75, 82, 110, 113, 140
creationist(s)
   author as a, 27, 32, 37, 44
   ideas and culture of, 28, 34, 60, 74, 133, 140, 149, 151, 154, 174, 176, 186
   individuals who were, 29, 35, 36, 39, 60, 62, 133, 138, 140, 149, 151, 174, 186, 201
   science and, 133
creativity and fundamentalist past, xv
Cretaceous Period, 139
Crick, Francis, 14, 198
crust of the earth, 128
Curry, Philip, 147–48
Cushing, Jim, 99
Cymothoa exgua, tongue-mimicking crustacean, 183

"Dangers of Early Schooling, The" (Moore), *Harper's Magazine*, 56
Darwin, Charles, 12, 48, 64, 184, 196
Darwin's Black Box (Behe), 177–78
dead organisms, recycling of, 166–67
death as a biological reality, 7, 162, 165–70, 179, 184, 186, 190, 192
Decan Traps, India, 153
deciduous forests of Michigan, 53
Declaration of Independence, 197
decomposers, 166–67
Deep Sea Drilling Project, 127
deep sea sediments and oxygen isotope ratios, 144–45
deep time, 46, 135, 146, 192
denial of evolutionary change, 109
Department of Biological Sciences, Walla Walla College, 42–43
Department of Biology, Andrews University, 55–56, 62, 64, 77
Descartes, Rene, 45
design argument, 7, 34, 64, 176–85, 199
detritivores and decomposers, 166–67

Devil's Coulee, Warner, Alberta, 90, 92, 147-48
Die Entstehung der Kontinente und Ozeane (Wegener), 125
dinosaur(s)
  author's research and writing related to, 80-81, 91-92, 139, 147, 202
  birds related to, 85, 156-157, 175
  creationism and, 27-29, 31-32, 38, 92, 201
  eggs and eggshell of, 84-85, 90-92, 139, 147
  fossils (bone) of, 149, 155, 158
  nests of, 84-85, 90-91, 139, 147
  people who study, 80-81, 91-92, 139, 147
  research on, 89-92, 139, 148
  tracks of, 27-29, 31-32, 38-39, 158
Dinosaur Eggs and Babies (Carpenter et al.), 90
Dinosaur Provincial Park, Alberta, 90, 147-48
Dinosaur Valley State Park, Texas, 28
distribution of organisms after Genesis flood, 31, 63
diversity of life, 6, 10, 18, 45-46, 63-64, 77, 95, 149, 154, 191, 198
DNA (deoxyribonucleic acid), 198-99
Dobson, James, 57
doubts, 193
duck-billed dinosaur, 90, 148

eagles, 92, 94-98, 148, 166, 168, 180-81
earth science, xii, 123-24
earthquakes, 111, 122, 128-29, 132-33
echidnas, 164
Ecological Animal Geography (Allee and Schmidt), 63
ecological zonation theory, 151
ecology, 6, 18, 36, 46-49, 65-66, 69, 85-86, 88, 92, 148, 151, 161-70
ecosystem recovery following Mount St. Helens' eruption, xii
education, xv, vi, 2, 46, 54, 81, 200
Egg Mountain, Choteau, Montana, 90, 139

eggshell fossilization, 85, 88-92, 95, 139, 148
electric guitar, important instrument for 1960s rock music, 24
Ellen G. White Estate, 72
"Ellen Gould White and Seventh-day Adventism" (Winslow), 8
"Ellen White and the Protestant Historians" (McAdams), manuscript, 76
Ellesmere Island, Canada, 176
Emlen, John T., 66
Emmanuel Missionary College, Michigan, 54
Emperor Seamounts, 129
endemism, 63
enzymes, 199
Episcopalian priesthood, 3
eruption, Mount St. Helens, first informed about, x, xi-xii, 66, 84, 121, 130
Eurasian Plate, 128
evangelistic meeting, 3, 9
Everson Formation, 136
evidence from multiple sources, important in science, 104
evil and suffering, 7, 10, 118, 146, 162, 168-70, 184-85, 190, 193
evolution, 12, 32-34, 44-46, 69, 84, 150, 171-87, 202
evolutionary biology, 48, 86, 185-86
evolutionary change, 109, 200
extinct organisms, increasing percent at deeper levels of geologic column, 153-55, 59, 160
extinction, 80, 153-55, 158, 160, 167, 186

faith, xiv, xvi, 11, 31, 46, 61, 75, 81-82, 85-86, 101, 106, 162, 165, 178, 194, 199, 200-202
Falls of the Ohio, 59
fanatical belief, 8, 22, 82
feathers, 66, 93, 156, 175-76
Field Guide to Birds, A (Peterson), 9
Field Museum of Natural History, Illinois, 59, 172
field research, 39, 87

firn, 142
flagellum, 177
Flaming Arrow YMCA Camp, Kerr County, Texas, 25
flood of Genesis. *See* Genesis flood
flowering plant fossils, 149, 154
Focus on the Family, 57
"Footprints in Stone," film, 28
form criticism, 109
Fort Worth Junior Academy, Texas, 14
fossil(s)
    author and, 13, 37, 61, 88-92, 135-36, 147-48, 175, 192, 202
    creationists and, 29, 31-37, 56, 60-61, 92, 139, 151
    distribution of, 13, 152, 157, 163-64
    eggs, 88-91, 148
    footprints, 27-29, 31-32, 38-39
    forests, 36-37, 60-61
    geologic column and, 59, 152-53, 155-59
    intermediate types of organisms found as, 156, 175-76
    record, 10, 92, 151, 154, 160, 163-64, 172, 174, 181, 187, 192, 202
    site(s), 28, 30, 89, 128, 148
Fossils (Rhodes, Zim, Shaffer), 13
Francis of Assisi, 195
Franklin, Rosalind, 14, 198
freshwater dune system of Lake Michigan, 53
friendship, 11, 52, 194-95, 201
fundamentalist(s)
    author's background as a, xii, xvi, 23, 31, 46, 71, 75, 87
    biblical interpretation by, 106, 109, 112, 192
    creationist views of, 23, 30-31, 46, 56, 63, 78, 87, 113, 170, 173, 191-92
    fragility of faith of, 82
    general characteristics of, xiii
Fundamentals of Ecology (Odum), 47

Galileo, 145
Galusha, Joseph, 93-94
Gandhi, Mahatma, 195
genealogies of Gen 5 and 11, 73-74, 109, 146
General Ecology course, 48
Genes and Genesis (Clark), 33
Genesis creation account, xiv, xv, 7, 12, 31-32, 44, 46, 64, 75, 82, 109-11, 116, 118-19, 140, 201
Genesis flood, the
    author's changing views on, 7, 13, 33, 37, 44, 46, 59-60, 71, 87, 92, 201
    biblical account of, 32, 109, 111, 113-17,
    creationist views about, xii, 28, 30-33, 36-37, 44, 46, 56, 61-63, 71, 75, 82, 87, 109, 113, 133, 139, 141, 150-51, 164, 200-201
    scientific evidence and, 59-60, 62-63, 71, 92, 113, 151-53, 155, 159, 164, 200
Genesis Flood, The (Whitcomb and Morris), 149
Genesis Vindicated (Price), 33
genetics, xvi, 15, 33, 45, 78, 81, 118, 163, 167, 182, 187, 197-99
geocentric universe and Christians, 145
geologic column, 31, 88, 122, 149-60, 187
geology, paleontology, and the vast sweep of history, 160
Geophysical Laboratory, Carnegie Institution, Washington, DC, 139
George McCready Price Hall, Andrews University, 62, 78
Geoscience Research Institute, 34, 36, 55, 60, 64, 75
Geraty, Lawrence, 73
geysers, 130
Gibson, L. James, 164
Glomar Challenger, 159
Glossopteris, fossil tongue fern 125
God
    author's views on, 75, 80, 146, 200-202

God (*continued*)
　belief in, xiv, 12, 22, 70, 166, 173-74, 186, 191, 200-202
　creator, 11-12, 33, 75, 80, 82, 116, 119, 168, 173-74, 177-78, 184, 186
　death and, 110-11, 166, 168, 180-85
　declarations by, 177-81, 183, 185
　design by, 177-85
　Genesis flood and, 31, 116-17
　ineffable nature of, 118, 146, 170, 201
　questions about, 107, 162-63, 168, 170, 179-184, 193
　suffering and, 22, 110-11, 118, 168-69, 179-85
　views about, 24, 80, 82, 110-14, 146, 166,
God, Man, and the Thinker (Wells), 45
Golden Nature Guides, 10
Gondwanaland, 125, 163
Gone with the Wind (Mitchell), 11
Goodness, Donald R., 3
"Grandma's dressing," E. G. White's "inspired" mulch formula, 26
Great Controversy, The (White), 33, 76
Great Depression, carving of "human" footprints during, 32
"greater light," Seventh-day Adventists' reference to Bible, 72-73
Greek Septuagint, 108
Greenwalt, Glen, 55
gull(s), 121, 153, 168, 180
　California gulls, ix, xi
　egg cannibalism in, 98-101
　egg-laying synchrony in, 98-101
　eggs of buried by Mount St. Helens' ash, xi, 84-86, 88-89, 91
　glaucous-winged gulls, 49, 64-66, 91-101
　ring-billed gulls, ix, xi
　signal for egg-laying synchrony in, 100
Guy, Fritz, 111-12

Haas, Gene, 37
Habenicht, Herald, 56
hadrosaur, 148
Haeckel, Ernst, 161
half-life concept, 137
half-lives of radioactive elements, 137-38
Hallam, Anthony, 123
Hammill, Richard, 62
Handel, George Frideric, 195
Hardy-Weinberg equilibrium theory, 45
Hare, Leonard, 64
Hare, Peter Edgar (Ed), 56, 138-40
Harper Island, Sprague Lake, Washington, 84
Harper's Magazine, 56
Hawaiian Island chain, 129
Hawaiian Islands 130
Hayward, Annette (grandmother of author), 7-8
Hayward, James L., Sr. (father of author), 3-12, 15-16, 18, 23, 25, 33-34, 48, 53, 55, 57-58, 71-72, 80, 115, 192
Hayward, Jane B. (mother of author), 6-10, 19, 53, 57-58, 72
Hayward, John L. (uncle of author), 4
Hayward, John William (brother of author), v, 6
healthcare system, Seventh-day Adventist, xv
healthful living, xv,
heat flow, mid-ocean ridges, 126
Hebrew, ancient, 64, 111-13
Henson, Shandelle, 95-99
Hess, Harry, 123
Hewitt Research Center, Michigan, 56
Hill Auditorium, University of Michigan, 195
Hill, Calvin, ix-x, 88, 121
Himalayan Range, 128
Hirsch, Karl, 88-90, 147
historical biology, 13
historical criticism, 109
Historical Geology (Dunbar and Waage), 59
hoarfrost, 142
Holy Land, 157-60
Horner, Jack, 90

hotspots, 129-30
How to Know the Mammals (Booth), 42
human fossils, 149
human value, 198
humanitarian organization of Seventh-day Adventist Church, xv
"human" fossil footprints, 27-29, 31-32, 38
human-like primate fossils, 149

ice cores, 142-45
ice layers, 142-44
ichneumon wasps, 183-85
"idols of fundamentalism," 202
index fossils in geologic column, 155
Indian Plate, 128
integrity, xvi, 2, 11, 22-23, 28, 40, 77, 87, 143, 191-92, 201, 203
intelligent design (ID), 7, 34, 64, 176-84, 199
Introduction to Paleontology course, 59, 63, 122
irreducible complexity, 177-78
islands, 87, 94, 122, 129, 163-64, 181, 186
Issues in Origins and Speciation course, 63-64, 77-78, 123

James White Library, Andrews University, 8
James, Harold E., 75, 122-23
Japan, 128
"Jesus Loves Me this I Know," 105
Jesus, Second Coming of, xiii-xiv, 3, 5, 76
Jewish diaspora, 107
Jewish Sabbath. *See* Sabbath
Jewish scribes, 107-108
Job, biblical story of, 22, 118, 169-70, 186
John Day fossil beds, 153
Jordan Hall of Science, University of Notre Dame, Indiana 202
Journal of Adventist Education, 81
joy, 7, 10-11, 20, 70, 85, 118, 166, 170, 197-98, 200, 203
Jung, Carl, 82

"Jurassic Park," movie, 80

kangaroos and other marsupials, 163-64
Keene, Texas, 26
Kellogg Company, Battle Creek, Michigan, 54
Kellogg, John Harvey, 53
Kellogg, Will Keith (W.K), 54
King, Martin Luther, 195
Kirby, William, 184
koalas and other marsupials, 163-64
Kuban, Glen J., 39
Küng, Hans, 200

"La Femme a l'ombrelle-Madame et son fils" (Monet), 196
land bridge between Old and New Worlds, hypothesis of, 124-25
Land, Gary, 79
larger reality, reasons to believe in, 193
Latin Bible, 108
lava flows, 153
Leopold, Aldo, 48
"lesser light," Adventists' reference to E. G. White's writings, 72-73
Liaoning Provence, China, 156
limestone, massive deposits of, 153
Linnaeus, Carolus, 173-74
"Little Bessie Would Assist Providence" (Twain), 184-85
Little Theater, Worcester, Massachusetts, 3
Living the Good Life (Nearing and Nearing), 48
lobe-finned fish, 176
Loihi Island, 129
Loma Linda University, California, 70
Lord, David and Eleazar, 151
Los Angeles Times, xiii
Lost World of Genesis One, The (Walton), 114
Lugenbeal, Edward N., 75-76
Luther, Martin, 145-46, 200

macroevolution, 174-77, 186
magnetic poles, 125, 127
magnetometer, 125

Maimonides, 115
malaria, 181-82
mammals, 6, 16-19, 29, 42-43, 59, 149, 154, 163-64, 172
Mammals of North America (Cahalane), 6
Mammals of North America (Hall and Kelson), 42
mammoth tusk, Protection Island, 137
mantle, 130-31
map-making and plate movement, 132
Marianas Trench, 128
marine birds and mammals, Protection Island, 136
Marsh, Frank Lewis, 55-56, 78, 140-41
marsupials, 163-64
mathematical ecologists, 36, 95-97
mathematical modeling, 95-97
Maxwell, Arthur S., 7
McAdams, Donald R., 75
McCampbell, John C., 31
McClarty, Wilma, 115
McCloskey, Lawrence R., 46-47
McCullough, David, xvi
McLean, Orlin R., 22-23
Meaning in Nature (Ritland), 34, 55
Mediterranean Sea, desertification of, 159
Megna, Libby, 69
Mesozoic birds, 156
Mesozoic rocks and fossils, 59, 149, 154-56
Messages to Young People (White), 106
"Messiah," 195
Messinian Salinity Crisis, 159
Micah 6:8, 202-3
Michigan Basin, 59
Mid-Atlantic Ridge, 126
Middle Eastern fossils, 157
mid-ocean ridges, 126, 130, 132
Miller, Don E., 66, 88
Miller, William, xiii
Millerite movement, xiii, xi
miracles, use of by creationists, 165
mollusk shells, 135-36, 139, 155
Moncrieff, Andre, 69-70
Monet, Claude, 196
Monotremes, 164

Moore, Dorothy, 56
Moore, Raymond S., 56-58
Morris, Henry M., 30-32
Mount Everest, 128
Mount Katmai, 121
Mount Krakatoa, 121
Mount Mazama, 121
Mount St. Helens, ix-xii, 66, 84, 87-89, 92, 120-21, 130, 153
Mount Vesuvius, 121
mountains and mountain ranges, 3, 41, 85, 90, 113, 122, 126, 128, 130, 132, 164, 195
Museum of Natural History, University of Colorado, 88
Museum of the Rockies, Montana State University, 90
Music and Seventh-day Adventists, 24
mustelids, 172
mutations, 187
Myers, Samuel, 35
Mytilus, 139

National Gallery of Art, Washington, DC, 196
National Geographic, 46
National Institutes of Health, 49, 62
National Museum of Natural History, Smithsonian Institution, Washington, DC, 68
National Science Foundation, 67, 97, 143
Natural History, 29
natural selection, 33-34, 45, 78, 99, 162, 167, 187, 194, 196, 198
Natural Theology (Paley), 177
Naugatuck High School, Connecticut, 4
Naugatuck, Connecticut, 4
Nearing, Helen and Scott, 48
Neotropical biogeographic region, 63
Neufeld, Berney, 38-39
New Bedford, Massachusetts, 25
New Diluvialism, The (Clark), 150
New England Sanitarium and Hospital, Massachusetts, 4, 6
New England, 6, 10-11, 13, 53

New Englanders, common sense realism of, 6
new habitats, formed as a result of tectonic plate movement, 122
New View of the Earth, The (Uyeda), 123
New York Academy of Art, 55
New Zealand, 163
Nightingale, Florence, 195
Niihau Island, Hawaii, 129
non-Christian fundamentalists, xiii
non-flowering plant fossils, 149
North American Plate, 130
Numbers, Ronald L, 70-72, 76, 79-80.
numbers, use of in Bible, 73-74, 115-17

Oak Hill Cemetery, Battle Creek, Michigan, 54
objectivity in science, 104
obnoxious, subjectivity of what is, 179
Odum, Eugene P., 7
oil, vast deposits of, 152
O'Keefe, Kathie, 120-21
Old Testament, laws, xiv
Origin of Species, The (Darwin), 48
Osborn, Karen, 68
oscillatory motion, 36
oxygen isotope ratios, 144
Ozark Academy, Arkansas, 19-25, 106

Pacific Ocean, 128
Pacific Plate, 129-30
Pacific Union College, California, 138
pageant of life, 149
pain and suffering, 7, 118, 162, 168-70, 179, 184-85, 192-93
Painswick, England, 5
"Paleobiochemistry" (Abelson), 138
paleontologists, 28, 55, 59, 89-90, 92, 147-48, 156-57, 160, 175
paleontology, 13, 29, 38, 45, 59-60, 63, 85, 87-90, 147-48, 151, 155, 160, 172
Paleozoic rocks, 59, 149, 151, 154, 176
Paley, William, 177
Paluxy River, Texas, 27-29, 31-32, 38-39

paradigm shift in geology, 132
Paradise Bay, Antarctica, 195
parasites, 64-65, 118, 179, 181-85
parasitoids, description, 183-85
patience, important component of scientific process, 86
Paul, the Apostle, 159
peat deposits, Protection Island, 135
peer-review in science, 86
Pentateuch, 108
Perry, Alfred E., 42
Peterson Guides, 10
Philo, 115
Philosophy of Origins and Speciation course, 48
physical reality, xvi, 85-86, 101, 146, 165, 200
Pierson, Robert H., 61
Pika Formation, Banff National Park, 152
pillow basalt, 153
plagiarism, Ellen G. White accused of, xiii
Planiceps hirsutus, 183
Plasmodium, 181-82
plate movement, 130
plate tectonics, 78, 120-34, 187, 202
Plato, 45
platypus, 164
Plumas National Forest, California, 34
polar wandering, 125-26, 130
Portuguese man-o-war, 30
Post, C. W., 54
potassium-argon dating, 142
predators, 65, 85, 98, 118, 147, 166, 168, 179-81, 185
prediction in science, 96-97, 123, 136, 139, 141, 143, 155-57
Price, George McCready, 31, 33-34, 62, 78, 86, 149-50, 154
Price, Ira Maurice, 107
proof, 86, 107, 178
Prophetess of Health (Numbers), 70-72
"Prosperity Gospel," an anti-Christian perspective, 201
Protection Island, Washington, 60, 69, 92-101, 135, 166, 180-81
protein translation, 199

Protestant opposition to Copernicus and Galileo, 145
proton-precession magnetometer, 126
Prum, Richard, 197
Pseudepigrapha, 108
pyramids of Egypt, composed of marine limestone, 158

radioactive decay, 137
radiometric dating techniques, 140
Ramm, Bernard, 31
Reader's Digest, 56
Real Happiness Is (White), 37
reasons to believe, 193-99
redaction criticism, 109
Reid, George, 75, 107, 109
replication of DNA, 199
reproduction and death, 162, 165-67, 170
restaurant sit-ins, 11
ridge-push force, 131
Rigby, Donald W., 38, 42, 49
Ring of Fire, 128
Ritland, Richard M., 6, 34, 55-56, 59-61, 63, 122
rival Greek Old Testament texts, 108
RNA transcription, 199
rodents in Australia, 164
Rollins, Fred, 121
Rollins, Margery, 121
Roman Catholic Church, xv, 4, 145-46, 200
Romer, Alfred Sherwood, 55
Rosario Beach Marine Lab, Washington, 18, 38, 49, 93
Roth, Ariel A., 75
Rutherford, Ernest, 137

Sabbath, xiv, 12-13, 33, 110-11, 116
sacred writings, xv, 105-119, 146, 200
sacredness of life, 11
sanctuary doctrine, xiii-xiv
Samaritan Pentateuch, 108
Sand County Almanac, A (Leopold), 48
Santayana, George, 45
sauropod tracks, Paluxy Riverbed, 28
scenic beauty and tectonic plate movement, 122

scientific discovery of physical reality, 85-86, 101, 200
scientific methodology limits bias, 86
Scripps Institution of Oceanography, California, 123
sea surface temperature, effect on gull egg cannibalism, 98
seafloor spreading, 127, 130
SEALAB Aquanaut program, U.S. Navy, 46
Second Coming of Christ, xiii, 3, 5, 76
sedimentary rocks, 13
seismic tomography, 128
self-categorization, limits a person's exploration, 201
selfless care for others, 195
Senckenberg-Museum, Frankfurt am Main, 125
Seventh-day Adventist Church, xiii, 2, 4, 11-15, 54, 70, 72, 80, 110, 150
Shark Bay, Australia, living stromatolites of, 152
"Should We Drift with the Drifting Continents" (James), 122, 133
Shubin, Neil, 176
Siberian traps, Russia, 153
sin, 22-23, 30, 44, 46, 66, 169
six-thousand-year-old earth, xii, 28, 73
slab-pull force, 131
Sloboda, Wendy, 90
Soddy, Frederick, 137
soils, rejuvenated as a result of tectonic plate movement, 122
Sojourner Truth, 54
sonic depth recorder, 126
source criticism, 109
South Lancaster Academy, Massachusetts, 9
South Lancaster, Massachusetts, 5-9
Southern Missionary College, Tennessee, 13
Southern New England Conference of Seventh-day Adventists, 7
Southwestern Union College, Texas, 9, 26, 28-40, 42-44, 57, 66, 75-76
Southwestern Union Conference of Seventh-day Adventists, 37

speciation, 44, 78, 173
species, new, formed as a result of tectonic plate movement, 122
Spectrum, 81
Sphinx, Egypt, 158
spiders, 19, 180-81, 183, 185
Spirit of Prophecy Treasure Chest, The, 23-24
Sprague Lake Resort, Washington, x
Sprague Lake, Washington, ix-xi, 21, 66
stars, creation of, 32
Steele and Johnson Company, 4
Steps to Christ (White), 37
storytelling in science, 87
Stout, John F., 49, 58-62, 65-66, 70, 93
Strait of Gibraltar, 159
stromatolite reefs, 152
subduction zones, 128
subspecies, questionable value of, 42-43
suction along subduction zones, 131
suffering and evil, 7, 10, 118, 146, 162, 168-70, 184-85, 190, 193
sun, 53, 112, 131, 142, 145-46, 161-63, 170, 193
Surfaris, The, musical group, 25
survival of Hebrew texts, 107
synthetic theory of evolution, 45
Syriac Bible, 108
systematics, 43

Talmudic rabbis, 115
talpid mutant, 157
Targums, 108
Taylor, Stanley E., 27-29, 39
technology, advances in, 86
tectonic plates, 111, 121, 128-31, 192
temperament, xvi
Ten Commandments, xiv, 110
tephra, 130
Teresa, Mother, 195
Terian, Abraham, 112, 114, 194
tetrapody, 175
Texas, 9, 15, 18-19, 25-26, 28, 30, 35, 38-39, 43, 75
textual criticism, 109
theodicy, 168

Theories of Satanic Origin (Price), 150
theory, 132
thermal probe, 126
thermodynamics, 32, 44
theropod dinosaurs, 28, 156-57, 175
Thompson, D'Arcy, 86
Thornton Quarry, Illinois, 151
tidal forces on tectonic plates, 131
Tiktaaltk roseae, 176
time and space, 145
Time magazine, xiii
Time of the End, The (Hayward, Sr.), 5
time, deep, 46, 135, 146, 192
Tinbergen, Niko, 93-94
tooth inductions in modern birds, 156
torture and doom, instruments of in nature, 184
tranlation of proteins, 199
transcription of RNA, 199
tree ring dating, 142
trilogy about Genesis by Bull and Guy, 111
truth, 171
tsunamis, from energy released by tectonic plate movement, 122
Twain, Mark [Samuel Clemens], 184
Tyrannosuarus rex, 147

ultimate reality, 200
Understanding Evolution (Volpe), 45, 122
understanding literature helps one understand Bible, 115
Union College, Nebraska, 9, 67, 76-77, 87
United States Air Force, 62
United States Geological Survey, 132
University of Southern California, 57
University of Tokyo, 123
upbringing, partly determines how one thinks, xvi
upright floatation of trees, 36-37, 44, 61
uranium-lead dating, 142
Ussher, James, 73
Uyeda, Seiya, 123-24

valleys and ridges province, Tennessee, 13
vast deposits of organic material represented in geologic column, 151
volcanic deposits, 153
volcanic ash-buried gull colony, xi, 84
volcanic eruptions, x, 128-29, 133, 153
volcanoes, xi-xii, 121-22, 128-30

Walla Walla College, Washington, 16, 38, 41-49, 55, 58, 94, 122
Wallace, Alfred Russel, 63
Walton, John, 114
Washington Post, xiii
Washington State University, 76
Watson, James, 14, 198
Wegener, Alfred, 124, 131
Wenham, Gordon J., 117
Whidbey Formation, 137
Whitcomb, John C., Jr., 30-32
White Cliffs of Dover, England, 151
White Oak Mountain, Tennessee, 13
White, Arthur L., 24-25

White, Ellen G.
admonitions, warnings, teachings of, 4-5, 14-15, 20, 22-24, 30, 33, 55, 57
authority of among Adventists, 4-5, 16, 23, 26, 55-57, 71-72, 75, 106
Seventh-day Adventist prophet, xii, xv, 44, 54
studies and critiques regarding, xiii, 8-9, 70-72, 76, 80
whooping cranes, Aransas National Wildlife Refuge, Texas, 30
Wilson, Edward O., 41
Winslow, Guy Herbert, 7-9
"Wipe Out," music, 25
wonderment, source of, 191
Woodmorappe, John, 164
World War II, 4

Yellowstone caldera, 130
Yellowstone hotspot, 130

Zelenitsky, Darla, 147

About the Author

James L. Hayward, Professor Emeritus of Biology at Andrews University, taught for thirty-seven years at the college and university level. He earned a PhD in zoology at Washington State University in 1982. His scholarly interests include community ecology, paleoecology, and the history of science. For more than thirty field seasons he researched the behavioral ecology of seabirds, bald eagles, harbor seals, and other animals at Protection Island National Wildlife in the Washington's Salish Sea. He has published more than sixty papers in the peer-reviewed, scientific literature, along with dozens of popular articles. His book, *The Creation-Evolution Controversy: An Annotated Bibliography* (1998), was selected by the American Library Association's journal *Choice* as an "Outstanding Academic Title, 1999." He served as editor of *Creation Reconsidered: Scientific, Biblical, and Theological Perspectives* (2000).

www.ingramcontent.com/pod-product-compliance
Lightning Source LLC
Chambersburg PA
CBHW062014220426
43662CB00010B/1324